Building Transnational Networks

Building Transnational Networks tells the story of how a large and diverse group of civil society organizations joined forces to contest free trade negotiations in the Americas. Based on qualitative research and social network analysis carried out in Brazil, Chile, Mexico, Peru, the United States, and Canada, it presents original data on twenty years of collective action within and across national boundaries. The author shows that the most effective transnational actors have strong domestic roots and that "Southern" organizations are key actors in trade protest networks. Such networks remain vulnerable to changes in national political contexts and to tensions stemming from enduring asymmetries among actors. These findings offer new understandings of the challenges of transnational collective action.

Marisa von Bülow is professor of political science and Vice-Director of the Political Science Institute at the University of Brasilia, Brazil. She is the author of numerous book chapters as well as articles in journals published in the United States, Europe, and Latin America. Professor von Bülow holds a Ph.D. from the Johns Hopkins University and has conducted research throughout the Americas, including in Argentina, Brazil, Canada, Chile, Mexico, Paraguay, Peru, the United States, and Uruguay.

Cambridge Studies in Contentious Politics

Editors

Mark Beissinger *Princeton University*
Jack A. Goldstone *George Mason University*
Michael Hanagan *Vassar College*
Doug McAdam *Stanford University and Center for Advanced Study in the Behavioral Sciences*
Suzanne Staggenborg *University of Pittsburgh*
Sidney Tarrow *Cornell University*
Charles Tilly (d. 2008)
Elisabeth J. Wood *Yale University*
Deborah Yashar *Princeton University*

Ronald Aminzade et al., *Silence and Voice in the Study of Contentious Politics*
Javier Auyero, *Routine Politics and Violence in Argentina: The Gray Zone of State Power*
Clifford Bob, *The Marketing of Rebellion: Insurgents, Media, and International Activism*
Charles Brockett, *Political Movements and Violence in Central America*
Christian Davenport, *Media Bias, Perspective, and State Repression: The Black Panther Party*
Gerald F. Davis, Doug McAdam, W. Richard Scott, and Mayer N. Zald, *Social Movements and Organization Theory*
Jack A. Goldstone, editor, *States, Parties, and Social Movements*
Joseph E. Luders, *The Civil Rights Movement and the Logic of Social Change*
Doug McAdam, Sidney Tarrow, and Charles Tilly, *Dynamics of Contention*
Sharon Nepstad, *War Resistance and the Plowshares Movement*
Kevin J. O'Brien and Lianjiang Li, *Rightful Resistance in Rural China*
Silvia Pedraza, *Political Disaffection in Cuba's Revolution and Exodus*
Eduardo Silva, *Challenging Neoliberalism in Latin America*
Sarah A. Soule, *Contention and Corporate Social Responsibility*
Sidney Tarrow, *The New Transnational Activism*
Ralph Thaxton, Jr., *Catastrophe and Contention in Rural China: Mao's Great Leap Forward Famine and the Origins of Righteous Resistance in Da Fo Village*
Charles Tilly, *Contentious Performances*
Charles Tilly, *The Politics of Collective Violence*
Charles Tilly, *Contention and Democracy in Europe, 1650–2000*
Stuart A. Wright, *Patriots, Politics, and the Oklahoma City Bombing*
Deborah Yashar, *Contesting Citizenship in Latin America: The Rise of Indigenous Movements and the Postliberal Challenge*

Building Transnational Networks

CIVIL SOCIETY AND THE POLITICS OF TRADE IN THE AMERICAS

MARISA VON BÜLOW

CAMBRIDGE
UNIVERSITY PRESS

CAMBRIDGE UNIVERSITY PRESS
Cambridge, New York, Melbourne, Madrid, Cape Town, Singapore,
São Paulo, Delhi, Dubai, Tokyo, Mexico City

Cambridge University Press
32 Avenue of the Americas, New York, NY 10013-2473, USA

www.cambridge.org
Information on this title: www.cambridge.org/9780521191562

First published 2010

Printed in the United States of America

A catalog record for this publication is available from the British Library.

Library of Congress Cataloging in Publication data
Von Bülow, Marisa.
    Building transnational networks : civil society and the politics of trade
in the Americas / Marisa von Bülow.
        p.   cm. – (Cambridge studies in contentious politics)
    Includes bibliographical references and index.
    ISBN 978-0-521-19156-2 (hardback)
    1. Free trade–Social aspects–America.   2. Civil society–America.
    I. Title.   II. Series.
    HF1745.V65 2010
    382'.71097–dc22   2010021483

ISBN 978-0-521-19156-2 Hardback

To Carlos and Luisa

Contents

List of Figures   *page* xiii

List of Tables   xiv

Acknowledgments   xvii

**Part One   Civil Society Organizations and Their Pathways
to Transnationality**

1.   INTRODUCTION   3
     What Is Transnational Collective Action?   5
     Why Trade?   9
     Why the Americas?   10
     Researching Networks in Political Contexts   13
     Disclaimers and Main Arguments   16
     The Plan of the Book   18

2.   MULTIPLE PATHWAYS TO TRANSNATIONALITY   20
     The National in Transnational Collective Action   22
     Pathways to Transnationality   25

Part Two   The Politicization of Trade

3.   THE CONTENTIOUS NATURE OF TRADE DEBATES   39
     The Creation of a Global Trade Regime and Civil Society
         Participation   42

4.   NEW REGIONALISM IN THE AMERICAS   49
     Different Civil Society Responses to NAFTA
         and MERCOSUR   51
     Lessons from NAFTA and MERCOSUR   63

Part Three   The Dynamics of Networks

5. TRADE PROTEST NETWORKS   67
    Who Are Your Closest Allies?   69
    Who Are Your Closest Allies in Other Countries?   76

6. THE ORIGINS AND DYNAMICS OF TRADE
    CHALLENGERS' NETWORKS   81
    The Power of Labor Organizations and Its Limits   81
    "We Want Our Own Space": The Rise of Rural
        Transnationalism   92
    The Potential Brokerage Roles of NGOs   103
    The Strength of Missing Ties   112

Part Four   Organizational Pathways to Transnationality

7. THE CREATION AND DEMISE OF TRANSNATIONAL
    COALITIONS   117
    Campaign and Affiliation Coalition-Building Modes   118
    The Creation of the Hemispheric Social Alliance   121
    The Continental Campaign against the FTAA   128

8. DIFFUSION AND DIFFERENTIATION
    OF NATIONAL COALITIONS   131
    The Cases of RMALC in Mexico and the
        ACJR in Chile   133
    Coalition Building in the United States and Brazil: Different
        Pathways within the Same Country   142
    National Coalitions: From Gateways to Gatekeepers?   149

Part Five   The Search for Ideational Pathways

9. ALTERNATIVES FOR THE AMERICAS   155
    Mechanisms and Ideational Pathways   158
    The Sovereignty Dilemma   161

10. TRANSNATIONAL COLLECTIVE ACTION
    IN DYNAMIC POLITICAL CONTEXTS   176
    Transnational Collective Action and
        Political Systems   179
    Are New Opportunities for Domestic Action New
        Threats to Transnational Action?   186

Contents

11. CONCLUSIONS: AGENCY, NETWORKS,
AND COLLECTIVE ACTION   190
The National Dimension   190
The Asymmetry Dimension   193
Have Trade Agreements Gone Too Far?   196

Main Abbreviations Used   201

Appendix A: Lists of Interviews   207

Appendix B: Social Network Questionnaire (United States)   219

Bibliography   235

Index   251

Figures

2.1	Four Pathways to Transnationality	*page* 26
2.2	Organizational Pathways to Transnationality	28
2.3	Ideational Pathways to Transnationality	33
3.1	NGOs Eligible to Attend WTO Ministerials	46
5.1	Closest Allies: Brazil	70
5.2	Closest Allies: Chile	70
5.3	Closest Allies: Mexico	71
5.4	Closest Allies: United States	71
5.5	Transnational Ties among Most Nominated (> 5%) CSOs	78
6.1	Closest Ties among Selected Labor Federations (Brazil, Chile, Mexico, and the United States)	87
6.2	Closest Ties among Selected Rural Organizations (Brazil, Chile, Mexico, and the United States)	97
7.1	Two Decades of Coalition Building on Trade in the Americas, 1986–2006	120
7.2	Organizational Pathways to Transnationality on Trade in the Americas	121
7.3	Members of the HSA Hemispheric Council (2006)	124
8.1	Gateways Used by Mexican CSOs to Reach U.S. CSOs	141
8.2	Gateways Used by Chilean CSOs to Reach U.S. CSOs	141
8.3	Gateways Used by U.S. CSOs to Reach Mexican CSOs	145
8.4	Gateways Used by Brazilian CSOs to Reach U.S. CSOs	150
9.1	Ideational Pathways to Transnationality on Trade in the Americas	160

Tables

4.1 Issues on the Agenda of Selected Agreements
(1989–2006)   *page* 52

5.1 Distribution of Organizations in the Closest
Allies' Networks, According to In-Degree   73

5.2 Civil Society Organizations Most Often Nominated
by Others as Their Closest Allies in Trade Mobilizations   74

5.3 Density of the Networks, within and across
Types of Organizations   75

5.4 Most Often Nominated CSOs in Transnational
Network of Closest Allies (> 10%)   77

5.5 Transnational Ties: Density of Ties within and across
Types of Organizations   79

6.1 Main National Labor Federations in the
Trade Debates (2004)   85

6.2 Rural Organizations' Participation in Trade
Debates – Main Challengers from Brazil, Chile,
Mexico, and the United States (2004)   99

6.3 Selected Multi-Issue NGOs in Trade Challengers'
Networks (2004)   105

8.1 Main Affiliation-Based Trade Coalitions in Brazil,
Chile, Mexico, and the United States   133

8.2 Coalitions Most Often Named as Closest Allies in Brazil,
Chile, Mexico, and the United States   134

Tables

9.1   "Alternatives for the Americas": Main Topics
and Proposals in Two Versions (1998, 2005)   168

A1   Total Number of Interviews, by Type of Interview,
Number of Individuals, and Number of Civil Society
Organizations   208

A2   Organizations That Answered the Social Network
Questionnaire in Brazil between February and May 2005   208

A3   Organizations That Answered the Social Network
Questionnaire in Chile between May and June 2005   209

A4   Organizations That Answered the Social Network
Questionnaire in Mexico in August 2004 and August 2005   210

A5   Organizations That Answered the Social Network
Questionnaire in the United States between May 2004
and January 2006   211

A6   Semistructured and In-Depth Interviews, by Country
Where the Interview Was Conducted, Name,
Affiliation, City, and Date   212

Acknowledgments

I became interested in the general questions put forward in this book twenty years ago. I met some of the key informants that feature in it quite early, at a time when they were just beginning to think in transnational terms about their own work and their organizations. The opportunity I had to witness the many ways in which these activists have changed their understanding of transnational collective action over the years helps to explain this book's theoretical concern with the impacts of time, uncertainty, and choice.

In Brazil, Maria Sílvia Portella de Castro and Rafael Freire, in the Unified Workers' Federation, never turned down the numerous requests for interviews and information about their efforts that I have made since they began to build transnational networks around trade agreements two decades ago, first in the Southern Cone and later across the hemisphere. In Mexico, I had the opportunity to meet some of the most important actors in the NAFTA debates in the early 1990s. Bertha Luján, Héctor de la Cueva, and many of the other founders of the Mexican Action Network on Free Trade provided me with unrestricted access both to meetings and to their thoughts, as Mexican civil society actors struggled to find their pathways to transnationality. I had the opportunity to analyze these very different experiences of transnationalism when I was accepted as a Ph.D. student at Johns Hopkins University in 2001. As a U.S.-born but Brazilian-raised scholar who had lived in Mexico, I proposed a broad study on transnational networks that crossed North–South boundaries in the Americas. This book certainly would not have been possible without Margaret Keck's unwavering support and enthusiasm for such an overly ambitious undertaking, support that continued for years after my dissertation was complete.

In addition to Mimi Keck, I would like to thank most especially the encouragement and intellectual inspiration of Sidney Tarrow, Ann Mische, and Mark Blyth. These wonderful scholars will recognize the many instances that I stand on their shoulders throughout the book. I hope they will forgive me if I have failed to do justice to their influence.

Rebecca Abers, Paula Duarte Lopes, and Ricardo Gutiérrez have been fundamental sources of emotional as well as intellectual support along every stage of this book. I am forever grateful for their friendship and amazed by their brilliance. Bill Smith, Jan Aart Scholte, L. David Brown, Boris Holzer, Daniel Kryder, Diana Tussie, Jonathan Fox, Velia Cecilia Bobes, Graciela Bensusán, Eduardo César Marques, Arnulfo Arteaga, Javier Iñón, Nizar Messari, Miguel Carter, Bilgin Ayata, and Jack Spence helped me along the way with friendly critiques, ideas, and suggestions of key books to be read and contacts to be interviewed. Two anonymous reviewers made important critiques that helped to refine my arguments.

I also want to recognize the generosity of scholars who helped me as I struggled to learn about social network analysis. Ann Mische and Marc Boulay gave me very useful suggestions on the initial drafts of the social network questionnaire. Peter Marsden opened the doors to his great graduate course on social network analysis at Harvard University. At Boston College, Steve Borgatti and his amazing group of graduate students welcomed me to their meetings and showed me that I still have a lot to learn about social network analysis. Special thanks go to Inga Carboni, who made the effort to understand where I wanted to go.

Preliminary versions of the argument in this book have been presented at many venues in North America, South America, and Europe: at the Berlin Roundtables on Transnationality organized in Germany in January 2004, at the Work-in-Progress Seminar sponsored by the Hauser Center for Nonprofit Organizations at Harvard University, at the Center of Social Studies (CES) at the University of Coimbra, at the 2008 Harvard Networks in Political Science Conference, at the Congress that commemorated the fiftieth anniversary of the Latin American Faculty of Social Sciences in Ecuador, and at various meetings of the Latin American Studies Association, the International Studies Association, the American Political Science Association, and the Brazilian International Relations Association. Fellow panelists and audiences made important suggestions and contributed ideas that helped me to further clarify my arguments, and I am grateful to them all. A previous version of the analysis of labor transnationalism that appears here, in Chapters 6 and 9, was published in

2009 as an article in the journal *Latin American Politics and Society*. I am grateful to William C. Smith, the editor of *LAPS*, for permission to use this previously published material.

Several institutions supported my research through the years. The Fulbright-Hays Doctoral Dissertation Research Award enabled me to spend six months in Brazil, Chile, and Mexico. The Brazilian Ministry of Education, through its agency CAPES, awarded me a scholarship that paid for most of the costs of graduate school, as well as for part of the field research. The Political Science Department at Johns Hopkins University generously covered other costs, and the University of Brasilia gave me a paid leave for the first four years of the Ph.D. program. The Program on Latin American Studies at Johns Hopkins University also helped fund my field research by awarding me a grant to spend one month in Mexico in August 2004, and the Brazilian National Research Council (CNPq) made possible a trip to the United States for further research in 2008.

I am very grateful for the support of my colleagues at the Political Science Institute of the University of Brasilia, most especially of its Director, Marilde Loiola de Menezes. My students at UnB have been a constant source of inspiration. In particular, I wish to thank the undergraduate participants of the Tutorial Educational Program (PET), which I had the pleasure to coordinate while writing this book. Their joyful interest in research and their amazingly sharp questions blurred the lines between those who learn and those who teach. I also thank José Roberto Frutuoso for his assistance in making a first draft of the index and helping to organize the bibliography.

Every person I interviewed for this book contributed in key ways to making this a better work, and I hope they will forgive me for not listing them. In Brazil, Maria Sílvia Portella, Rafael Freire, Gonzalo Berrón, Iara Pietricovsky, Átila Roque, Graciela Rodríguez, Luiz Vicente Facco, and many others went out of their way to help me get the information I needed. In Chile, Etiel Moraga and Coral Pey helped me to understand the Chilean civil society and provided me with all the contacts for the interviews. In Mexico, Maria Atilano and the staff of the Mexican Action Network on Free Trade once more gave me unrestricted access to their documents, analysis, and opinions. In the United States, Stan Gacek, Timi Gerson, and Tom Loudon helped open many doors and gave me wonderful interviews. Other people made me feel at home, most especially Marcela Fernández and her friends and Marcela Ríos and her family in Chile; Velia Cecilia Bobes and her friends and Gabriela Balcazar and her family in Mexico; and Márcio Aith, Daniela Araújo, and the little Marina in São Paulo.

I thank my editors at Cambridge University Press, Eric Crahan and Jason Przybylski, for their enthusiastic belief in this undertaking, their efficiency, and their patience. I am also grateful to David Anderson for making this a better book by doing an excellent editing job.

My husband, Carlos, my mother, my sisters, and my friends supported me in my moments of pessimism and understood my frequent absences. Most of all, Carlos patiently endured my seemingly unending need to do more interviews in more countries, at the same time that he nudged me toward finishing this book. His support and love during all these years have helped make this a wonderful journey.

This book was finished as we await the arrival of our first child. In trying to juggle with nausea and deadlines, I follow the pathway taken before by many of my colleagues, who wish, as I do, to face the challenges and rewards of being both a scholar and a mother.

Brasilia, April 2010

PART ONE

Civil Society Organizations and Their Pathways to Transnationality

1

Introduction

When civil society organizations (CSOs) enter the realm of international relations, they make a decision that is fraught with uncertainty. Not only is there no blueprint for going global, but doing so requires skills and resources that are scarce for most actors. Different choices are available, and which is the best may not be obvious. The results often are ambiguous because actors become neither local nor global, and sometimes are both. This book is about the uncertainty and ambiguity that permeate collective action across different scales. It offers an analysis about when, and how, actors choose among multiple possible pathways to transnationality.

In 1969, James Rosenau called for the development of a *linkage theory*, supported by a research agenda on national–international flows of influence. The absence of such a theory was, according to the author, due both to the lack of communication between those who specialize in national politics and those who specialize in international relations, and to the radical revision of the standard conception of politics that this theoretical approach would entail (Rosenau 1969a: 8–10). Twenty-five years later, another prominent international relations scholar, Robert B. J. Walker, made a similar appeal to understand the *politics of connection* across spatial boundaries and the *politics of movement*, which should consider the changing contexts of political action through time (Walker 1994).

A key premise of this book is that we have not yet been able to answer these calls for a dynamic, multiscale, and multidisciplinary approach in studies about transnational collective action. Doing so remains a relevant task. It is true that, since the publication of the pioneering analyses on transnationalism (Kaiser 1969, 1971; Keohane and Nye 1971), this research field has gained increased relevance and sophistication. What began as an attempt to incorporate the roles of nonstate actors – mainly, at the time, multinational corporations – in studies of international relations has become a vast literature that considers an increasingly diverse set of actors, strategies, and processes. The contributions of the last four decades have been truly welcome innovations in a traditionally state-centric literature on international relations.

However, most analyses have focused on trying to understand why nonstate actors have become so important – the problem of origin – and what kinds of impacts they have had – the problem of outcome. By emphasizing either the relevance of structural factors to explain the emergence of transnational collective action or its short-term results, scholars have paid insufficient attention to understanding how these actors decide with whom to build ties, the sustainability or fragility of these ties through time, and the dilemmas they have to face when engaging in action across scales.

This book contributes to fill these gaps. Its main goal is to provide a better understanding of the variety and dynamics of transnational collective action. It presents the results of a study on the ways in which CSOs that have challenged free trade negotiations in the Americas linked the national and international scales of activism. The book covers two decades of collective action, which allows me to analyze the formation, development, and, in some cases, demise of the ties created among CSOs within and across national borders. This period goes from the incipient transnationalization of actors' strategies, networks, and discourses, during the debates about the constitution of the Common Market of the South (Mercado Común del Sur – MERCOSUR) and the North American Free Trade Agreement (NAFTA), to the more institutionalized and diverse repertoire of action that characterized the mobilizations around the hemispheric negotiations of the Free Trade Area of the Americas (FTAA).

How and why did a wide variety of actors, ranging from tiny nongovernmental organizations (NGOs) to million-member unions and social movements, from countries with very different levels of economic development and cultural backgrounds, find a common agenda and mobilize together? Are these agreements sustainable through time? In what instances do actors fail to collaborate? The book adopts a theoretical and methodological framework that is especially sensitive to two characteristics of transnational collective action: its potential mutations through time and its variation across scales.

What Is Transnational Collective Action?

When CSOs want to influence international negotiations, some reach out to allies beyond national boundaries, launch joint campaigns, and create common agendas, whereas others prioritize lobbying domestic institutions. Some CSOs focus on influencing states' behavior, and others target public opinion, officials of international organizations, or other CSOs. More often than not, actors do not choose between a national versus a global level of collective action, but are present intermittently on both scales.

I propose to define transnational collective action as *the process through which individuals, nonstate groups, and/or organizations mobilize jointly around issues, goals, and targets that link the domestic and international arenas.* This mobilization is not necessarily continuous through time. On the contrary, most instances of transnational collective action will not breed institutionalized or stable relationships, but will instead be made up of contingent and temporary connections among actors. As much as domestic collective action, transnational collective action is a *dynamic process of configuration and reconfiguration of interactions.*[1]

This understanding of transnational collective action does not subsume it in the broader process of internationalization that CSOs have undergone since the 1970s. Activities such as the exchange of information among actors located in different countries, sign-ons, international seminars, visits of foreign delegations, and contact with foreign donors and agencies all have become part of the daily tasks of an increasing number of NGOs, trade unions, and business associations. However, these activities, by themselves, do not imply a commitment to joint mobilization.

At the same time, this definition of transnational collective action purposefully implies a larger universe than other scholars would allow. For example, it differs from that proposed by Donatella della Porta and Sidney Tarrow, who use the definition "to indicate coordinated international campaigns on the part of networks of activists against international actors, other states, or international institutions" (della Porta and Tarrow 2005a: 7), thus inadvertently excluding action oriented toward changing domestic institutions and policies. It also differs from the definition

---

[1] Similarly, Ludger Pries has proposed defining transnationalization as a process that consists "of relations and interactions that in some cases strengthen for a while and then dilute again" (Pries 2005: 180).

of transnationalism proposed by Alejandro Portes, Luis Guarnizo, and Patricia Landolt, who see it in terms of regular and sustained cross-border activities (Portes et al. 1999), thereby ignoring less structured forms of interaction.

The range of actors that engage in transnational collective action is extremely diverse. The analysis offered in this book focuses on a specific subset: CSOs from Brazil, Chile, Mexico, and the United States, which have challenged free trade negotiations in the Americas. As will be made clear throughout the book, the notion of civil society that I use does not imply the emergence of a new or homogenous actor. It is an internally heterogeneous category, which includes social movements, NGOs of various types, faith-based initiatives, professional organizations, and business associations. Civil society is best understood as "a space of contested power relations where clashing interests play themselves out through analogous but unequal modes of collective agency" (Colás 2002: 23). Thus, CSOs are not inherently benign (or malicious) forces in the international arena. I see them broadly as institutionalized political actors that seek, from outside political parties and the state, to shape the rules that govern social and political life.[2]

Through time, CSOs may change goals, strategies, and discourses significantly, and they may use a variety of paths that criss-cross scales to carry their messages and organize common action. I analyze this variety through the idea of *pathways to transnationality*, understood here as the routes built by CSOs to link debates and actions across scales. These routes may be temporary or sustained, and, contrary to more enthusiastic accounts, I argue that they are not unidirectional: CSOs have not grown steadily from being domestic to becoming global.

What is new, then, is not the emergence of a global civil society, but the increased internationalization of organizations that, for the most part, remain rooted at the local or national scale. The result is not the creation of a unified front, but an increasingly relevant process of articulation of differences across scales. The boundaries between action in the domestic and international arenas are still relevant for CSOs, but not in the same ways as in the past.

This book proposes to explain the pathways to transnationality taken by CSOs by studying actors' positions in social networks and the specific political contexts in which action takes place, both of which have changed

---

[2] This definition is similar to the one offered by Scholte (2003: 11).

significantly throughout the last two decades. The *double embeddedness of actors in social networks and political systems* is the analytical key used to understand the strategies, goals, and frames adopted by challengers of trade agreements at different points in time. By emphasizing both the network and the political embeddedness of CSOs, I bridge the literatures on social networks and social movements.

The focus on social networks relies on a tradition of thought that argues that how actors interact with one another may influence the ways in which they see their roles and their self-interest. Thus, social network analysts agree that there is no way of knowing in advance how social positions come about, and overall relations must be analyzed in an inductive attempt to identify behavior patterns (Wasserman and Faust 1994; Degenne and Forsé 1999). The "argument of embeddedness," as presented by Mark Granovetter, sustains that action is neither the result of atomized actors outside of a social context nor the consequence of adhering to previous scripts determined by the social categories that actors occupy (Granovetter 1985).

However, much social network analysis has focused on the consequences of network structures for collective action, rather than on the process of creation and rupture of social ties, and has not given sufficient attention to specific contexts in which ties are constructed.[3] This bias often has led networks to "take on a substantial, reified quality, removed from the actual dynamics of interaction" (Mische 2003: 262; Emirbayer and Goodwin 1994). The approach advocated here builds upon these sympathetic critiques and proposes to define social networks both as a precondition of collective action – because action is affected by actors' pre-existing networks – and as an outcome of collective action – because actors create new linkages that in turn constrain (or enable) future action.[4]

By considering the capacity of actors to create ties, this book also promotes a bridge between the constructivist approach in social and political theory and social network analysis. In order to explain collaborative ties among actors, it is not enough simply to reveal their common interests, but it is also necessary to identify the mechanisms by which they

---

[3] According to Borgatti and Foster, this has been changing, as more network analysts have tried to understand networks' causes, not only their consequences, and as scholars have developed new approaches to consider change. See the discussions in Borgatti and Foster (2003: esp. 1000), Emirbayer and Goodwin (1994), and Friedman and McAdam (1992).

[4] For a defense of such a dual understanding of networks, see, for example, Diani (2003a) and Mische (2003).

are able (or unable) to overcome their differences and construct common purpose.[5] Such a perspective moves toward an agency-centered view of networks as the product of choices of their members and as processes of meaning attribution.[6]

Furthermore, the creation and demise of social networks cannot be understood apart from the specific political contexts in which actors live. By emphasizing the relevance of the *political embeddedness* of actors, I am borrowing from the political process tradition in social movement theory, which has demonstrated that the emergence of social movements is impacted by the relationship between actors and the political environment (Tilly 1978; Kriese et al. 1995; McAdam 1999). A great deal of attention has been given in this literature to the concept of "political opportunities," defined as "consistent – but not necessarily formal or permanent – dimensions of the political environment that provide incentives for collective action by affecting people's expectations for success or failure" (Tarrow 1998: 76–77). The analysis of the impacts of political opportunities in this book pays special attention to how actors may differ in their interpretations of these opportunities, in agreement with the critique of the overly structural and static use of the concept in part of the literature.[7] Actors do react to changes in the political environment, but often not in the same way.

The relationship between actors and the political environment assumes a clearer importance if we consider that challengers of trade negotiations are not necessarily challengers of governments, political parties, or legislatures, either in their own country or elsewhere. Quite the contrary, in fact. Most of the CSOs studied in this book had some kind of collaborative tie or participation in the institutional arena, domestically and – increasingly – also abroad. As the political context changes, for example, through the election of a new president or the launching of another trade agreement negotiation, actors change their perceptions of opportunities and threats to collective action. In the last decade, debates

[5] For a call to shift from the search of general models to the study of mechanisms, processes, and episodes, see McAdam et al. (2001). These authors define mechanisms as "a delimited class of events that alter relations among specified sets of elements in identical or closely similar ways over a variety of situations" (24).

[6] Harrison White made an important contribution to social network analysis by defining social ties as processes of meaning attribution and shared discourse (White 1992).

[7] For this debate, see Goodwin and Jasper (1999a, 1999b), Tilly (1999), and Tarrow (1999). Sidney Tarrow (2005) has argued also in favor of a more dynamic treatment of the concept.

8

about trade agreements became linked to discussions among CSOs about how to deal with the increasing electoral power of the Democratic Party in the United States and the new center-to-left governments that many of them helped elect in Latin America. In various countries, individuals who led campaigns against trade agreements became a part of the new administrations, somewhat muddling the line between government and challengers of trade negotiations.

As suggested above, these interactions with political allies and foes are not only domestic. In part, tensions among challengers of trade agreements arose because activists in various countries had an opinion about everyone else's governments, and often a direct relationship with them. For example, during the FTAA negotiations, the Venezuelan government established close ties with U.S. challengers of trade agreements. Organizations such as the California-based NGO Global Exchange participated in meetings with Venezuelan negotiators and received information from them that was not available through the U.S. delegation.[8]

Social movement scholars have tended overwhelmingly to study political opportunities domestically, whereas international relations scholars have focused on the international scale (Klotz 2002: 54–55; Tarrow 2005: 24; Sikkink 2005: 156). The analysis of the political embeddedness of actors in this book considers the interplay of changing political opportunities at both scales and their impacts on actors' pathways to transnationality.

By considering the double embeddedness of actors in social networks and political environments domestically and beyond national borders, this study assumes not only that theories of social movements, comparative politics, and international relations are all useful for understanding transnational activism, but also that the boundaries among these fields are increasingly porous. Adopting a multidisciplinary approach provides the best way to enhance our understanding of transnational collective action.

Why Trade?

Many CSOs have moved from working on single to multiple issues, progressively broadening their goals and alliances (Pianta 2001: 191; Smith

---

[8] This was true, for example, during the Free Trade Area of the Americas Ministerial Meeting, held in Miami in 2003, when I attended a meeting between Venezuelan negotiators and U.S. CSOs.

2005: 234). That being true, it has become more relevant to understand how actors with various policy interests may (or not) come together in collective action. Perhaps more than any other negotiating arena, trade offers the possibility of studying the dynamics of interaction among differently situated actors. In the process of creation of a global trade regime, the agendas of negotiations have expanded greatly, and new actors have become interested in challenging or supporting these efforts. In fact, international trade negotiations have become increasingly prominent stages for the battle of ideas over the future of globalization and global governance, going much beyond traditional discussions about quotas and tariffs.

These changes require a new approach to the study of trade-related collective action. Because of the distributive impacts of trade policies, traditionally scholars have emphasized the tendency toward domestic polarization between those that expect to gain and those that expect to lose from negotiations. Thus, the political economy literature on trade coalition building argues that productive forces gather around their particularistic demands and agendas at the national scale (see, for example, Rogowski 1989; Hiscox 2002).

However, the usual polarization between "protectionists" and "free traders" or between "winners" and "losers" that lobby domestic negotiators is not as useful anymore, for two main reasons. First, civil society participation in trade debates has gone far beyond productive forces (such as labor and business). These forces now compete for seats at the table with environmental organizations, human rights NGOs, consumer rights movements, and development organizations, which do not necessarily orient their actions according to protectionist or liberal positions on trade. Second, a purely economic and static interest-based account does not explain the collaborative linkages created between actors in developed and developing countries, nor does it allow us to understand how organizations that compete for similar pools of jobs, such as the different national labor federations, sometimes can collaborate. A domestic approach to trade coalition building based on actors' fixed short-term interests tells us only a small part of the story, and not the most interesting one.

Why the Americas?

The process of politicization of trade negotiations happened first in the Americas, diffusing from there to the rest of the world. The street protests during the Ministerial Meeting of the World Trade Organization (WTO), held in Seattle in 1999, are mentioned often as a defining moment in the history of transnational collective action. However, what happened in Seattle should be analyzed in light of the previous decade of contention around free trade agreements in the Americas.

CSOs in the Americas began to pay greater attention to trade negotiations in the mid-1980s, but they did not really engage in the transnational collaboration efforts that characterized the following decade. A few of them became interested in the negotiations within the General Agreement on Tariffs and Trade (GATT), the precursor of the World Trade Organization. However, the earliest precedent of the mobilizations that characterized the 1990s were the actions of Canadian CSOs that challenged the Canada–United States Free Trade Agreement (CUSFTA) negotiations. The Canadians were the pioneers in organizing a broad coalition, which brought together NGOs of various types, labor unions, gender organizations, and family farmers to criticize a free trade agreement. This initial period was one of raising awareness about the potential impacts of trade agreements and, as will be shown in this book, was characterized by a few largely unsuccessful attempts at transnational collaboration.

A second period was initiated with the launching of two key subregional negotiations at the beginning of the 1990s: the NAFTA and the MERCOSUR. As CSOs began to pay greater attention to trade negotiations, they realized how ill-prepared they were to deal with this new issue. First, many actors in the region did not speak to each other because of political grievances inherited from the Cold War era. Furthermore, there were few hemispheric or even subregional spaces in which to exchange ideas and information. This period was one of learning about how to build transnational collaboration and of diffusion of organizational repertoires and frames across national borders.

From the mid-1990s to the mid-2000s, a third period began, as the mobilizations shifted to the hemispheric scale, prompted by the negotiation of the FTAA. Challengers of trade agreements created new coalitions, launched campaigns, lobbied negotiators and legislatures, held multitudinous protests, and built common critiques and demands across countries. Never before had so many different CSOs from the region come together to debate and mobilize transnationally around a hemispheric agenda.

During this period, challengers of free trade agreements had to combine collective action on various scales, as a series of negotiations followed one another, in various formats and involving different subsets of countries. Thus, at the same time that Brazilians were discussing the FTAA at the hemispheric level, they were engaged in the ongoing MERCOSUR negotiations, they debated other South American integration initiatives, analyzed the proposed MERCOSUR–European Union agreement, and followed the Doha Round of negotiations at the WTO. CSOs from other countries had to face a similar set of simultaneous negotiations.

This book focuses on the second and third periods of mobilizations in the Americas but situates them in the context of earlier challenges to trade negotiations. It also provides an analysis of the post-FTAA period, which sheds light on the dilemmas faced by hemispheric activism when there is no common target.

The issues raised by challengers of trade agreement negotiations across the hemisphere during these periods were surprisingly similar, given the different types of CSOs involved and the many political, social, economic, and cultural differences between, for example, the United States and countries such as Chile or Brazil. These issues touched on the decision-making processes, the agenda of negotiations, and the impacts of the implementation of agreements. Some of the key critiques presented by challengers were related to the lack of transparency during negotiations, the absence of channels of dialogue between CSOs and negotiators (the so-called problem of the "democratic deficit" of negotiations), the disregard for social, environmental, and cultural issues in the agendas of negotiations and in the analysis of impacts, the unfair distribution of benefits and costs of agreements, the "race to the bottom" promoted by agreements (which, it is argued, act as an incentive to competition that is based on declining wages and on the weakening of environmental and labor rights legislation), and the undemocratic limitations on the power of nationally and locally elected authorities to design and implement public policies.

By studying trade protests in the Americas, we can analyze transnational collective action as it unfolded through time within and across countries and, more specifically, across the North–South divide. This book reveals that organizations from the South have come to acquire greater centrality in trade protest networks in the region. Such a finding goes counter to much of the transnationalism literature, which has tended to focus on the role of organizations headquartered in North America and Western

Europe.[9] This research casts a broader net than most, not only because it includes Southern organizations, but also because it brings to the analysis the roles of grassroots CSOs and how these interact with NGOs.

Researching Networks in Political Contexts

A theoretical approach that emphasizes the dynamics of the double embeddedness of actors, as proposed above, requires a research strategy that focuses on relationships at various sites, and at different points in time. Bringing together social network analysis techniques and qualitative methods, as this book does, is especially useful for accomplishing this task.

Two choices limited the number of actors whose roles and interactions I analyze in this book. The first was to focus on the group of challengers of trade agreements, which includes not only CSOs that decided to oppose negotiations, but also those that wanted to reform the contents of at least one agreement in significant ways. These actors defy the common labels that often are slapped on them, such as "anti-trade," "protectionists," or "anti-globalization," which reflect a distorted and simplified view of collective action on trade. In fact, challengers of trade negotiations present a wide variety of agendas and perspectives on public policies, global governance, and globalization in general.

The second choice that narrowed the empirical focus of the study was to apply a social network questionnaire to challengers of trade negotiations in four countries of the Americas: Brazil, Chile, Mexico, and the United States. This selection was based on two main criteria. First, countries had to be involved in different regional experiences of trade negotiation, including (but not only) the FTAA. This allowed me to assess the variation of pathways to transnationality across different kinds of contexts and negotiations. Furthermore, at least one of the countries studied had to be a developed country, because of the focus of this research on power relations within networks and North–South interactions.

---

[9] For example, the editors of the influential *Global Civil Society Yearbook* have emphasized the concentration of "global civil society" in northwestern Europe and in OECD countries (Anheier et al. 2001; Anheier and Themudo 2002). For a critique of this argument that is very much in tune with the empirical findings of this book, see Friedman et al. (2005: esp. 159). See also Pianta (2001, 2002) for data that show a geographical shift in the organizing of transnational parallel summits, from Western Europe and North America to the South.

Bearing in mind these general criteria, more specific reasons informed the selection of each country. The United States was preferred as the developed country to be studied (over Canada) because of its importance as the main promoter of the new round of free trade negotiations.[10] Brazil was chosen because of its leadership role in both South–South and FTAA negotiations.[11] Brazilian CSOs have taken very different positions in these arenas, thus providing insights into the variety of reactions and strategies pursued within the group of challengers of free trade agreements. Chile was chosen because it was the first country in the hemisphere to sign a bilateral agreement with the United States after NAFTA, and Chile negotiated several others in its aftermath,[12] also having associated member status in MERCOSUR. Interestingly, of the four countries studied, Chilean CSOs were the ones that faced the greatest mobilization and coordination difficulties. Finally, Mexico was chosen because challengers have accumulated over fifteen years of experience in dealing with free trade agreements and because it was the first Latin American country to negotiate an extensive agreement with the United States.[13] Mexican actors have been particularly influential among challengers of trade agreements in other Latin American countries.

As will be made clear throughout the book, these countries are not self-contained units, to be compared by using the most similar or the most

[10] At the beginning of 2008, the United States was involved in a large number of regional and bilateral trade initiatives, in force or under negotiation, such as the Central American Free Trade Agreement, the Association of Southeast Asian Nations Initiative, NAFTA, the Middle East Free Trade Area Initiative, the Asia-Pacific Economic Cooperation Forum, and free trade agreements with Canada, Australia, Chile, Israel, Jordan, Morocco, Singapore, Peru, and Colombia, among others. See www.ustr.gov, last accessed February 8, 2008.

[11] As part of MERCOSUR, Brazil has participated in trade negotiations with the European Union, the Southern Africa Customs Union, India, Egypt, Israel, and Morocco, among others. Brazil has also been a long-standing member (since 1980) of the Latin American Integration Association (ALADI). More recently, it has participated in launching a new initiative for South American integration. See www.mre.gov.br, last accessed February 8, 2008.

[12] Besides the free trade agreement negotiated with the United States, Chile signed various bilateral agreements, for example, with Canada, Japan, Korea, Mexico, and Central America. It also is a participant in the Asia-Pacific Economic Cooperation (APEC) forum and ALADI. See www.direcon.cl, last accessed February 8, 2008.

[13] After the negotiation of NAFTA, Mexico signed free trade agreements with the European Free Trade Association, Guatemala, El Salvador, Honduras, the European Union, Israel, and Chile, among others. The country is also a member of ALADI. See www.sre.gob.mx, last accessed February 8, 2008.

different comparative methods. The multiple pathways to transnationality taken by Brazilian, Chilean, Mexican, and U.S. CSOs are a mixed outcome of influences originating from beyond and from within national borders. A methodological approach that focused on the causal powers of particular variables by comparing countries taken as separate "cases" would be misleading[14] because it would ignore the impacts of transnational diffusion and influence.

One hundred and twenty-three CSOs answered the social network questionnaire in Brazil (29), Chile (23), Mexico (30), and the United States (41) (see the lists of organizations in Appendix A). This "n" is not representative of all challengers of free trade negotiations. It does include, however, the core organizations in each country. To reach this number, a combination of strategies was implemented in three consecutive steps. The first was the creation of a preliminary roster of organizations, based on the lists of members of trade coalitions, sign-ons, and participants in trade-related events. It included organizations from various sectors that sponsored different goals and strategies. The second step was "snowballing" from this initial list. Interviewees were asked to name other groups that were missing from the roster. When three different informants mentioned the same organization not on the list, an attempt was made to include it.[15] This combination of strategies avoided missing important actors, which were added during the study. At the same time, it prevented having a list that was too homogeneous, which may happen in social network studies that rely only on interviewees' responses.

Dozens of semistructured and in-depth interviews with key CSO members helped to clarify and make sense of the network data uncovered (see Appendix A). Most importantly, these interviews provided information on changes in organizations' interactions and pathways to transnationality. They were undertaken in two rounds: the first, between May 2004 and September 2005, and the second, between January and

---

[14] World-historical scholars have made this point clearly (for example, Silver 2003, esp. 25–31). Charles Tilly argues more broadly that the results of strict cross-national analysis may be misleading (Tilly 1984).

[15] Approximately 5 percent of the organizations interviewed were added through snowballing, and 10 percent from the initial roster were excluded, either because they had ceased to exist at the time of the interview or because they were no longer active on trade debates. For a review of the advantages and disadvantages of different boundary-specification strategies in social network research, see Marsden (2005).

August 2008. Furthermore, key civil society actors were interviewed in Canada, because of the significant influence they had on how trade protests later were organized in other countries in the hemisphere, and in Peru, to gather information on their reactions to the U.S.–Peru Free Trade Agreement.

In addition to CSO members, I conducted in-depth and semistructured interviews with government officials, legislators and their staff, and key informants from international organizations (see Appendix A). The research strategy also included participant observation in dozens of events (civil society meetings, rallies, debates, seminars, meetings between negotiators and civil society representatives, etc.), informal conversations, and the analysis of documentation produced by the different actors involved in the debates about trade agreements.

Disclaimers and Main Arguments

In this book, readers will learn that changes in the way CSOs debate trade agreements are related to the creation of a global trade regime and to the vertical (to more countries) and horizontal (to new issues) proliferation of trade negotiations. However, it does not seek to explain the increased relevance of transnational collective action in terms of broad structural changes. Having made the connection between global changes and their impacts on collective action, this study moves on to analyze a more intriguing side of the story: the variety of responses that CSOs have given to these broad changes.

It is also important to note that this study does not examine transnational activism in all its forms. Excluded from a systematic analysis are the role of individuals and the relevance of more informal relationships, which are undoubtedly important to understanding transnational collective action in general. Finally, the analytical framework used does not pretend to propose strong laws that predict the future of collective action, but admits that researchers are capable of focusing on specific processes and relational mechanisms that help to explain the dynamics of collective action.

Five interrelated arguments, summarized below, constitute the common thread that unites the different parts of this book:

1. *Interaction among actors is relevant*, because it may lead to changes in the way actors see their roles and their self-interest in transnational

collective action. Thus, in order to understand transnational collective action, it is not sufficient to analyze the costs and benefits each actor may have because of their isolated actions. It is necessary to map their positions in social networks, to understand the origins of the ties, and to study how these change through time.

2. *National collective action has tended to become less autonomous from international politics.* It would be misleading, however, to simply blur the lines between the national and the international, or to argue that actors are simultaneously present on both scales. CSOs choose different pathways to transnationality that entail varying degrees of internationalization, and these may change through time.

3. *Emerging forms of transnational collective action cannot be understood as independent of political contexts.* Even among those CSOs that have struggled to build common pathways to transnationality since the 1990s, the fragility of agreements is clearest when actors perceive that new windows of opportunity for negotiating concrete proposals on their own have opened. An approach that is sensitive to the political embeddedness of actors helps in further understanding the different choices made by similar organizations across countries and through time, and in exploring the potentialities and pitfalls of transnational collective action.

4. *New organizational forms linking the local and the global scales represent a reconfiguration of the organizational repertoire available for CSOs.* Power relations and asymmetries have not disappeared in this new organizational repertoire. They are a constitutive part of these new initiatives. Transnational coalition building often depends, however, on the role of a few actors that can be gateways among different sectors and issue areas, and across national boundaries. This is most relevant in cases of long-term initiatives.

5. *Relational mechanisms such as extension, suppression, diffusion, and transformation may strengthen ties among heterogeneous allies internationally, but may also lead to a decline of collective action at the domestic level,* because political attention and resources are spread out instead of focused on specific demands, because key demands are sometimes ignored, and because new organizational forms and ideas have to be adapted to different social and political realities. For the same reasons, transnational agreements among CSOs are often fragile and remain valid for short periods of time.

The Plan of the Book

The book is divided thematically and functionally into five parts and eleven chapters. Part I sets out the objectives, methodological choices, and theoretical framework that informed the research. Part II focuses on the transformation of the contents of trade negotiations, from being mainly discussions about quotas and tariffs to becoming key arenas for the broader debates about global governance at the beginning of the twenty-first century. Chapter 3 underscores the novel aspects of the agendas of negotiations and the institutions created around them. Having put current trade negotiations in a historical context, Chapter 4 focuses specifically on how these transformations have been felt in the Americas and how CSOs from the region increasingly became interested in debating their impacts.

Following the discussion about the progressive politicization and increased scope of trade debates, Parts III through V present the analysis, from different empirical angles, of the multiple pathways to transnationality taken by CSOs from Brazil, Chile, Mexico, and the United States. Chapter 5 lays out the maps of relationships of challengers of trade agreements within each of these countries, as well as the transnational ties among them. Chapter 6 presents an analysis of the pathways to transnationality from the perspective of three types of actors that occupy the core of these networks: labor organizations, rural movements, and a subset of NGOs. Having explained the positions occupied by these actors, this part ends with a discussion of organizations that are *not* part of the networks, or that are not as central in the networks mapped as one would expect them to be.

The remaining chapters focus on the responses given by actors to two key challenges in transnational collective action. Part IV offers an analysis of the attempts to create new common spaces for coordinating action, or the *organizational pathways* taken by actors. More specifically, one of the goals in this part is to understand the relevance of brokerage roles across national and sectoral boundaries. It tells the stories of actors that became successful brokers, as well as stories of actors that contributed to block, instead of facilitate, the flow of information and resources.

Part V focuses on a second key challenge that CSOs have had to face: how to build common frames in very heterogeneous relational settings, or their *ideational pathways*. Thus, this part focuses not on what actors have mobilized *against*, but what they have mobilized *in favor of.* It presents examples of how the choices of pathways and their sustainability are often impacted by the actors' perceptions of the opportunities and obstacles of dynamic political contexts.

In the conclusion, the initial arguments are reexamined, and the importance of the proposed framework is reiterated. This book ends with a reflection on what still needs to be done in order to better understand the dynamics of collective action in a globalizing world. As will be argued, what is most relevant and interesting theoretically and empirically lies not at the local or global scale, but at the crossroads, where actors meet, negotiate, and clash.

2

Multiple Pathways to Transnationality

In 1997 a coalition of more than 600 organizations from seventy countries launched a transnational campaign that aimed at stopping the negotiations of the Multilateral Agreement on Investment (MAI). Debates about this treaty had begun a couple of years earlier within the Organisation for Economic Cooperation and Development (OECD), in view of the difficulties to negotiate a global agreement on investments at the World Trade Organization (WTO). The goal was to establish a set of rules on liberalization and investor protection, based on a broad definition of investment. Among the most contentious provisions included in the draft of the treaty were the possibility of compensation for expected profits in cases of expropriation, and a dispute settlement system that enabled investors to sue states before international tribunals.[1]

Participants in the anti-MAI Campaign framed their resistance to the proposed agreement largely in terms that would resonate with domestic public opinion. More specifically, issues such as the defense of national autonomy and democracy were at the forefront of discourses. For example, in a joint statement, publicized by over a hundred CSOs from all over the world in 1997, it was argued that the agreement's intention "is not to regulate investments but to regulate governments" and that "the MAI did not respect the rights of countries … including their need to democratically control investment into their economies" (Alternate Forum for Research in Mindanao et al. 1997). Interestingly, this common framing was adapted to the reality in each country. When Canadian activists Maude Barlow and Tony Clarke published their book on the

---

[1] For an overview of the treaty's characteristics and its negotiation, see, for example, Kobrin (1998) and Tieleman (2002).

agreement in the United States, they changed the subtitle from "the threat to Canadian sovereignty" to "the threat to American freedom." Similarly, when U.S. and Canadian activists visited Germany, "national sovereignty" was replaced by "popular sovereignty" in their speeches (Laxer 2003: 176, 182).

The campaign against the MAI overlapped with the mobilizations of challengers of free trade negotiations, as happens with so many transnational initiatives. For example, in Canada, the strength of the mobilization and the rapidity with which it spread is explainable, in part, because Canadians were under the impact of the threat by Ethyl Corporation to use the North American Free Trade Agreement's (NAFTA) investment regulations against the country (Laxer 2003: 179). The fact that a U.S. corporation could obligate the Canadian government to pay a fine because of domestic restrictions on gasoline additives that were characterized as being harmful to human health provided activists with a very clear example of the possibility that the MAI provisions would prevail over domestic environmental and health regulations. Unable to come up with a consensual alternative, participants in the Campaign opted for opposing any agreement and, based on this common denominator, built a coalition that brought together "internationalists" and "isolationists" that framed their objections in terms of the threats that the agreement posed to national autonomy (Desai and Said 2001: 61).

I begin this chapter with the story of the anti-MAI Campaign because it nicely illustrates the relevance of analyzing new instances of transnational collective action in light of previous initiatives and debates. It also underscores the need to focus on the embeddedness of actors in social networks and in political contexts to understand their strategies and discourses. Although the anti-MAI Campaign often is presented as a prime example of the capacity of a global civil society to quickly react to new threats,[2] the story is best understood as the successful establishment of a temporary coalition of heterogeneous groups of actors at the subnational, national, and global scales, built on a flexible framing of national sovereignty and on previously established networks and debates. It is not an isolated case, as similar stories throughout this book will attest.

---

[2] For example, Stephen Kobrin talks about the importance of "an electronically networked global civil society" in explaining the failure of the MAI negotiations (Kobrin 1998: 99), and John Ruggie talks about it as "the iconic case of civil society action to redress imbalances in global rule making," through a coalition that "sprang into 'virtual existence' on the World Wide Web almost overnight" (Ruggie 2004: 511).

The National in Transnational Collective Action

A key question in the transnationalism literature is: where is mobilization likely to be most effective? For some authors, given the weakening of the authority and power of national states, the global scale has become more relevant. In this perspective, even if civil society actors were to focus on national sovereignty claims, this would be a mistake.[3] For others, states still hold considerable power, and thus actions at the national and local scales are most likely to succeed (Akça 2003; Halperin and Laxer 2003).

By structuring the debate in either/or terms, both sides lose sight of the current dilemmas of coordination actors face – how to interact across boundaries – and the challenges scholars encounter – how to analyze the combination of collective action initiatives at these different scales. As the example of the anti-MAI Campaign made clear, transnational activists are not necessarily willing to declare the end of the era of sovereign states. Although some wish to "deglobalize" the world,[4] restoring decision-making powers to national political institutions, others want further globalization in specific arenas and issue areas. Often, civil society actors from the North *as well as* from the South[5] feel that they defend their country's sovereignty and interests better than their own governments. Their ultimate goal is to strengthen national states, not to weaken them. Furthermore, many NGOs, social movements, and labor unions view with mistrust any attempt to create global civil society arenas that would undermine their own autonomy and flexibility.

In their contributions to the 2005–2006 *Global Civil Society Yearbook*, Marlies Glasius, Mary Kaldor, and Helmut Anheier admit that "since the turn of the century, there appears to be a renewed interest in national politics" (Glasius et al. 2005: 19). However, the authors limit this interest to mobilizations that aim at democratization and emphasize that none of

---

[3] For instance, Mary Kaldor and colleagues have argued that "The price that was paid for national sovereignty was the existence of repressive undemocratic governments" and "to the extent that civil society remains wedded to old fashioned notions of sovereignty, the end result may not be democracy but continuing insecurity" (Kaldor et al. 2005: 16).

[4] See, for example, the argument in favor of "deglobalization" made by the founding director of Focus on the Global South (Bello 2002a).

[5] Sandra Halperin and Gordon Laxer argue that critics of what they call "globalism" from the North tend to view its antidote as global civil society, while critics from the South tend to see the solution as greater sovereignty, not global civil society (Halperin and Laxer 2003: esp. 3). In fact, however, this book shows that these different reactions to the negative effects of globalization span the North–South divide.

these were exclusively national in their concerns. When actors that defend the capacities of nation states are considered, the authors relegate them to the negative categories of "rejectionists" or "regressives" (Kaldor et al. 2005: 3–4).

In their efforts to go beyond state-centrism and "methodological nationalism" (Beck 2003; Ezzat 2005), scholars of global civil society have tended to overlook the importance of the embeddedness of actors in political systems. This is an important issue, because, among other things, different views on how to deal with state authorities have been a key source of divisions among civil society organizations (CSOs) that seek to influence policy making.

Paradoxically, the cosmopolitan literature on global civil society tends to hide the capacity of actors to change states' behaviors.[6] Such an approach runs the risk of falling into an inverted version of "the territorial trap." John Agnew coined this phrase in his critique of the ontological presumption in international relations theories that social, economic, and political life are contained within the territorial boundaries of states in contradistinction to processes going on outside state boundaries: "Politics, in the sense of the pursuit of justice and virtue, could exist only within territorial boundaries. Outside is danger, *realpolitik*, and the use of force" (Agnew 1994: 62). The global civil society literature tends to do the opposite, by thinking in terms of the "outside," or the global scale, as the privileged space for "the pursuit of justice and virtue."

James Rosenau's assertion, made four decades ago, still holds true: "transnational politics are a long way from supplanting national politics and, if anything, the world may well be passing through a paradoxical stage in which both the linkages and the boundaries among polities are becoming more central to their daily lives" (Rosenau 1969b: 47). Most importantly, considering this paradox allows us to understand that "transnational activists are often divided between the global framing of transnational movement campaigns and the local needs of those whose claims they want to represent" (Tarrow 2005: 76). Thus, a key challenge for many CSOs has been to uphold commitments made with domestic and transnational allies, while at the same time profiting from the opening of political opportunities to negotiate their particular agendas.

---

[6] Robert B. J. Walker has pointed out that claims about an emerging global civil society "usually reveal the reproductive powers of statist discourse more than they do the capacity of social movements to challenge that discourse" (Walker 1994: 674).

Some of the main contributions in the scholarly literature on transnational collective action that address the challenge of studying linkages, without blurring the lines between the domestic and the international scales, have been studies about the relationships between domestic and global opportunity structures and the tactics deployed by actors,[7] the new organizations created to coordinate action transnationally,[8] changes in repertoires of contention,[9] the emergence of new forms of citizenship,[10] and the impacts of global issues and negotiations on locally rooted organizations.[11] This literature represents a sustained effort to understand how and why actors sometimes "domesticate" international grievances and issues, and sometimes "externalize" them (Imig and Tarrow 2001; Rootes 2005; Tarrow 2005).

The Dynamics of Collective Action

An important part of the empirical analysis offered by the literature on transnationalism has focused on case studies of single-issue campaigns and protest events. Although this literature has taught us much of what we know about transnationalism, its case-study approach leads to a fragmented view of collective action. These studies lack a broader sense of the multi-organizational field within which cases fall (Taylor 2002).[12] Besides, they may lead to overly optimistic analysis about the sustainability and the impacts of transnationalism. By definition, campaigns are structured

[7] One of the first systematic contributions to understanding links created among local actors from different countries was the widely-quoted "boomerang pattern," defined as a tactic used by domestic actors who are faced with closed domestic channels and hope to achieve their goals by directly contacting international allies (Keck and Sikkink 1998: 12–13; Sikkink 2005).

[8] There is no consensus on how to name the different forms of transnational coalition building (see, for example, Fox 2002: 352; Tarrow 2005: esp. ch. 9).

[9] The literature has focused on the interaction of local and transnational actors with international institutions (Fox and Brown 1998; O'Brien et al. 2000), on the analysis of international events (a small sample includes Adler and Mittelman 2004; Bédoyan et al. 2004; della Porta 2005; Juris 2008), and the organization of transnational campaigns (see, for example, Keck and Sikkink 1998; Hertel 2006).

[10] There is an ample literature on this topic, developed by scholars of immigration. See, for example, Aihwa Ong's proposal to speak of "flexible citizenship" (Ong 1999), and Nina Glick Schiller's work on "transmigrants" (Glick Schiller 1997). See also Jonathan Fox's work on "transnational citizenship" (Fox 2005).

[11] See the contributions in della Porta and Tarrow (2005b).

[12] By proposing the concept of "multi-organizational field," Curtis and Zucher called the attention of social movement scholars to the relevance of multiple affiliations of members of social movement organizations to explain collective action, but their research focused on domestic linkages (see Curtis and Zurcher 1973).

around narrowly defined common goals and are set against specific targets. Similarly, transnational protest events, although they typically gather a heterogeneous crowd, are short-term arenas that bring actors together around broad demands.

Recent contributions, based on the analysis of protest events, argue that individuals that are capable of putting aside their specific identities have become increasingly important in transnational collective action (Bennett 2005; della Porta 2005; Giugni et al. 2006). For example, in the study of participants in the European Social Forum, Donatella della Porta sees a shift from a single-movement identity to multiple and "tolerant identities," characterized "by inclusiveness and positive emphasis upon diversity and cross-fertilization" (della Porta 2005: 186).

We still need a better understanding, however, of how individuals and organizations engage in transnational collective action without suppressing their national identities, and how their interaction with actors from other issue areas and countries produces an impact on their goals, tactics, and interpretations. Only recently have there been efforts by scholars to understand how actors involved in the protests studied may be embedded in more established and settled patterns of relations (see, for example, Diani 2005). A longer-term approach to the study of collective action, which goes beyond specific campaigns and/or events, can help in this task.

Pathways to Transnationality

The expression "pathways to transnationality" captures the different trajectories taken by CSOs as they engage in transnational collective action. These trajectories are the responses given by actors, in a context of uncertainty, regarding the most appropriate organizational repertoires, targets, demands, and frames. Figure 2.1 combines two key dimensions in differentiating schematically among four possible pathways: the variation of action across scale (the degree of internationalization) and through time (the degree of endurance).

By establishing actors' degrees of internationalization, this typology incorporates Sidney Tarrow's argument that "not all activism that is relevant to transnational politics takes place in the international arena" (Tarrow 2005: 30). The fact that sometimes civil society organizations actively internalize, or "domesticate," strategies or claims is an important part of what has been defined here as transnational collective action. Temporal variation, in turn, relates to the degree to which action is or not

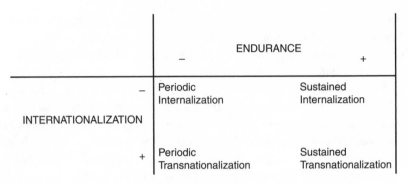

Figure 2.1. Four Pathways to Transnationality.

continuous. As Kathryn Sikkink has argued, many actors privilege domestic political change, but often maintain transnational activism as a complementary and compensatory option that is used intermittently (Sikkink 2005: 165). Others have a more sustained transnational presence.

Periodic Internalization is the pathway used by CSOs when they try to influence international decisions, or debate cross-border issues, by focusing on domestic targets, strategies, and coalition-building initiatives. For instance, many of the Brazilian CSOs that were active in the Campaign against the Free Trade Area of the Americas (FTAA) limited their activities to the participation in the domestic chapter of that Campaign and did not actively build ties with allies in other countries. Many also did not make an effort to participate in international meetings or events. Some of these were key actors in the mobilizations against the FTAA, but, as the Campaign withered away, so did the interest of these actors in participating in trade-related activities.

Other CSOs have a more sustained participation, situating themselves farther to the right of Figure 2.1, or closer to a *Sustained Internalization* pathway. For these actors, engagement in transnational collective action is mostly a matter of domestic politics but is not limited to specific campaigns. They move from one campaign to another, but spend most of their resources in coalition building at the domestic level and at targeting domestic actors.

Periodic Transnationalization can be described as a yoyo-like movement, whereby CSOs go back and forth across the domestic and international scales. This is perhaps the most familiar of the four pathways. The majority of the organizations studied for this book could be located somewhere around the bottom left-hand corner of Figure 2.1. They maintained their national roots, but participated intermittently in international campaigns, coalitions, and events, as these moved to the forefront or to the background of political agendas.

Sustained Transnationalization refers to the route taken by those CSOs that see the international arena not just as an intermittent option to further their immediate goals, but as a long-term site of political action. These organizations engage in the construction of sustained coalitions and in efforts to negotiate transnational frames with allies from other countries. In the case of challengers of trade agreements, the CSOs that have spent the most resources in trying to create the Hemispheric Social Alliance (HSA), a long-term coalition that brings together challengers of trade agreements from all over the Americas, present the best example of this type of pathway.

The proposed typology of pathways is useful in giving visibility to the contrasts and similarities among actors that too often are labeled simply as "anti-globalization" actors or as part of a "global civil society." It is most useful, though, if we consider the location of actors in Figure 2.1 as dynamic, in the sense that the choices of pathways are not fixed, but "contingently reconstructed by actors in ongoing dialogue with unfolding situations" (Emirbayer and Mische 1998: 966). As argued in the introduction, they change as a result of the embeddedness of actors in social networks and in political contexts, for example, through negotiated interactions with other actors, and/or as new opportunities or threats may be perceived by them. Furthermore, the four possible pathways sketched above are not necessarily in contradiction with one another, but, in practice, they can be combined. CSOs may use more than one at a time in different issue areas. However, as the next chapters of this book will show, the change of pathways and their combination entail dilemmas and tensions that are not easily resolved.

In sum, this study is about the agentic role of CSOs in constructing a politics of place and a politics of time in a context of uncertainty about how to respond to a new international situation. The multiple pathways that result are analyzed empirically in this book according to the responses given by CSOs to two key challenges of transnational collective action: the search for answers to the problem of coordination and coalition building – the *organizational pathways* – and the search for common frames, policies, and ideas – the *ideational pathways*.

The Challenge of Organizing Transnational Collective Action

Institutionalizing transnational collective action has become an increasingly complicated challenge in the last two decades. In part, this is

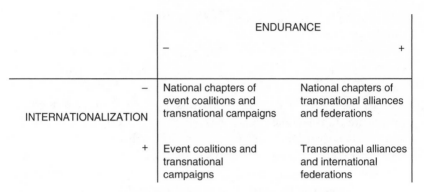

		ENDURANCE	
		−	+
INTERNATIONALIZATION	−	National chapters of event coalitions and transnational campaigns	National chapters of transnational alliances and federations
	+	Event coalitions and transnational campaigns	Transnational alliances and international federations

Figure 2.2. Organizational Pathways to Transnationality.

because of the success of transnational coalition building, which has led to a confusing overlap among numerous initiatives. CSOs have come to participate in a myriad of types of alliances at various scales, ranging from the creation of loose ties to more sustained efforts. For example, the Brazilian Unified Workers' Federation (Central Única dos Trabalhadores – CUT) participates in the World Social Forum's International Council, is a member of global and regional labor organizations and of the HSA, participates in numerous issue-based campaigns, and belongs to dozens of local and national-level coalitions that, in turn, also have their own international connections. In such a context, being able to differentiate among these initiatives, and better understand how actors choose among them, has become more relevant.

Coalition building is the process of creation of political spaces in which differently situated actors negotiate the meanings of their joint enterprise and elaborate common strategies.[13] Coalitions, therefore, "can include a broad variety of negotiated arrangements of two or more organizations coordinating goals, demands, strategies of influence, and events" (Meyer and Corrigall-Brown 2005: 331). The variety of possible negotiated arrangements is analyzed below along the two dimensions defined above: their endurance and the degree of internationalization. Figure 2.2 presents a schematic overview of the resulting organizational pathways.

This typology owes much to the one proposed by Sidney Tarrow (2005: ch. 9). As Tarrow argues, with respect to the endurance of coalition-building initiatives, actors may participate in campaigns or event

---

[13] This definition is based on the one provided by Keck and Sikkink (1998: 3).

coalitions that have a limited lifespan, or they may become a part of more continuous coalition-building efforts. In the first case, they may engage in what Tarrow calls "instrumental coalitions," united by a short-term common cause or interest (Tarrow 2005: 167–168). The participation in transnational alliances and federations, on the other hand, requires routinized communications, internal division of tasks, and procedures for making decisions. A few transnational campaigns, such as the International Landmine Campaign or the campaign to boycott Nestlé, are also closer to the bottom right of Figure 2.2, because they endure over the years (173–175).

In terms of degree of internationalization, actors can become part of international federations or global social movements, or they can restrict their participation to the domestic scale of transnational coalition building. For example, an important part of the mobilizations against the FTAA occurred within national borders, through the actions of the national chapters of the Continental Campaign against the FTAA. As mentioned above, many of the participants in national chapters did not engage in similar activities at the transnational level, an option that was possible because of the high level of autonomy held by these domestic arrangements.

Different pathways have various political requirements and consequences. It is not clear which one can be considered the most effective or desirable. Whereas at least a part of the domestic collective action literature has emphasized the positive impacts of the creation of institutionalized social movement organizations,[14] the transnational collective action literature has tended to celebrate the informal, diffuse, and flexible linkages among actors. In fact, there is a broad agreement that transnational campaigns, which do not have permanent staff or offices and are focused on specific demands and issues, are the most feasible form of coalition building across borders (Anheier and Themudo 2002; Tarrow and della Porta 2005).

Authors have relied often on the use of the term "networks" to describe this trend toward less hierarchical and more flexible forms of transnational collective action. This usage builds on the difference that organizational

---

[14] More specifically, the resource mobilization approach has seen the creation of organizations as an asset for social movements, and has argued that more resources, such as the appointment of professional staff, render social movement organizations more visible and more capable of reaching their goals. See, for example, McCarthy and Zald (1977).

sociologists establish between network forms of organization and market or hierarchically based governance structures (Powell 1990). In this conception, networks are distinct from centralized hierarchies because they are more horizontal, they have no chain of command or control, and therefore they are much more flexible and adaptable than hierarchical forms of organization. This understanding is similar to how activists have used the term, calling many coalitions "networks" as a way of emphasizing their horizontality, flexibility, and internal democracy. For these authors and practitioners, network forms of social organization represent "a superior social morphology for all human action" (Castells 2000:15) and are "becoming a signature element of global organizing" (Anheier and Themudo 2002: 191).

However, this metaphorical treatment of the concept of "networks" aprioristically establishes a superior form of organization and as a result turns our attention away from power relations, asymmetries, and conflicts among actors.[15] "Social networks" and "social network analysis," when used in this book, refer to the tradition of study of interactions in the social sciences over the last fifty years.[16] According to this tradition, whether transnational networks are formed by horizontal or by hierarchical relationships, and whether these lead to flexible governance arrangements or not, are empirical questions. Social network analysis tools, combined with qualitative information, help in determining whether actors have been successful in their efforts to build horizontal coalitions.

The fact remains, however, that CSOs have no clear organizational blueprint to follow at the transnational scale. They are torn between the need to ensure the continuity and efficiency of collective action by creating rules (and asymmetries) and the pressure to maintain horizontal relationships that entail respect for the autonomy and equality of participants. This is not, of course, a new dilemma.[17] In his classic study of the German Social Democratic Party, Robert Michels equated organization with oligarchy and linked routinized political engagement to political

---

[15] This critique has been made more in general to the turn in the sociology of organizations away from the Weberian model of bureaucratic organization and the analysis of relationships of domination, toward an emphasis on flexible organizations that can constantly redefine their outputs and internal structures, which ignores tensions among actors. See, for example, Melucci (1996: esp. 251).

[16] For an overview of the history of the development of social network analysis, see Freeman (2004).

[17] For an interesting review of debates that go back to nineteenth-century feminism, see Clemens (2005).

moderation. This remained a key issue of debate in the lives of socialist and communist parties throughout the twentieth century. In the period that preceded the Soviet Revolution, Vladimir Ilyich Lenin argued in favor of the creation of a hierarchical organization that would take the lead in the revolutionary struggle (Lenin 1969 [1902]). Current debates draw on these older discussions, but it is true that there is a growing disappointment with traditional forms of organizing in leftist organizations. The rise of so-called new social movements in the 1970s best illustrates this disillusionment.[18]

The same unresolved questions gain new contours in the more complex organizational environment of contemporary transnational collective action. For global civil society advocates, the focus is on the dilemmas faced by organizations "going global." In this respect, an important issue is internal democracy – for example, how to represent different regions of the world – and the impacts of globalization in organizational arrangements. These are certainly relevant questions, but the creation of global organizations is only a small part of the universe of transnational coalition-building initiatives. As Helmut Anheier and Nuno Themudo have demonstrated, although the number of international nongovernmental organizations increased steadily between 1981 and 2001, the most numerous organizational forms were found in the category "internationally-oriented national organizations" (Anheier and Themudo 2002: 194).

The case of challengers of trade agreements in the Americas illustrates the expansion and diffusion of new organizational pathways that vary considerably according to the site of activism and its duration. The participation in domestic chapters of transnational campaigns that focus on specific issues and are limited in time, such as the Campaign against the FTAA, provides great autonomy to members through loose structures and informal boundaries. On the other hand, coalitions that are based on campaigns tend to die as the issue that motivated their creation fades away from the agenda, or as their demands are met. Longer-term initiatives, such as the HSA, have to make tough decisions concerning membership and internal division of labor. However, these initiatives can provide sustained platforms for transnational collective action.

---

[18] The literature on "new social movements" argued that part of the novelty of these forms of collective action was the (commendable) rejection of hierarchical forms of organization and centralized decision-making structures. See, for example, Dalton (1994: esp. 8–9).

In sum, coalition building is not a linear process, whereby organizations are created and strengthened at the domestic level, only to, in a second stage, *spill over* into the transnational arena, moving toward the bottom right of Figure 2.2. There is no deterministic trend that goes from participating in an event coalition to becoming part of a global social movement or a transnational alliance. The choice of organizational pathways is less predictable than a progressive and unidirectional approach would make it, in part because these efforts often require the institutionalization of relationships simultaneously at both levels.

Making Claims and Building Projects in Transnational Collective Action

When CSOs participate in foreign policy debates, they are pressured to present alternative proposals and specific demands. This is true regardless of whether they act mainly at the domestic level or whether they populate the international arena. The pressure comes from parliamentarians, government officials, the media, and other CSOs. Of course, no single answer has been provided, for example, when activists are asked what should be the future of the WTO, or what kind of reforms would make the FTAA an acceptable agreement to them.

As much as coalition building, crafting common understandings is also a classic collective action challenge. In the 1980s, David Snow and his colleagues introduced the concept of "framing" into the study of social movements to understand how organizers present ideas in order to attract supporters and convey their messages (Snow et al. 1986; Snow and Benford 1988). In general terms, transnational framing has been easier as part of campaigns that rally opposition to a specific multilateral agreement, such as the MAI, than in cases when CSOs try to explain what they stand for and come up with alternative proposals.

True as this may be, however, attempts have been made to go beyond specific claims, reproaches, complaints, and accusations, in order to reach a coherent set of demands and norms that target longer-term changes in global governance. The ideational pathways shown in Figure 2.3 represent the different degrees to which actors participate in the debates about alternatives by domesticating frames, or by orienting them primarily to the international arena, and whether these consist of short-term claims or longer-term projects.

Actors may limit their role to supporting demands on short-term issues, which I call "claims." A good example is provided by the 2003

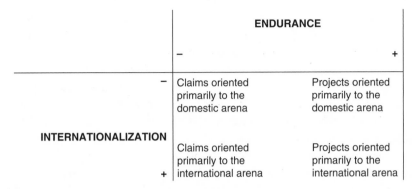

Figure 2.3. Ideational Pathways to Transnationality.

social movement against the Iraq War, which united a heterogeneous set of actors from various countries around an "extraordinarily simple platform" (Meyer and Corrigall-Brown 2005: 338) that opposed going to war at that moment. Alternatively, CSOs may decide to invest their resources in generating common ideational platforms aimed at more long-term changes, which I call "projects." As much as choosing among organizational pathways, different ideational choices also have specific political consequences. Claims and projects represent different sets of concerns, in terms of their depth as well as the degree of collaboration among actors that they demand. Project making implies negotiating and constructing common values, interests, and beliefs through time within a predefined set of actors. Claim making, on the other hand, implies finding common ground on more specific issues in a broader and often heterogeneous group of actors, as in the case of the Campaign against the MAI.

The debate about which is the best ideational pathway to be followed goes well beyond trade mobilizations. The largest global gathering of civil society actors, the World Social Forum (WSF), offers a good example. Since its first edition, most of the Forum's organizers have been opposed to the launching of final declarations and the drafting of a common agenda or list of demands. Their main argument has been that it is too hard to find relevant agreements in such a heterogeneous setting. Trying to do so would only generate fragmentation (Whitaker 2005). According to this perspective, having no common project is a good sign, and attempts to find one would lead the WSF to reproduce the model of the old Communist Internationals (Klein 2003; Adamovsky 2006). Thus, it is argued, it is best to maintain the Forum as a decentered space for debate and encounters that does not speak with one voice on any single issue. Both specific claims and projects are to be constructed by participants, but not in the name of the whole WSF.

This choice remains, however, very much at the core of the contentious debates about the future of the WSF, as some of the participants question its efficacy solely as a convener of movements and individuals. Proposals have been put forward for the Forum to establish a "minimum platform," which "would provide meaning and design for alternatives to neoliberal proposals" and escape the destiny "of becoming a showpiece for civil society" (Ramonet 2006). Whatever the result of this debate, it is certain that even if the WSF as such can withdraw from making claims and creating projects, the individuals and organizations that participate in it cannot.

The document *Alternatives for the Americas*, analyzed in the last part of the book, represents a rare example of an effort at building a common project at the transnational level within a heterogeneous coalition. Written by a group of organizations affiliated with the HSA, it is a "living document" that, in its various editions, put into writing alternative visions and proposals related to the debates about trade agreements, regional integration, and development. Although no necessary tendency exists for actors to go from making specific claims to building common projects, when a transnational alliance attempts to do so, as in the case of the HSA and its *Alternatives for the Americas*, scholars have a window of opportunity to look into the mechanisms through which actors try to achieve common ground in the long term, as well as their limits.

Pathways in Flux

In his historical analysis of labor internationalism, Eric Hobsbawn argued that "in the debate of political people, or ideologists, for whom nationalism or internationalism imply major political choices, the two concepts are regarded as mutually exclusive. ... But as a description of political behavior this is simply misconceived ... the development of mass working-class movements paradoxically creates both national consciousness and international ideology *simultaneously*" (Hobsbawn 1988: 13–14, emphasis in the original). Ronaldo Munck has made a similar point, arguing that actors often "strategize and operate simultaneously on the local and global levels, and 'in between,' refusing any debilitating binary oppositions" (Munck 2002: 359).

Although I accept the general argument made by these authors, it is also important to understand that CSOs do not always operate at various scales at the same time. They prioritize different sites and make choices with respect to the durability of their actions in specific contexts. Simply blurring the boundaries does not help us to understand why and how they make these choices.

Choices made are informed by each organization's history, but the pathway prioritized at a given point in time is also the result, as emphasized in this book, of the dynamic relational and political embeddedness of actors. Thus, choices and their impacts are not always predictable. However, it is possible to differentiate among four main types of relational mechanisms that help us analyze how actors attempt to make different choices compatible.

First, the *extension*, or amplification, of coalition-building strategies and frames, achieved by adding new allies and/or by incorporating other actors' grievances to one's claims or projects. It implies the coexistence of issues and tactics, but not necessarily a construction of enduring consensus or a transformation of previous interests. It allows actors to broaden their networks and do "multiple targeting" (Mische 2003), that is, aim toward different audiences and adversaries at the same time. Second, the opposite move, the *suppression* of allies, topics, goals, or tactics. "We agree to disagree" is the phrase that best summarizes this mechanism, when actors maintain their collaborative ties but refuse to discuss specific topics. It implies the construction of a minimum common denominator.

Third, the *diffusion* of organizational forms and ideas. New coalition-building strategies are emulated from one site to another, and with them come visions about what collective action should look like. Although diffusion can be nonrelational (such as through the media), in this book the focus will be on what Tarrow has called mediated and relational diffusion, variants that focus on the role played by social networks and brokers across space (Tarrow 2005: esp. ch. 6). Fourth, the *transformation* of coalition-building strategies and/or the content of claims and projects. This is the least common result of interactions, because it implies not only an adaptation, but also a change in the perception of agendas, goals, and self-interests, and the incorporation of new visions that were not present earlier for the actors.

These four mechanisms build partly upon the typology of frame alignment processes proposed by David Snow and his colleagues. According to them, frame alignment is defined as "the linkage of individual and social movement organizations' interpretive orientation, such that some set of individual interests, values and beliefs and social movement organizations' activities, goals and ideology are congruent and complementary" (Snow et al. 1986: 464). The typology proposed above is also an outcome of efforts by a group of people to fashion shared understandings of the world. However, the results of extension, suppression, diffusion, and transformation are not necessarily "congruent" and "complementary." These negotiated changes do not cancel out all conflicts, nor do they erase the power asymmetries among actors. Organizations still belong to multiple networks at different sites and social contexts, and these do not necessarily reinforce each other. Sometimes they generate contradictory pressures.

In this respect, the proposed typology is closest to the one developed by Ann Mische, who defined relational mechanisms "as means by which actors jockey over the multiple dimensions of their memberships, identities, and projects in order to build relations with other actors" (Mische 2003: 269). The difference between the mechanisms presented above and the ones proposed by Mische is that whereas she focuses her attention on "conversational mechanisms," the ones I identify are seen in a broader perspective, as constitutive of the pathways taken by actors. As the following chapter will show, extension, suppression, diffusion, and transformation can be seen not only through the analysis of discourses, but also through coalition-building strategies, the tactics implemented, and the ways in which CSOs frame their grievances and proposals.

PART TWO

The Politicization of Trade

3

The Contentious Nature of Trade Debates

Arguably, transnational collective action goes back as far as the creation of national borders themselves, but more immediate historical precursors of advocacy transnationalism include campaigns for women's suffrage (between 1888 and 1928) and the movement against foot binding in China (from 1874 to 1911) (Keck and Sikkink 1998: ch. 2). Other precedents include transnational political and ideological movements such as those led by organizations of anarchists, communists and socialists, faith-based movements and organizations, and labor collaboration that crossed national borders before and after Karl Marx and Friedrich Engel's famous call for the workers of the world to unite (Marx and Engels [1847] 1998).

The trade policy arena itself has historically been a contentious one, so much so that recent mobilizations cannot be seen as entirely innovative. It has also been a multifaceted arena. Because of the potential impacts of trade policies on productive systems, on the labor market, prices of goods, and technological innovation, decisions about trade have always been a part of broader economic and political debates about development models, international relations, and the role of the state. More specifically, the interfaces between trade and other policy arenas, such as the environment, food safety, or human rights, have not been ignored in the past. Furthermore, because of the fact that gains and losses from trade are unevenly distributed, the moral implications of trade have been an inseparable part of policy debates.[1]

Historical examples of the tensions arising from these interfaces abound, especially in debates about trade and human rights, trade and

---

[1] For a recent review of these debates and the proposal of a liberal theory of just trade, see Garcia (2003).

environmental protection, and trade and health issues. As early as 1890, the United States banned traded goods made by convict labor, a move that was followed by other countries. In 1880, European countries banned meat from the United States, based on food safety arguments, and the Fur Seal Treaty of 1911 regulated the hunting and importation of seals to avoid extermination (Aaronson 2001: 43–46).

Sometimes more than one of these issues intersected, as in the case of the London Matchgirls' Strike, which linked trade in a specific product to labor rights as well as to health issues. In 1888, 1,400 teenage girls and women from the Bryant & May match factory in London held a strike that was prompted by poor working conditions and health issues resulting from the use of a type of phosphorous in the production of the matches. This substance caused yellowing of the skin, hair loss, and phossy jaw, a form of bone cancer, eventually leading to death. Although phosphorous was banned in Sweden and in the United States, the British government argued that following their example would be an undue restraint on free trade.[2] Finally, in 1901, the factory announced that it had stopped using white phosphorous, and in 1906 signatories to the Berne Convention prohibited international trade in white phosphorous matches.

Governments officially acknowledged the link between the ability of countries to compete with each other and labor rights in the 1919 Preamble to the Constitution of the International Labor Organization (ILO), which stated: "the failure of any nation to adopt humane conditions of labour is an obstacle in the way of other nations which desire to improve the conditions in their own countries." Although the ILO has not had the necessary tools to effectively enforce the international harmonization of labor conditions, the need to promote a balance between competitiveness and respect for labor rights was in fact one of the motivations behind its creation (ILO 2006).

Perhaps the best-known instance of early trade-related transnational collective action did not deal with trade in goods, but with trade in persons: the transnational abolitionist movement that lasted from the end of the eighteenth century through the nineteenth century. It brought together antislavery activists in Europe and in the Americas, who engaged in intensive dialogue and collaboration. Much the same way as with current protests about trade, it is hard to understand that

---

[2] The summary of this story is based on the article by Peytavi (2003).

transnational movement without considering that it was based on previous connections between groups in different countries, most prominently the transnational religious ties between England and the United States.[3]

Other civil society groups, such as the environmentalists, mostly became interested in trade negotiations indirectly, through the filter of specific issues such as the trade in furs, or the protection of an animal species. Some of these negotiations had the participation of conservationists and naturalists who lobbied state officials at the domestic *as well as* at the transnational level (Aaronson 2001: 45).

In sum, trade has never been a purely economic issue, trade debates have never been limited exclusively to the establishment of tariffs and quotas, and, at specific moments, trade negotiations have sparked collective action and transnational alliances. In spite of these precedents, however, as early as about thirty years ago international trade had been an issue of interest mostly limited to government officials, international organizations (in the twentieth century), and – unevenly through time –those directly involved in manufacturing tradable products: farmers, business owners, and industrial workers. No global rules were in place to regulate international trade until after World War II.

In the mid-1970s, a new period began in the way states and civil society organizations (CSOs) perceived and debated international trade negotiations. The consolidation of a global trade regime changed dramatically the way in which international trade negotiations are carried out. Since then, notwithstanding the initiatives mentioned above, collective action on trade has been unprecedented, in terms of the amounts of collaboration as well as the amplitude of civil society sectors involved. This change happened in parallel to overall increasing levels of transnational collective action directed at various institutions and around specific issue areas. What is most interesting, as this chapter and the next will show, is that trade negotiations have become a pivotal arena, intersecting and overlapping with many of these other transnational mobilizations, and luring more and more CSOs that had not previously been interested in trade policies.

---

[3] Margaret Keck and Kathryn Sikkink explain that the backbone of the movement in the United States and in Britain was formed by Quakers, Methodists, Presbyterians, and Unitarians, who drew on a tradition of transatlantic ties that originated from before American independence (Keck and Sikkink 1998: 44).

The Creation of a Global Trade Regime and Civil Society Participation

The 1944 Bretton Woods Conference proposed the constitution of an International Trade Organization (ITO) to establish rules for multilateral trade. However, this proposal never passed the U.S. Senate. Instead, a much weaker organization, the General Agreement on Tariffs and Trade (GATT), became the institutional framework for global negotiations between 1947 and 1994.[4]

For most of the history of the GATT, groups of business organizations were almost the sole nonstate actors that followed its activities closely. Other sectors – labor and rural organizations, for example – focused their attention mainly at the domestic level. In spite of the fact that nongovernmental organizations (NGOs) participated in the conference that drafted the ITO Charter, and that this document included a provision for consultation and cooperation with NGOs, deliberations under the GATT were secretive (Charnovitz 2000). Moreover, during its first three decades, participation was limited because this was not truly a global organization. Developing countries considered the GATT mainly to be a forum controlled by developed nations. Although countries such as Brazil and Chile did become members early on, developing countries in general felt that the United Nations Conference on Trade and Development (UNCTAD), created in 1964, was the appropriate institutional channel to discuss trade policies and to voice their demands for a "New International Economic Order."[5]

Through the interface between trade and development, a few CSOs gained an early interest in the GATT and UNCTAD negotiations. One of them was GATT-Fly, an ecumenical coalition created in Canada in 1973 that was named after its desire to be a "bug" flying around governments, campaigning for trading prices that would benefit producers in developing countries. However, it focused less on monitoring these international organizations and more on direct action work in poverty and human rights projects in Southern countries, as one of its participants explained: "we came to realize that it wasn't enough to convert the powerful, but rather

---

[4] For an analysis of the unsuccessful history of the International Trade Organization, see, for example, Diebold (1993 [1952]).

[5] For different analyses of what the calls for a New International Economic Order represented, see, for example, Doyle (1983), Murphy (1984), and Krasner (1985).

we needed to begin trying to empower the powerless ... we realized that changing the price of sugar wasn't enough ... and that unless sugar workers in Brazil had the freedom to organize and freedom from repression, they weren't going to benefit."[6] The realization that siding with the governments of developing countries in demanding fairer prices for agricultural commodities was not necessarily going to bring effective results in terms of poverty reduction helps to explain the very limited interest of many civil society groups in trade negotiations during this period. Furthermore, most of CSOs' transnational linkages in the Americas between the mid-1960s and the mid-1980s focused primarily on the issue of human rights abuses in the dictatorships that plagued many Latin American countries.

Starting with the Kennedy Round of trade negotiations (1964–1967), members of the GATT began a progressive process of expansion of the negotiating agenda, which had, until then, been limited to reductions of tariffs. The Tokyo Round (1973–1979) introduced the negotiation of non-tariff barriers such as subsidies, national procurement, and health and regulatory standards, and the Uruguay Round (1986–1994) subsequently deepened this trend and broadened the agenda even more. This expansion of the scope of the negotiations coincided with the transitions to democracy in Latin America, and with a greater awareness on the part of CSOs of the domestic impacts of international trade negotiations.

The Uruguay Round represented a "wake-up" call to many actors, whereby "what had been sort of an apathetic attitude towards trade agreements quickly became a central issue."[7] In the United States, one of the first organizations to react was Public Citizen, a consumer rights organization. What first attracted its attention was the impact of trade agreements on what until then had been domestic public policy issues:

The original thing that actually did it was food issues. I went to a hearing in Congress on pesticides. My job was to say that the decent but not great bill was weak – because the opponent from the chemical company would testify that the bill was ridiculously strong. The bill would thus be positioned as a compromise. So, I said it was an outrageous bill, too weak, and the business guy ... simply said: "Well, you can't do what's in this bill, not under the Codex Alimentarious." Like two months later, I was working on a bill on beef labeling, something totally

---

[6] Dennis Hewlett, one of the participants of GATT-Fly, quoted in Laurie (1990: xx).
[7] Interview with John Dillon, representative of the Ecumenical Coalition for Economic Justice to the first Canada-Mexico Encuentro (organized in Mexico City in October 1990), Toronto, September 2004.

untrade related, theoretically. At a hearing, a Congressman argues that it's ridiculous that we don't have rule of origin labeled on beef ... and someone said "you can't do that, not under the GATT sanitary and phitosanitary protocols." And I said to myself: "why the fuck do the industry guys we are fighting keep talking about trade agreements?" ... People thought I was crazy ... because up until then trade only dealt with tariffs and quotas. Trade agreements had never dealt with domestic regulations. But in fact, the new agreements contained terms that provided a really powerful backdoor attack on almost everything we had been doing, on environment, consumer rights, safety.[8]

Perhaps the issue that best symbolized the possible regulatory impacts of this expanded agenda at the beginning of the 1990s was the tuna-dolphin dispute between Mexico and the United States, nicknamed by critics the "GATTzilla ate Flipper" moment in global trade governance (Wallach and Woodall 2004). This case was brought by Mexico against the United States because the U.S. Marine Mammal Protection Act set dolphin protection standards that were valid not only for its fishing fleet, but also for countries exporting fish caught in the Pacific Ocean to the United States. Because Mexico did not meet the protection standards, the United States embargoed all tuna imports from that country. Although the dispute panel ruled against the United States in 1991, this decision was not enforceable under the GATT rules.[9] It did, however, spark a discussion about the relationship between trade rules and domestic (and extra-territorial) environmental regulations that also became a part of the debates around the North American Free Trade Agreement (NAFTA) and, in fact, remains an important theme in current discussions about the global governance of trade.

Thus, when the World Trade Organization (WTO) was created in 1995, a wide group of civil society actors from developed and developing countries alike had come to the conclusion that trade negotiations must be

---

[8] Interview with Lori Wallach, Director, Global Trade Watch, Public Citizen, Washington D.C., September 2005. Other organizations working on food safety issues also point to the discussions about a new law on food labeling in the U.S. Congress in 1990, and the subsequent complaints by the European Union that it represented a trade barrier, as the moment in which they began to follow international trade negotiations. See Silverglade (1999). The U.S.-based International Agricultural and Trade Policy (IATP) was one of the first organizations to call the attention of organizations in the United States and in other countries to what was being discussed in the GATT negotiations.

[9] Under the GATT dispute settlement rules, a report was only adopted if there was consensus among all members. Under the new WTO Dispute Settlement Body, on the contrary, rulings are automatically adopted, and a consensus is required in order to reject them.

closely followed. The greater powers of the WTO, its expanded agenda, and its broader membership,[10] in comparison with the GATT, helped to justify this attention. Not only did this new organization continue the expansion of its agenda to other policy areas, but it also gained new regulatory powers through the creation of a more efficient and stronger dispute settlement mechanism than the one that existed under the GATT, the extension of the Trade Policy Review Mechanism (which, under the GATT, was limited to reviewing members' policies on trade in goods but under the WTO also reviews public policies on services and intellectual property), and the development of a set of mandatory codes (Williams 2005). The transition from the GATT to the WTO represented the culmination of the process of creation of a global trade regime, with established sets of rules, rights, and practices that changed the interaction dynamics between states and nonstate actors.

The increased scrutiny of trade negotiations and the critiques about the lack of transparency and accountability made during the Uruguay Round of the GATT led governments to include a provision that allowed for consultation and cooperation with nongovernmental organizations (Charnovitz 2000; Wilkinson 2005). In 1996, the WTO General Council decided to allow NGOs to attend the biannual Ministerial Conferences, after going through an accreditation process.

Figure 3.1 presents the evolution of participation in the six WTO Ministerials that were organized between 1996 and 2005. It is based on official lists of NGOs accredited by the WTO to participate in each Ministerial, which include business organizations, labor unions, consumer organizations, environmental groups, academic institutions, development NGOs, and human rights NGOs. It is clear from the figure that interest in participating has grown exponentially over time. Although only 108 organizations were accredited to participate in the Singapore Ministerial in 1996, almost ten times more – 1,066 – were accredited to participate in the Hong Kong Ministerial in December 2005. This growing trend was interrupted only momentarily by the Doha Ministerial, in 2001, but that can be explained by the greater obstacles to travel there (if compared to the meeting organized in Seattle, for example) and by the fact that it happened only two months after the terrorist attacks of 9/11 in New York and

---

[10] The GATT was originally signed by twenty-three countries; at its last meeting in 1994 it had 128 signatories. In 2009, the WTO had 153 members (www.wto.org, last accessed September 24, 2009).

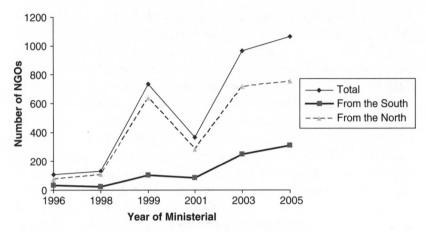

Figure 3.1. NGOs Eligible to Attend WTO Ministerials.
Source: Author's elaboration, based on lists of NGOs eligible to attend Ministerials provided by the WTO (www.wto.org/english/forums_E/ngo_E/ngo_E.htm, accessed March 1, 2006).

Washington, D.C., and not because of a decrease in interest (Wilkinson 2005: 170).

Figure 3.1 also shows that most of the organizations eligible to attend WTO Ministerials came from developed countries. Nonetheless, in the period studied there was a clear tendency for this gap to narrow: whereas in Seattle (1999) the relative participation of organizations from developing countries was of only 13.68 percent of the total, in Doha (2001) it increased to 23.28 percent, in Cancun (2003) it was 25.82 percent, and, finally, in Hong Kong (2005) it reached 29.17 percent of the total number of NGOs. It remains to be seen whether this trend will continue as strongly, especially if future Ministerials are organized in developed countries (with greater obstacles in terms of distance and the financial resources necessary for Southern organizations to participate).[11] However, if analyzed together with the findings in this book, which show an increased level of activism on the part of Latin American CSOs, it becomes clear that the tendency for Southern actors to have a more important presence in trade negotiations is not a temporary phenomenon.

---

[11] The facts that the WTO headquarters are located in Geneva and that most of the negotiations between Ministerials are held in that city also restrict the ability of Southern organizations that have scarce resources to follow up on these negotiations.

Beyond their place of origin, there is great heterogeneity among CSOs with respect to the positions advocated in these fora. As argued before, the traditional distinction between two antagonistic sets of actors, protectionists and free traders, does not reflect the reality accurately, simply because it oversimplifies and distorts the debate (Destler and Balint 1999; Aaronson 2001; Kelly and Grant 2005). Other dichotomies, such as pro– and anti–free trade, or pro- and anti-globalization, suffer from similar shortcomings.

In terms of their support or opposition to the WTO, CSOs are roughly divided into four groups: (1) those that support the global agenda of negotiations in general (but from various positions and based on different motivations); (2) those that are critical of some aspects of the WTO's role but are broadly supportive of the notion of a multilateral organization that regulates trade liberalization; (3) those that are highly critical of the WTO but seek to engage with it and with member states in an effort to bring about change; and (4) the so-called abolitionists, who argue that there is no solution other than abolishing the WTO and creating something new in its place (Said and Desai 2003; Wilkinson 2005; Williams 2005). Even this last group, however, does not present its position in "anti–free trade" terms. Furthermore, actors' positions with respect to the WTO are not necessarily reproduced in other negotiating arenas. As will be discussed in the following chapters, many CSOs that are highly critical of the WTO are at the same time broadly supportive of specific regional negotiations.

In this new context of trade negotiations, the traditional scholarly focus on the role of labor, capital, states, and international organizations became insufficient to analyze collective action around trade. The increased politicization of trade debates makes theories in the political economy literature that try to explain the formation of domestic coalitions based on factor endowments incomplete, at best.[12] Similarly, explanations of

---

[12] For example, Rogowski's model purports to explain domestic coalitions based on the different factor endowments across countries. The three factors he takes into consideration are labor, capital, and land. See Rogowski (1989). Midford argued that Rogowski's model failed to make adequate predictions, but limited his critiques to the way factors are measured, not going beyond the basic model (see Midford 1993). Similarly, Hiscox contributed to the sophistication of the model by focusing on the impacts of inter-industry factor mobility to better understand variation in coalition building; in the analysis presented about the passage of the NAFTA in the U.S. Congress, however, the author does not even mention the participation in the debates of groups other than labor, farm, and business (see Hiscox 2002: esp. 69–70 for the analysis of NAFTA debates).

collective action that ignore the impacts of actors' embeddedness in social networks in the constitution of interests can hardly explain how heterogeneous groups of actors have come together to influence trade negotiations and the variety of positions that coexist.

Nowhere has this new period in the history of trade negotiations and collective action been lived more intensely than in the Americas. The parallel negotiations of NAFTA and the Common Market of the South (MERCOSUR), analyzed in the next chapter, illustrate the different pathways to transnationality taken by actors during the early period of these debates in the region.

4

New Regionalism in the Americas

At the end of the 1980s, the Americas became an important laboratory for new trade negotiations. Debates about trade liberalization were not, however, unknown to the region. The idea of free trade between the United States and Canada was over a century old when the two countries signed their free trade agreement in 1989. Similarly, the history of Latin America is punctuated by failed attempts to fulfill what many saw – at least rhetorically – as its "historical calling," that is, to become united as one country. The first round of attempts at integration in the nineteenth century – some of which included the United States –collapsed under the weight of geographical distances, the power of *caudillos* (local strongmen), and the differing interests of the subregions.[1]

A second round of attempts to integrate the region began in the 1950s, as part of a development strategy that aimed at industrializing Latin America. Between the 1950s and the mid-1980s, the United States and Latin America pursued antagonistic trade policies. Whereas in the United States the years following the Second World War inaugurated a period of trade liberalization, in Latin America this was the age of protectionism. Both of these strategies were influenced by the Cold War. In the United States, free trade was perceived as an important part of its anticommunist strategies, whereas in Latin America protectionist policies were considered a key tool in reaching autonomous economic development.

The technical justifications for Latin America's protectionism were provided by the Economic Commission for Latin America and the Caribbean

---

[1] There is a large literature that discusses this "historical calling" and the causes of the ultimate fragmentation of Latin America in several countries after the wars of independence. See, for example, Furtado (1976, esp. the first part), Lambert (1968), and Bethell (1985).

(ECLAC), which, based on a critique of classic trade theory inspired by Keynesianism, argued that the specialization of the region in primary products was detrimental to its development because of the tendency of the terms of trade of these products (in relation to manufactured products produced by developed countries) to deteriorate through time. This critique led the ECLAC group to propose autonomous development policies based on a strong role of states in promoting the industrialization of the region, through the extensive use of protectionist measures. This development model, known as the import-substitution industrialization strategy, became dominant in Latin America between the 1950s and 1970s.[2] The many regional integration initiatives dating from this period[3] were considered an essential part of it, because greater regional integration would provide incipient industries with access to the larger markets that they needed. In spite of the progress made by some initiatives in liberalizing trade in the region, by the end of the 1970s negotiations were stalled.[4]

Civil society participation varied considerably across the region during this period. Even if most U.S. citizens remained oblivious of trade negotiations, labor and business organizations did participate actively in the debates promoted by Congress (Aaronson 2001: 85). In Latin America, however, trade negotiations remained a black box, accessed almost exclusively by a small circle of national bureaucrats and international organization officials. This would change only with the transitions to democracy in the region.

Between the mid-1980s and the end of the 1990s, trade policies in the United States and Latin America increasingly converged, and a new wave

[2] For the most important documents outlining the import-substitution industrialization strategy and its interface with regionalization in Latin America, see CEPAL (1949, 1959), and Prebisch (1964). For a review of ECLAC's economic and political thought in its first fifty years of history, see Bielschowsky (1998).

[3] In 1960, Guatemala, El Salvador, Honduras, and Nicaragua launched the Central American Common Market (later joined by Costa Rica); also in 1960, Argentina, Bolivia, Brazil, Chile, Colombia, Ecuador, Mexico, Paraguay, Peru, Uruguay, and Venezuela signed the Montevideo Treaty that created the Latin American Free Trade Association; in 1969 the Andean Pact was signed by Bolivia, Colombia, Chile, Ecuador, Peru, and Venezuela; and in 1973 the Caribbean Community and Common Market (CARICOM) was established by Barbados, Guyana, Jamaica, and Trinidad & Tobago (and later expanded to Antigua, British Honduras, Dominica, Grenada, Saint Lucia, Montserrat, St. Kitts/Nevis/Anguilla, and St. Vincent).

[4] There is a large literature on these initiatives and why they failed. See, for example, Urquidi (1993).

of agreements was negotiated within an ideological framework given by neoliberal economic policies. Under the U.S. leadership, the "new regionalism" consisted mainly of the negotiation of free trade areas, but with extended agendas that went much beyond trade liberalization. In this context, the traditional understanding of free trade areas in regional integration theory as the first phase of trade liberalization in an ever-widening process that would lead to the formation of a customs union, a common market, and eventually an economic union (Balassa 1961) was no longer useful.

Free trade agreements negotiated in the 1990s in the Americas liberalized trade at the same time that they included specific elements of domestic policy harmonization that are typical of the formation of a customs union or of a common market. As shown in Table 4.1, since the North American Free Trade Agreement (NAFTA) these agreements have included clauses on investor-state dispute settlement, intellectual property rights, labor rights, and environmental protection. They have remained silent, however, with respect to issues such as freedom of movement of labor and a common external tariff.

The exceptions to this trend were a few South–South initiatives that maintained the ambition to follow the European Union example and eventually constitute a common market. The Common Market of the South (MERCOSUR) and older integration processes that governments tried to reactivate in the 1990s, such as the Andean Community, relied, if not on the economic reasoning, at least on the political arguments advocated by ECLAC to justify Latin American integration as a way of strengthening the region's autonomy and political power in the international system. In an attempt to bring together these initiatives, in 2008 twelve South American governments signed a treaty creating the Union of South American Nations (Unión de Naciones Suramericanas – UNASUR). Civil society organizations (CSOs) did not react in the same way to these different models of regional liberalization.

Different Civil Society Responses to NAFTA and MERCOSUR

The first of the new wave of free trade agreements signed was the Canada–U.S. Free Trade Agreement (CUSFTA), negotiated between May 1986 and October 1987. For the first time, a broad set of CSOs followed these negotiations closely. The Pro-Canada Network, created in 1987, brought together an unprecedented variety of sectors to challenge this free trade

Table 4.1. *Issues on the Agenda of Selected Agreements (1989–2006)*

Agreement and Date of Entry into Force	MERCOSUR 1991	Canada–U.S. FTA 1989	NAFTA 1994*	U.S.–Chile FTA 2004	CAFTA 2006**
Type	Common market	Free trade agreement	Free trade agreement	Free trade agreement	Free trade agreement
Tariff elimination	■	■	■	■	■
Common external tariff	■				
Rules of origin	■	■	■	■	■
Technical barriers to trade	■	■	■	■	■
Investment	■		■	■	■
Investor-state dispute settlement	■		■	■	■
Services	■	■	■	■	■
Migration	■				
Intellectual property rights	■		■	■	■
Public procurement	■	■	■	■	■
Dispute settlement	■	■	■	■	■
Labor			SA***	■	■
Environment			SA	■	■

* North American Free Trade Agreement; ** Central American Free Trade Agreement; *** Side Agreement.

Sources: Table adapted from Devlin and Giordano (2004: 150); OAS Foreign Trade Information System; www.aladi.org; www.ustr.gov.

negotiation: women's organizations, faith-based groups, labor unions, environmentalists, artists' groups, and human rights organizations (Ayres 1998; Bleyer 2001).

The debate about the CUSFTA remained, however, mainly confined to the domestic arena. Canadian activists did try to reach out to U.S. CSOs, but they failed to convince them of the importance of the agreement. As one of the participants at the time explains, Canadian organizations relied on their previous ties to their institutional equivalents in the United States to try to find allies:

We simply used historic relations … like in any human endeavor, one goes with the networks that one is familiar with. So, with the obvious links, CLC [Canadian Labour Congress] and AFL-CIO [American Federation of Labor–Congress of Industrial Organizations], environmental movements, as you know, are international, so they would talk to each other, and, for research groups like us, the Institute for Policy Studies (IPS) and Development-GAP were in many ways allies that we knew from other work.[5]

These attempts were frustrating, however, as John Cavanagh, director of the Washington-based Institute for Policy Studies (IPS), recounts:

In the mid-1980s I began to receive calls from Canadian groups saying "there's this terrible thing being proposed, that will be the CUSFTA. We want to come to the U.S., have meetings about it. Can you convene people?" So they would come, these big delegations of Canadians, and I would try to convene people, and nobody was interested.… I spent a great deal of time being embarrassed.[6]

Around the same time that Canadians were traveling to the United States in exasperating attempts to find partners to fight against the CUSFTA, in South America labor organizations that would later on become key actors in the MERCOSUR negotiations were also looking for transnational allies. Even though Argentina, Brazil, and Uruguay had signed agreements to reduce tariffs in 1986, trade was not on their agenda at the time. The primary goal of organizations that formed the Coordination of Southern Cone Labor Federations that same year was to push transitions to democracy forward, especially in Paraguay and Chile. Their second goal was to develop common actions against the payment of developing countries' foreign debts. Not much thought was given to the

---

[5] Interview with John Dillon, representative of the Ecumenical Coalition for Economic Justice to the first Canada-Mexico Encuentro (organized in Mexico City in October 1990), Toronto, September 2004.

[6] Interview with John Cavanagh, Director of the IPS, Washington, D.C., July 2004.

trade agreements that had been signed. The new organization had the support of the International Confederation of Free Trade Unions (ICFTU) and of its regional affiliate, the Inter-American Regional Organization of Workers (Organización Regional Interamericana de Trabajadores – ORIT), which were interested in gaining more presence in the region but did not consider trade agreements one of their priorities either.[7]

Between the end of the 1980s and the launching of the NAFTA and MERCOSUR negotiations at the beginning of the 1990s, an important change happened, which led to increased mobilization of CSOs in both regions. In spite of the coincidence that different CSOs in different countries mobilized at roughly the same time, the processes that explain this common movement differ. In North America, change is linked to the existence of the CUSFTA precedent (especially the accumulated experience of Canadian civil society), to the early alarms sounded by U.S. and Canadian CSOs on the GATT negotiations, and, perhaps most importantly, to the widespread fears triggered by the inclusion of Mexico in the U.S.–Canada free trade area. In South America, change is linked to the new opportunities for participation that were brought about by the transitions to democracy, to the need to find new development strategies, and to the precedent of regional collaboration among labor organizations through the Coordination of Southern Cone Labor Federations.

In fact, these initiatives represent very different instances of the same impetus toward the creation of regional blocks. The stories of civil society participation in the two regions allow us to consider the origins of ties among CSOs and to compare the narratives and strategies that inform action on trade at different sites.

The Search for Allies in the NAFTA Region

When the proposal to include Mexico in the Canada–U.S. free trade area was made known, in 1990, Canadian CSOs once again called John Cavanagh at IPS in Washington. This time, Cavanagh succeeded in bringing together two strands of organizations that had up to then worked on separate tracks: environmental and agriculture groups that had become interested in the GATT negotiations, and labor, human rights, and religious groups that had worked together on debt-related issues

---

[7] At that time, the only ICFTU affiliate in the region was the Argentinian CGT. Interview with the then Secretary General of ORIT, Víctor Báez Mosqueira, Belo Horizonte, December 2004.

and/or on peace negotiations and human rights in Central America during the 1970s and 1980s.[8] By then, interest in free trade negotiations was already growing because of the greater awareness of the impacts of the proposed extended agenda, and because the inclusion of a developing country represented a great source of anxiety for various sectors in the United States. As Brooks and Fox have argued, "NAFTA put a specifically *brown* face on the perceived trade threat" (Brooks and Fox 2002: 4, note 7, emphasis in the original).

In spite of a common interest in the negotiations, however, transnational coalition building in the region was not an easy task. The support given by sectors of U.S. civil society to the U.S. government's Cold War policies in Latin America had created a general distrust among potential allies. Thus, when U.S. organizations looked to the South for collaboration in their challenges to the NAFTA negotiations, they encountered some of the same difficulties the Canadians had a few years earlier, for different reasons. Many actors felt as if they were looking around for the first time:

I will never forget our first meeting without the Canadians. We sat there and said: "OK, who knows people in Mexico?" And basically we did not know anyone in Mexico. ... It was shocking. Here we were, in 1990, and with some of the best non-profits in the country, and people didn't know anything about our two neighbors.[9]

There were previous ties among actors in the three countries, but these were limited to a relatively small group of organizations and individuals in specific issue areas that, at least until then, had not been trade related. Of the seventy-one CSOs from Mexico and the United States included in this study, less than one-third had collaborative ties with organizations in the other country before the 1990s.[10]

The most institutionalized pre-NAFTA ties were those among labor organizations that shared membership in the International Confederation of Free Trade Unions (ICFTU), which linked the three key national labor federations: American Federation of Labor–Congress of Industrial Organizations (AFL-CIO), the Confederation of Mexican Workers (Confederación de Trabajadores de México – CTM), and the Canadian Labour Congress (CLC). A second network existed around organizations

---

[8] Interview with John Cavanagh, Director of the IPS, Washington, D.C., July 2004.
[9] Ibid.
[10] See Appendix A for the list of organizations.

that were working on human rights issues and democracy in Latin America, which brought together faith-based organizations, human rights organizations, and groups of exiles. A third network was constituted by organizations working on development and debt issues in Latin America, a fourth linked organizations in Mexico working on immigration issues with Latino groups in the United States,[11] and, finally, a fifth involved a variety of forms of collaboration among independent labor organizations.[12] There were also a myriad of contacts among organizations on the U.S.–Mexico border,[13] and, of course, informal relationships among academics, friends, and political leaders from the three countries.

The first network turned out to be a deterrent, instead of a facilitator, in this first effort at relationship building, because of the strong disagreements among ICFTU members on how to respond to NAFTA. The CTM and others linked to the Mexican Labor Congress decided to support the negotiations, in spite of many attempts by their counterparts in the United States and Canada to convince them otherwise. In this context, other links among labor organizations proved to be more fruitful. Most importantly, the Confederation of National Unions (Confédération des Syndicats Nationaux – CSN) in Québec had a long-standing relationship with a small independent Mexican organization, the Authentic Labor Front (Frente Auténtico del Trabajo – FAT), which became the only Mexican labor organization to side with other Mexican, Canadian, and U.S. CSOs in their critique of NAFTA (Hathaway 2000).

Other types of preexisting ties also were fertile. Canadian faith-based groups, some of which had been debating the impacts of international trade since GATT-Fly was created in the 1970s, played an important role in activating previous ties. Their relationships in Mexico, however, had been built in the context of their work on human rights and peace

---

[11] Interview with Juan Manuel Sandoval, Seminario Permanente de Estudios Chicanos y de Fronteras, Mexico City, August 2005.

[12] For example, some independent unions from the auto sector in Mexico had solidarity ties with United Auto Worker locals in the United States that were in opposition to the UAW national leadership.

[13] Some of the oldest ties in the Mexico–U.S. border were those between the American Friends Service Committee, a Quaker-founded organization from Philadelphia, and border groups working on community development and immigrant and *maquila* workers' rights since the 1930s. During the Canada–U.S. Free Trade Agreement negotiations, a group of labor, environmental, and ecumenical actors created Common Frontiers, a Canadian organization that investigated the impact on Canada of the *maquiladoras* in the Mexican northern border. When the NAFTA negotiations began, they had established relationships with different groups on the border (Ayres 1998: 123).

negotiation processes in Central America and did not touch on trade or economic issues. In the early 1990s, they reached out to a former Mexican Jesuit, whom they knew because a member of the Canadian Jesuit Center attended the Marxist course he used to teach to Guatemalan exiles in Mexico City on Saturday mornings.[14] This former Jesuit had also begun to shift agendas, becoming an active participant in the early debates about NAFTA in Mexico. Through him and his Canadian friends, at least part of the network built around human rights was redirected to trade negotiations, and reconfigured to link different actors.

This mixture of both formal and informal ideological, religious, and category-based ties allowed CSOs to establish initial contacts to talk about NAFTA in the three countries. When Presidents Carlos Salinas de Gortari and George Bush formally announced that they would begin negotiations, in June 1990, groups of organizations from the three countries were already meeting.

Even among actors that had a similar approach to the negotiation of NAFTA, however, consensus and trust were hard to reach. Although most Canadian CSOs simply opposed the negotiations, their Mexican allies argued that the best strategy, in light of their country's specific political situation, would be to propose changes to the agreement and to demand greater transparency in the negotiations (RMALC 1993). Furthermore, many U.S. and Canadian organizations chose a domestic strategy that alienated potential friends, especially in Mexico, because it was based on a nationalist discourse that often "failed to even consider how their harsh and categorical criticisms sounded to the people of Mexico" (French 1994: 121).

In contrast with the Southern Cone, in the NAFTA region the networks built by challengers of the agreement did not lead to institutionalized forms of transnational coalition building. There was, however, innovation in the repertoire of organization, which was possible because of the diffusion of the Pro-Canada Network coalition mode to the other two countries. Its first offspring were the Mexican Action Network on Free Trade (Red Mexicana de Acción Frente al Libre Comercio – RMALC) and the U.S. Alliance for Responsible Trade (ART). As will be seen later on in this book, similar coalitions would be created in other countries during the Free Trade Area of the Americas (FTAA) negotiations. Although

---

[14] Interview with Joseph Gunn, Director of Social Affairs at the Canadian Conference of Catholic Bishops, Ottawa, September 2004.

these organizations were unable to stop the implementation of NAFTA or even to change the agreement in significant ways, they provided an organizational blueprint that inspired many other actors.

Innovative (but Limited) Transnational Collaboration in the Southern Cone

The literature on trade and civil society in the Americas has paid most of its attention to NAFTA and its lessons. However, the case of the Common Market of the South (MERCOSUR) is also important, for three main reasons. For the first time, a group of labor organizations built and sustained transnational ties to try to influence a regional integration process in the Southern Cone. Differently from how most of the labor movement dealt with NAFTA in North America, in the MERCOSUR region labor decided to support the integration process. Finally, and, again, in contrast with what happened in North America, labor and business organizations were able to open spaces of participation in an unprecedented way in the history of trade negotiations in Latin America.[15]

CSOs from the MERCOSUR countries stood against a new political and economic background as negotiations began. The mid-1980s were characterized by the transitions from military dictatorships to democracy, and thus by a greater opening for the participation of CSOs in public debate. At the same time, the 1980s are known in all of Latin America as "the lost decade" in terms of economic progress. This context of political transition and economic crisis helped build a basic consensus among labor leaders, one that was also shared by government officials and many business representatives: that a Southern Cone integration process could bring more development to the region, could help consolidate the newly reborn national democracies, and could strengthen the political and economic positions of the region in the international system.[16]

---

[15] As early as 1991, the three governments approved the participation of "the private sector," that is, the representatives of organizations "with direct interest in any of the phases of the process of production, distribution and consumption" (article 29 of the Internal By-Law of the Common Market Group), as observers in the preparatory meetings of the negotiating subgroups. Labor and business representatives also participate in the tripartite Social-Laboral Commission that was created as an outcome of the MERCOSUR Social-Labor Declaration of 1998. Furthermore, CSOs constitute the Economic and Social Consultative Forum, established in 1995 as an official MERCOSUR forum.

[16] Maria Sílvia Portella, an advisor to CUT/Brazil for MERCOSUR since 1991, argues that one of the motivations of labor organizations participating in the MERCOSUR

This basic consensus was not, however, an automatic reaction to the integration process by CSOs from the region. Even though previous ties existed among actors in Argentina, Brazil, Uruguay, and Paraguay, at first organizations that became interested in the integration process had as much difficulty finding transnational allies as those in the NAFTA region. As one of the advisors on MERCOSUR to the Unified Workers' Federation (Central Única dos Trabalhadores – CUT), the main Brazilian labor federation, recalls:

> The embryo of the MERCOSUR labor network was formed during the dictatorships, because Uruguayan exiles created a labor coordination that functioned in my office in São Paulo. ... In 1982, we sent a labor mission to Uruguay ... to protest against the lack of freedom of association. It was the first international experience for most of those involved. ... I think it was the first MERCOSUR political action. In Argentina we could not do the same, because we did not have the same political relationships. The political exiles that I met from Argentina in Brazil were not from labor unions, they were from political parties. Even so, through them I was able to find people with whom we could establish ... more permanent and trustworthy relationships.[17]

In the new context of democratization, there was a shift from transnational work that tied together human rights activists, pro-democracy actors, and militants in political parties that opposed dictatorships, to transnational work based on a broader agenda that included trade agreements and that brought together a set of actors that did not necessarily overlap consistently with these previous networks. In 1990, the same year that a trilateral group of CSOs challenged the NAFTA negotiators for the first time, the Coordination of Southern Cone Labor Federations consolidated the change in its agenda, from focusing on the fight against authoritarian regimes to influencing the Southern Cone regional integration.

Labor Collaboration in "Critical Support" of MERCOSUR

In December 1991, the Coordination of Southern Cone Labor Federations issued its first official declaration on MERCOSUR, signed by the most

---

debates was to strengthen the transitions to democracy; this challenge, parallel to the economic challenges that came with neoliberal reforms that were being implemented in different rhythms in the four countries, provided labor organizations with a common agenda. See Portella de Castro (2002).

[17] Interview with Maria Sílvia Portella de Castro, CUT-Brazil's consultant, Washington, D.C., January 2005.

important labor federations in six countries (Argentina, Bolivia, Brazil, Chile, Paraguay, and Uruguay).[18] This declaration spelled out the position of "critical support" at which the labor organizations had arrived at the national level: they criticized the way governments were handling the process but simultaneously reaffirmed the confidence in the potential of the integration for the development of the region (broadly defined to include social and cultural aspects). Indeed, these labor organizations presented themselves as "the true defenders" of Latin American integration (Smith and Healey 1994: 84).

This position was the result of a contentious debate, however, both within domestic borders and among the national labor federations themselves. The need for regional integration has been part of the rhetoric of the labor movement in Latin America for a long time, presented as a means of achieving greater autonomous development for the region. In the MERCOSUR case, labor organizations argued that the integration process could be an effective means of guaranteeing less dependence for the region in the international system. This is precisely the reverse of the framing used by the CLC and by the Mexican FAT, which portrayed the integration in North America through NAFTA as a threat to their countries' national sovereignty and domestic growth. Furthermore, labor leaders in the Southern Cone knew that the integration process could lead to further transnationalization of firms, and were afraid of losing power by ignoring this trend.[19] The fact that MERCOSUR was proposed as a future common market, and not merely as the creation of a free trade area, gave labor organizations a horizon of many years of negotiation on delicate issues such as labor mobility, a process they felt they could not be excluded from.

Supporting MERCOSUR, however, meant supporting a process with no guarantee that unions would be heard, or have any kind of influence. It also meant supporting an initiative that was seen by some actors as beneficial only to big corporations. The Uruguayan national labor organization PIT-CNT was probably the first to put MERCOSUR on its agenda, to affirm its critical support, and to demand a seat at the negotiating table

---

[18] The signatories were the Argentinian General Workers' Confederation (CGT), the Bolivian Workers' Federation (COB), the Brazilian Unified Workers' Federation (CUT) and General Workers' Confederation (CGT), the Chilean Unitary Workers' Federation (CUT), the Paraguayan Unitary Workers' Central (CUT), and the Uruguayan Interunion Workers' Assembly–National Workers' Confederation (PIT-CNT).

[19] Interview with Maria Silvia Portella de Castro, CUT-Brazil's Consultant, Washington, D.C., January 2005.

(Portella de Castro 1994). Even in this case, though, an important minority within Uruguay's labor movement argued that MERCOSUR could not be changed from within because of its inherent "neoliberal logic." A vote on the organization's critical support stance won by a small margin against the proposal to oppose the agreement.[20]

A similar debate happened within CUT-Brazil as well, but there was a weaker opposition to the MERCOSUR project in the Brazilian labor movement. Thanks to previous bilateral ties, PIT-CNT's position had an influence on CUT's first reactions to the integration treaty (Portella de Castro 1994). Both, however, denounced the antidemocratic character of the negotiations and the privileging of trade liberalization deals to the detriment of the implementation of policies that would favor the economic and social development of the region. They also argued that the proposed integration model benefited mainly transnational corporations, and that negotiators did not consult national business representatives properly before making decisions. According to these actors, the potentially negative consequences of the integration process for workers were: rise in unemployment, worsening of working conditions, further threats in terms of violations of labor rights, and deregulation of collective relations (CUT 1991).

In Argentina, the main national-level labor organization, the General Workers' Confederation (Confederación General de Trabajadores – CGT), was the first to propose the inclusion of labor representatives in decision-making arenas, through the creation of a negotiating group dedicated to debating labor issues.[21] Its initial reaction to MERCOSUR reflected the preoccupation with the asymmetries between Argentinean and Brazilian labor costs, and thus it demanded that the issue of harmonization of labor laws be included in the agenda of negotiations (CGT 1992). Only in the case of Paraguay did the national labor organizations, led by the Unitary Workers' Central (Central Unitaria de Trabajadores – CUT-Paraguay), demand the temporary exclusion of the country from MERCOSUR. This position was based on the perceived absence of protective measures to prepare its (much smaller) economy to compete with its neighbors. Even in this case, though, CUT-Paraguay estimated that, in general terms, MERCOSUR was a positive initiative (Pecci 1994).

[20] Interview with Álvaro Padrón, PIT-CNT, Montevideo, Uruguay, November 1999.
[21] Interview with Maria Sílvia Portella de Castro, advisor to CUT-Brazil, Washington, D.C., January 2005.

A second regional labor coalition that participated in the MERCOSUR debates was formed by the Christian Democrat unions, gathered around the Latin American Workers' Federation (Central Latinoamericana de Trabajadores – CLAT), which was affiliated to the World Confederation of Labor. This organization had members in the four MERCOSUR countries, but it had much less of a presence than ORIT. A few other civil society sectors followed MERCOSUR negotiations in a less sustained way throughout the 1990s, without creating common transnational spaces.[22] In fact, the one regional process in the Americas that had an ambitious integration agenda and that opened limited but important spaces for civil society participation did not capture the attention of a diverse set of civil society groups. Until the first years of the twenty-first century, groups of labor and business organizations remained the civil society actors with the most sustained and institutionalized participation in MERCOSUR fora.

This lack of interest by organizations whose counterparts in North America were at this point highly involved in the NAFTA debates, such as environmental organizations, is partly due to the haunting of past failures of Latin American integration initiatives. Few believed that MERCOSUR would succeed, and the fact that recurrent crises have led to successive postponements of integration goals have given these skeptics some reason. Furthermore, participating in such a long-term negotiation required from CSOs a considerable amount of resources, both financial and human. The lack of financial resources to travel to meetings organized in four different countries and the understanding that the governments of the region could not find consensus on a significant agenda with civil society participation were the main reasons given by environmental organizations to justify their very limited participation.[23] The next parts of this book will show

---

[22] The partial exception to that are Uruguayan consumers' organizations, which have participated in a sustained way but mostly at the domestic level (Padrón 1998). For some time, women's organizations became involved in the negotiations for the creation of a Specialized Women's Meeting, and environmental organizations went to the Environmental Subgroup meetings, but this participation was not sustained. More recently, small farmers' organizations have begun to participate actively in the Specialized Meeting on Family-Based Agriculture, and to coordinate positions transnationally.

[23] A few CSOs from Brazil, Argentina, and Uruguay participated in the subgroup in charge of discussing environmental policies during the 1990s, but not in a sustained or coordinated way. From Brazil, the most active participants were CUT-Brazil, the National Industry Confederation (CNI), and World Wildlife Fund–Brazil, and, for a limited period, there was a representative from the Brazilian Forum of NGOs and Social Movements for the Environment and Development. From Argentina, the CGT, Natural

that, more than a decade later, when Brazilian CSOs from a great variety of sectors incorporated trade debates into their agendas, MERCOSUR remained a rather distant topic for many.

Lessons from NAFTA and MERCOSUR

A first lesson from this analysis of the early attempts to create transnational collective action around trade negotiations is that the transferring of collaborative ties across different issue areas is not always successful. Although previous relationships of trust and friendship had been established among groups of organizations in North America and in the Southern Cone, these did not automatically generate collaboration on trade. Previous ties are important, but not a sufficient condition to create new transnational collective action.

A second finding is that actors' decisions need to be understood in the specific social and political context that informs their perception of the opportunities and threats of regional trade agreements. Global changes, such as the end of the Cold War, and domestic changes, such as the transitions to democracy in the Southern Cone countries, affected actors' answers as to whether or not they should participate in the trade debates, and with whom. These impacts were not homogeneously felt by all actors, though, which brings us to the third lesson learned.

As argued in the introduction to this book, social interaction is important in shaping actors' interests and beliefs. The diffusion of organizational forms in the NAFTA case – the emulation of the Canadian experience of coalition building to Mexico and the United States – and the diffusion of ideas in the MERCOSUR case – the influence of PIT-CNT's position on the Brazilian CUT's decision making – show the importance of a relational approach to understand the dynamic character of civil society participation in trade debates. These outcomes were not predetermined from the start as a result of the new opportunities opened by NAFTA or MERCOSUR.

The NAFTA and MERCOSUR experiences developed in parallel, with scarce dialogue or collaboration among CSOs across these two regions. On the contrary: there was much mistrust and disinformation that separated similar types of organizations. Thus, actions by challengers

Resources and the Environment Foundation (FARN), and the Vitae Foundation participated in a few meetings, as well as the Eros Foundation and the Latin American Center of Social Ecology (CLAES) from Uruguay (von Bülow 2003a: 99–100).

of NAFTA were perceived as based on disapproval and resistance, and actions by critical supporters of MERCOSUR were perceived as based on collaboration with national governments. Ironically, the two strategies had similar results. In both cases, CSOs have been able only to extract a few concessions from negotiators. In the NAFTA case, the Side Agreements on labor and environment negotiated by the Clinton administration are the best example. In the MERCOSUR case, labor and business organizations opened participatory channels in official negotiating processes, but with little power to influence the governments' agenda and change the integration model (von Bülow 2009).

PART THREE

The Dynamics of Networks

5

Trade Protest Networks

This chapter lays out the networks created among challengers of trade agreements in the Americas in the last twenty years of mobilizations and debates. Based on a combination of data gathered through social network questions answered by informants, document analysis, and semistructured interviews, it presents an analysis of how actors relate to each other, within and across national borders. The embeddedness of actors in these networks tells us much about their strategies and goals, and helps us understand changes in their pathways to transnationality.

Informants from one hundred and twenty-three civil society organizations (CSOs) in Brazil (29), Chile (23), Mexico (30), and the United States (41) answered the same questionnaire (see the lists of organizations in Appendix A and a copy of the questionnaire in Appendix B). This was not meant to be a representative sample of the literally hundreds of CSOs that became involved in challenging free trade agreements at one point or another. However, they do include the major challengers in each country, until the freezing of the Free Trade Area of the Americas negotiations in about 2004.[1]

---

[1] As explained in the Introduction, and more fully in Appendix A, a roster of organizations was created before data collection began. The goal was to generate a list as broad and heterogeneous as possible. A first version was created based on the analysis of documents such as membership lists in coalitions, lists of attendants at events, lists of organizers of events, sign-ons, and various documents published by CSOs. This list was then complemented by references found in a review of the literature. During field research, it was expanded by the interviewees themselves, based on the snowball procedure: actors were asked if there were other organizations missing from the roster. However, addition only occurred if an organization was mentioned more than three times. Some names were excluded, because a few organizations had ceased to exist at the time of the interview, and others were not active in the trade debates any longer. Approximately 5 percent of the organizations interviewed were added through snowballing, and 10 percent from the

The mapping of ties among trade agreement challengers focused primarily on the strongest relationships among them, based on the perceptions of intensity of relations among informants at the time of the interview. Thus, the social networks presented in this chapter do not represent all forms of interaction among actors. This approach to mapping relationships resulted from the choices I made with respect to two related methodological challenges: how to distinguish between ties in general and the strongest ties among actors in dense relational environments, and whether to map actually existing ties, or ties that reflect the perceptions of actors.

In dense relational environments, by definition most actors have some form of interaction among themselves, ranging from occasional exchanges of information to long-term collaboration. This is certainly the case of CSOs challenging trade agreements within the four countries studied. Although many did not collaborate closely before engaging in debates about trade agreements, nongovernmental organizations (NGOs), labor unions, and faith-based organizations, to mention only a few of the actors, had a previous history of being at the same meetings, exchanging information, and engaging in debates about various topics. In such a dense environment, general data about interactions among CSOs, such as who speaks to whom, would have yielded an uninformative set of ties, one that would have shown only the most visible facet of relationships. As we will see below, this is mostly true at the domestic scale. At the international scale, ties are much scarcer.

A second challenge was to decide whether to measure actually existing relations or relations as perceived by the actors (Marsden 1990). Studies that seek to analyze relationship building, such as this one, will profit more from data based on perceptions. Therefore, instead of gathering only quantifiable data on interactions, such as co-membership in coalitions and co-presence at events, I focused most of my attention on asking key informants about the strength of ties. They were questioned about the most significant relationships their organizations had in mobilizations related to trade agreements, at the domestic and at the international scale. This "snapshot" information on ties at a given moment is complemented in the analysis that follows by answers given to questions about the longevity of these ties, how actors established their first contacts in other countries, and their proximity/distance to key CSOs.

initial roster were excluded. This combination of strategies avoided missing important actors, at the same time that it avoided having a list that is too homogeneous, based solely on snowballing from an initially small number of key informants.

Who Are Your Closest Allies?

In order to map significant interactions within each country, informants were asked: *Who are your organizations' closest allies in the trade debates, the ones you talk most often to?* The answers resulted in four square matrices of organizations by organizations, which are presented in the form of sociograms in Figures 5.1 through 5.4.[2] In each the nodes represent CSOs. A line links organizations if one identified the other as a close ally in trade debates, and an arrow shows the direction of the link.[3] The shape of nodes varies according to the different types of organizations, and their size varies according to the number of times the organization was identified by others as a close ally. Because of lack of space, acronyms or name reductions were used (for the full names, see Appendix A).

These sociograms help us visualize a set of important characteristics shared by the four domestic networks. First, the most striking common characteristic is the diversity of actors involved. Nodes were given different shapes according to the types of organizations and the issues they prioritize. This classification yielded six different groups, which are asymmetrically represented in the networks: (1) labor unions, labor federations, and NGOs working primarily on labor issues; (2) environmental organizations; (3) rural organizations (landless workers' and small farmers' organizations) and NGOs specializing in rural issues; (4) faith-based organizations; (5) business organizations; and (6) a residual but important group that brings together other NGOs, as well as foundations and think tanks. The networks show a similarly broad variety of types of organizations across the four countries, ranging from labor unions to NGOs from different issue areas to rural organizations. As will be analyzed in further detail below, this heterogeneity is the result of a process of diversification of actors' collaborative ties through time. This finding confirms what was argued in Part 2 of this book: that collective action on trade has changed significantly in the last few decades, becoming an increasingly plural arena.

[2] Actor-by-actor matrices were manipulated using the social network analysis software UCINET, and the sociograms were produced using NetDraw (Borgatti et al. 2002).

[3] These are "directed graphs," meaning that the direction of the tie, represented by the arrows, is an important part of the information provided, because ties were not necessarily reciprocated. The absence of a line does not indicate an absence of relationship, but only the absence of a "closest ally" type of relationship. Informants were allowed to name as many organizations as they wanted, which explains the variation in the number of organizations nominated by each.

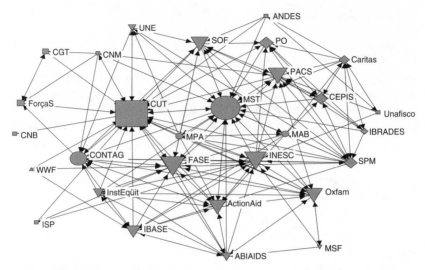

Figure 5.1. Closest Allies: Brazil.
Types of organizations: labor (■), environment (▲), rural (●), NGOs, founda-
tions, and think tanks (▼), faith-based (◆), business (▢).
Sources: Interviews (see Appendix A).

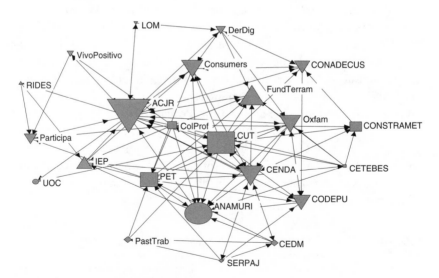

Figure 5.2. Closest Allies: Chile.
Sources: Interviews (see Appendix A).

Trade Protest Networks

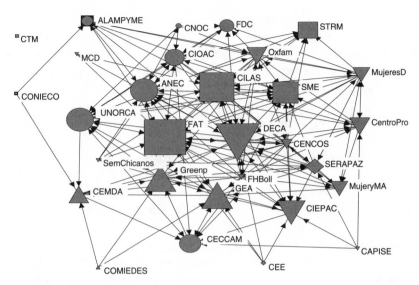

Figure 5.3.   Closest Allies: Mexico.
Types of organizations: labor (■), environment (▲), rural (●), NGOs, foundations, and think tanks (▼), faith-based (◆), business (▯).
Sources: Interviews (see Appendix A).

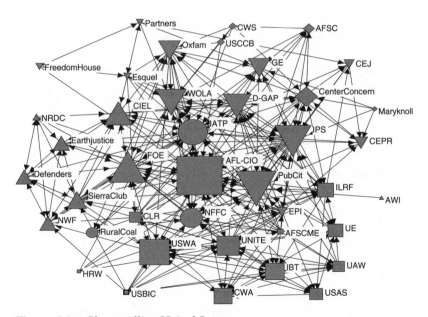

Figure 5.4.   Closest Allies: United States.
Sources: Interviews (see Appendix A).

Another shared characteristic in all four networks is that no single organization or type of organization dominates them, as can be seen from the differences in sizes of nodes. Instead of a single large node, around the core of the networks we see a few nodes that are larger than the others, with different shapes, a result that allows us to say that actors differ considerably in terms of whom they consider to be their closest allies. Finally, in the four countries most nodes represent well-established organizations that are rooted at the domestic scale and are engaged in multiple transnational initiatives. Although a few international NGOs are present in the networks, notably the national and regional offices of Action Aid, Oxfam International, Oxfam America, and Oxfam Great Britain, most of the organizations depicted operate primarily at the domestic scale. These actors are a mix of member-based (one-third) and non–member-based organizations (two-thirds), varying from tiny NGOs and think tanks to organizations with millions of members. As will be seen in greater detail in the next chapter, these CSOs are among the most influential ones in each country. This, again, confirms the relevance that the issue of trade has gained.

The comparison of the four domestic networks of closest allies also indicates some interesting differences in terms of the presence and positions of the different types of actors. For example, environmental NGOs appear in larger numbers and occupy a more central position in the U.S. network than in the other three countries; business organizations were named only in the U.S. and Mexican networks, and even so they are at the periphery of the sociograms; finally, faith-based organizations seem to be more relevant in Brazil and in the United States than in Chile and Mexico. These variations are best explained by each country's specific civil society history. What is most striking, however, are the similarities across the four networks in spite of important differences in the four countries' history and development levels.

Relationships among Organizations

By stating that the networks mapped are heterogeneous and that no single actor dominates them, I do not mean that they are horizontal or devoid of asymmetries. On the contrary: the different sizes of nodes portrayed in the sociograms indicate a highly asymmetrical distribution of responses as to who each CSO has as its closest allies within the four countries. The distribution is three-tiered, based on the number of times organizations

Table 5.1. *Distribution of Organizations in the Closest Allies' Networks, According to In-Degree*

Percentage of Total Possible Nominations Received	Country, Number, and % of Organizations in Each group			
	Brazil (*n* = 29)	Chile (*n* = 23)	Mexico (*n* = 30)	U.S. (*n* = 41)
First tier: > 50%	3 (10.3%)	1 (4.3%)	2 (6.7%)	3 (7.3%)
Second tier: 20–49%	10 (34.5%)	10 (43.5%)	16 (53.3%)	17 (41.5%)
Third tier: < 19%	16 (55.2%)	12 (52.2%)	12 (40.0%)	21 (51.2%)

were nominated by others as their closest allies (in social network terms, their "in-degree") (see Table 5.1). The first tier is of the largest nodes, those that were identified as closest allies by over half of the informants; the second is of the intermediate-sized ones, named by over 20 percent but less than 49 percent; and the third is of the more peripheral ones, the smallest nodes, which are those organizations that were nominated by less than 19 percent of the respondents.

This uneven distribution suggests that informants perceive a few organizations as crucial references for them in trade mobilizations. Others are less central but still play important roles, and a third group is much more marginal. Table 5.2 focuses on the first group. It presents a list of the three organizations most often identified by others as close allies in each country, corresponding to the largest nodes located around the core in sociograms 5.1 through 5.4. Interestingly, the list includes a mix of membership and nonmembership organizations. Three different types of actors received most nominations: labor federations, a select group of NGOs, and, especially in the cases of Brazil and Chile, rural organizations. Again, this confirms the asymmetrical distribution of ties and that this distribution is not concentrated around a single type of actor.

A second common relationship pattern relates to the density of ties among groups of organizations. In Table 5.3 organizations were partitioned in blocks according to the classification of groups made above, and the density of ties (the proportion of all possible ties that are actually present) was measured within each block and among all blocks for the networks in the four countries. The numbers in bold indicate densities higher than the overall network density. This information should be interpreted cautiously, because the absence of specific types of organizations (for

Table 5.2. *Civil Society Organizations Most Often Nominated by Others as Their Closest Allies in Trade Mobilizations (By Country, in-Degree, and Type of Organization)*

Country	Civil Society Organization	In-degree (%)*	Type of Organization
Brazil	CUT (Unified Workers' Federation)	75	Labor federation
	MST (Landless Rural Workers' Movement)	68	Rural workers' movement
	FASE (Federation of Organizations for Social and Educational Assistance)	54	NGO
Chile	ACJR (Chilean Alliance for a Just and Responsible Trade)	64	NGO
	ANAMURI (National Association of Rural and Indigenous Women)	41	Rural women's organization
	CUT (Unitary Workers' Central) – Chile	41	Labor federation
Mexico	DECA-EP (Equipo Pueblo)	60	NGO
	FAT (Authentic Labor Front)	57	Labor federation
	CILAS (Center for Labor Investigation and Consulting)	47	Labor NGO
United States	AFL-CIO	65	Labor federation
	Public Citizen	57	NGO
	IPS (Institute for Policy Studies)	50	NGO
	FOE (Friends of the Earth)	50	Environmental organization

* Percentage of total possible nominations. In-degree counts the number of times each organization was nominated by the others as one of their closest allies in trade-related activities.
Sources: Interviews (see Appendix A).

instance, business organizations in Brazil and Chile) or the very small number of cases (for instance, environmental organizations in Brazil and faith-based organizations in Mexico) limits the possibility of comparisons and the conclusions that can be derived from them.

Table 5.3. *Density of the Networks, within and across Types of Organizations**

Country	Type of Organization	Average Density					
		Rural	Labor	Environment	Faith-Based	NGOs	Business
Brazil	Rural	**0.58**	0.12	0.00	0.10	**0.43**	—
	Labor	0.12	0.21	0.00	0.05	0.12	—
	Environment	0.00	0.12	—	0.00	0.18	—
	Faith-based	**0.40**	0.07	0.00	**0.75**	0.18	—
	NGOs/think tanks/foundations	**0.36**	0.12	0.00	0.11	**0.44**	—
Chile	Rural	0.00	0.00	0.17	0.17	0.10	—
	Labor	**0.50**	**0.50**	**0.40**	**0.33**	0.20	—
	Environment	0.00	0.07	0.17	0.00	0.10	—
	Faith-based	0.17	0.20	0.00	**0.50**	0.10	—
	NGOs/think tanks/foundations	**0.25**	0.20	0.20	0.20	**0.25**	—
Mexico	Rural	**0.47**	**0.23**	**0.29**	0.08	0.09	0.00
	Labor	0.23	**0.55**	0.10	0.00	0.20	0.20
	Environment	**0.25**	0.00	**0.67**	0.00	0.02	0.00
	Faith-based	0.00	**0.40**	**0.38**	0.00	**0.27**	0.00
	NGOs/think tanks/foundations	**0.23**	**0.42**	**0.23**	**0.23**	**0.29**	0.04
	Business	0.08	**0.30**	0.12	0.00	0.14	**0.50**
United States	Rural	**1.00**	0.17	0.12	0.00	**0.33**	0.00
	Labor	0.17	**0.43**	0.12	0.15	**0.24**	0.00
	Environment	0.12	0.12	**0.21**	0.00	**0.28**	0.00
	Faith-based	0.13	0.17	0.07	0.15	0.18	0.00
	NGOs/think tanks/foundations	**0.42**	**0.25**	0.16	0.05	**0.25**	0.08
	Business	**0.33**	**0.33**	**0.25**	0.00	0.17	—

* Numbers that are higher than the total average density of the network are in bold.

In spite of these limitations, two interesting findings from the density data are worth noting. First, the highest proportion of ties is found usually within the same group, rather than across them, suggesting that close ties are best explained by the specialization of organizations in specific issues and/or their sectoral identities. Second, there are some important exceptions to this pattern. The group with the most ties to others is the one made up of "NGOs, foundations, and think tanks." Since this is the most internally heterogeneous group, this finding is hardly surprising. However, this information becomes relevant when complemented with document analysis and qualitative interviews (see Chapter 6). It provides interesting suggestions in regard to the possibility of overcoming obstacles in the collaboration across different types of CSOs and the potential roles of specific actors as brokers in these heterogeneous networks.

Who Are Your Closest Allies in Other Countries?

Informants from CSOs answered the social network questionnaire at a time when the Free Trade Area of the Americas (FTAA) negotiations were losing steam, after a period of intense mobilizations and relationship building across the hemisphere.[4] In spite of that, approximately two-thirds of the 123 organizations from Brazil, Chile, Mexico, and the United States included in this study did not have trade-related ties to organizations in all of the other three countries.[5] What was true at the domestic scale – that most of the CSOs included in the study had some kind of interaction with one another – was *not* true at the transnational level.

In order to gather data on transnational linkages, informants were asked to indicate their proximity/distance to some of the most prominent organizations in other countries, with respect to their goals and strategies in trade debates (see the questionnaire in Appendix B). They were also prompted to name unlisted allies. The networks mapped show a high concentration of strong ties among a small number of organizations. Only nine organizations, listed in Table 5.4, received over 10 percent of the total number

---

[4] Most of the interviews based on the social network questionnaire were conducted between May 2004 and September 2005(see Appendix A).

[5] One-third of the 123 organizations from Brazil, Chile, Mexico, and the United States had trade-related ties with CSOs in every one of the other three countries; almost half had ties in only one or two; and the remaining had no ties, or informants were unable to answer the question.

Table 5.4. *Most Often Nominated CSOs in Transnational Network of Closest Allies (> 10%)*

Country	Civil society Organization	In-degree (%)*	Type of Organization
Brazil	Landless Rural Workers' Movement (MST)	23.4	Rural movement
U.S.	Public Citizen	21.9	NGO
Brazil	Unified Workers' Federation (CUT)	21.3	Labor federation
U.S.	American Federation of Labor–Congress of Industrial Organizations (AFL-CIO)	20.7	Labor federation
Chile	Chilean Alliance for a Just and Responsible Trade (ACJR)	19	NGO
Mexico	Authentic Labor Front (FAT)	17.2	Labor federation
Mexico	National Union of Autonomous Regional Rural Organizations (UNORCA)	16.1	Rural organization
Chile	Institute of Political Ecology (IEP)	14	NGO
Brazil	Brazilian Institute of Social and Economic Analysis (IBASE)	12.8	NGO

* Percentage of total possible nominations by CSOs from the other countries.
Sources: Interviews (see Appendix A).

of possible nominations as "close" or "very close" allies of others. Thus, not only are transnational trade protest networks less dense than domestic ones, but strong ties are much rarer across than within national borders.

Other differences between the domestic and the transnational networks are worth pointing out. Although, as at the domestic scale, the most central organizations also include different types of CSOs, these are not necessarily the same as in domestic networks of organizations' closest allies. These differences become clearer when we expand the group of the most central organizations listed in Table 5.4 to include those that received over 5 percent of total possible nominations and map their ties. The result can be visualized in the network presented in Figure 5.5. The colors of nodes in this figure (gray, white, or black) vary according to the country of origin, and the shapes vary, once again, according to the differentiation among types of organizations.

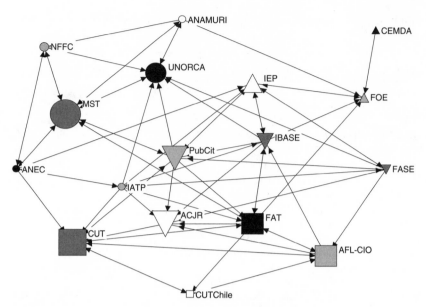

Figure 5.5. Transnational Ties among Most Nominated (> 5%) CSOs.
(Size of Nodes by In-degree, Shape by Type of Organization, Color by Country)
Types of organizations: labor (■), environment (▲), rural (●), NGOs, founda-
tions, and think tanks (▼)Countries according to node colors: Chile (white), U.S.
(light gray), Brazil (dark gray), Mexico (black)
Sources: Interviews (see Appendix A).

Figure 5.5 shows that there is a greater salience of rural organizations in
transnational networks. Whereas in the Brazilian and Chilean networks
these were among the three most central organizations, at the transnational scale this prominence is even clearer. In the figure we can visualize
the presence of this type of organization in the upper left corner. Of these
rural organizations, only the Brazilian Movimento dos Trabalhadores
Rurais Sem Terra (MST – Landless Rural Workers' Movement) was
also among the most central organizations in the domestic network.
Furthermore, ties among environmental organizations are also more visible at the transnational scale than in domestic networks. In Figure 5.5,
three environmental NGOs occupy the right upper corner: the Chilean
Institute of Political Ecology (Instituto de Ecología Política – IEP), Friends
of the Earth (FOE-U.S.), and the Mexican Center for Environmental Law
(Centro Mexicano de Derecho Ambiental – CEMDA). Of these, only
FOE-U.S. was among the most central organizations in the domestic networks of closest allies.

Table 5.5. *Transnational Ties: Density of Ties within and across Types of Organizations*

Type of Organization	Rural	Labor	Environment	Faith-based	NGOs
Rural	0.195	0.011	0.012	0.000	0.015
Labor	0.009	0.059	0.006	0.000	0.011
Environment	0.008	0.004	0.083	0.000	0.008
Faith-based	0.004	0.002	0.000	0.024	0.003
NGOs	0.032	0.018	0.011	0.001	0.035

These differences indicate that at the transnational scale there are fewer ties and that they are less strong. The ones that do exist tend to follow more closely affinities based on the types of organizations. The data on density, displayed in Table 5.5, confirm this finding, if we compare the density intragroup with ties across groups. It is especially true in the case of rural organizations, which have a much higher intragroup density of international ties than the other types of organizations.

Finally, the data on the centrality of organizations at the transnational scale indicate the visibility of those originating from the Southern countries (Brazil, Chile, and Mexico), which confirms the increased relevance of South–South ties in trade debates (see Table 5.4 and Figure 5.5). As explained above, if these data had been gathered in the early 1990s, at least two of the most central organizations – MST and CUT (the Brazilian Unified Workers' Federation) – would have been absent from the networks, or would be in a much more peripheral position.

In sum, the ties mapped show that networks of trade agreement challengers are not horizontal, in the sense that all actors occupy similar positions. Strong relationships tend to be concentrated in a small number of organizations, especially at the transnational scale, with a myriad of other organizations occupying semiperipheral and peripheral positions. The data also show the heterogeneity of participants. More specifically, labor unions, rural organizations, and a small number of NGOs tend to share the most central positions in the networks. Differentiating among types of organizations helps in visualizing these patterns of relationships, indicating that at the transnational scale these boundaries are more important in explaining the configuration of networks than at the domestic scale.

However, how much – and in what sense – are these data a reflection of new patterns of relationship, and how durable have they proven to be?

Do they reflect different pathways to transnationality taken by actors? Network analysis measures such as centrality and density can be extremely useful to visualize what would otherwise be invisible interactions, and to better understand their complexity. However, in order to show how actors came to occupy their positions in the networks, how these have changed through time and the impacts they have, we must move from the primarily descriptive use of social network measures to an analysis of the dynamics of interaction. As Ann Mische has argued, this requires that "we view the topographical maps produced by formal techniques as the result of many local, contingent, and intersecting relational processes" (Mische 2003: 265). The next chapter undertakes this challenge.

6

The Origins and Dynamics of Trade Challengers' Networks

How did a select number of labor, rural, and nongovernmental organizations (NGOs) come to form the core of the networks of trade challengers, within and beyond national boundaries? In order to answer this question, it is necessary to put the social network data presented in the last chapter in a historical context. The analysis presented below provides a detailed account of the origins of transnational ties within these three groups of organizations, and the pathways to transnationality taken by civil society organizations (CSOs) from each of these sectoral domains, as they responded to changes in their relational and political environments.

This approach makes sense if we consider that transnational ties have tended historically to be stronger among similar types of organizations, a trend that, according to the network data uncovered, seems to still hold true. At the same time, the data also showed some evidence for what the literature on transnationalism has been arguing: that cross-sectoral, multi-issue ties have become more common in the last few decades. An analysis that focuses on both intra- and intersectoral ties, such as the one presented below, shows that the construction of domestic and transnational networks among trade challengers has been full of tensions and ambiguities.

The Power of Labor Organizations and Its Limits

In total, informants from eight national labor federations and eighteen key sectoral unions answered the social network questionnaires in Brazil,

Chile, Mexico, and the United States (see Appendix A).[1] Although they represented only around 20 percent of the total number of CSOs, they were among the most nominated in every country (see Table 5.2).

Arguably, this result is not surprising. Labor organizations enjoy more access to financial and human resources than many other CSOs, and, in general, their membership perceives itself as directly affected (positively or negatively) by trade agreements. Furthermore, as has already been noted in Part 2, unions have participated in debates about international trade for many decades, and some of the most contentious disagreements over the benefits or dangers of trade liberalization have concerned the consequences on labor markets.

On the other hand, labor organizations in the Americas, a few notable exceptions notwithstanding, have had traditionally weak collaborative relationships with other types of organizations at the domestic as well as at the transnational scale. Labor's international relations, moreover, are characterized by diplomatic ties among labor federations, and international relations secretariats are usually weak in comparison with those in charge of domestic affairs (Costa 2005a). Sustained collaboration between workers' organizations from the North and South that compete for scarce jobs and investments is especially difficulty to produce. Despite more than a century of internationalist rhetoric, labor organizations have retained deep national roots.[2] This being true, their current centrality in domestic and cross-national trade protest networks represents an interesting puzzle.

In order to understand this puzzle, it is important to consider the changes in the relational and political embeddedness of labor organizations since the end of the 1980s. The demise of the Cold War and the transitions to democracy in Latin America inaugurated a new political context, in which, for the first time in the history of the Americas, hemispheric-level collaboration seemed to be possible.[3] However, this new context was plagued with uncertainty.

---

[1] This section is partially based on von Bülow (2009). Given that labor federations are not homogenous organizations, it made sense to include at least a few key labor unions in the initial roster of organizations interviewed, which do not necessarily share the same perspective as the federations' leadership on trade negotiations.

[2] For the historical debate on labor internationalism, see, for example, Hobsbawn (1988) and Stillerman (2003).

[3] CUT-Brazil's former Secretary of International Affairs has gone even farther and argued that, in spite of previous instances of cross-border labor collaboration, it is only with the process of globalization and technological progress that it is really possible to speak of labor internationalism (Jakobsen 1999: 234).

Labor in Dynamic Relational and Political Contexts

The first attempts at hemispheric collaboration among labor organizations in the Americas date from the end of the nineteenth century but were short-lived. During the Cold War, initiatives fell under the ideological polarization between "free unionism," sponsored mainly by the AFL-CIO in the United States, and unions that were linked to the communist-led World Federation of Trade Unions. A third, nonaligned, group existed, but its transnational activities were limited often to diplomatic exchanges. Furthermore, unionism in Latin America was stifled by the military dictatorships that dominated the region between the 1960s and the 1980s. Transnational mobilizations during this period were mainly "transitory, responding to repression of domestic labor movements" (Keck and Sikkink 1998: 15).

The convergence of major national labor federations that emerged in the mid-1990s in opposition to the Free Trade Area of the Americas (FTAA) and other trade agreements would not have been possible before. However, this convergence hides important differences. Not all labor actors have sponsored the same strategies or presented the same arguments at every negotiation table. The social networks mapped in Chapter 5 show that not all occupy the same positions in the three tiers of the domestic networks of closest allies: a few occupy the core, while others are on the semiperiphery and periphery of the sociograms. At the transnational scale, only three federations were among the most nominated actors (see Table 5.4). These different positions are the result of the various perceptions of the opportunities and challenges of the 1990s, which, in turn, led to a variety of pathways to transnationality.

We can differentiate three groups among the labor federations according to their choices of pathways. First, there are those that have sustained participation in transnational coalitions, that have built a diverse array of trade-related ties with other types of organizations at the domestic and transnational scales, and that have made attempts to create common projects with their allies (CUT-Brazil, the AFL-CIO, and the Authentic Labor Front [Frente Auténtico del Trabajo – FAT] in Mexico). Second, there are those that have only a subregional presence and few trade-related ties with other types of organizations at the domestic and transnational scales, with limited attempts at creating common projects (the other two Brazilian federations, the General Workers' Confederation [Confederação Geral dos Trabalhadores – CGT] and Labor Force, along with the Chilean Unitary

Workers' Central [Central Unitaria de Trabajadores – CUT], and the Mexican National Union of Workers [Unión Nacional de Trabajadores – UNT]). Third, there is the isolated case of the Confederation of Mexican Workers (Confederación de Trabajadores de México – CTM), which has a domestically oriented approach to trade debates, while at the same time maintaining its regional and global diplomatic ties with other labor federations (see Table 6.1).

Studies of labor transnationalism have emphasized the role of structural variables to explain these different choices.[4] Generally speaking, they have not explored the impact of labor organizations' relations with other actors. Transnational action is seen *ex post* as the product of a single, previously taken autonomous decision, as if organizations existed in closed bubbles and did not change their views through time as a result of interactions with others. For example, Michael Dreiling and Ian Robinson can successfully explain the variation of union strategies in regard to the North American Free Trade Agreement (NAFTA) based on their differentiation of union types, defined "in terms of the inclusiveness of union collective identities and the degree to which union conceptions of a just political economy are at odds with the existing system" (Dreiling and Robinson 1998: 164). However, it is difficult to generalize this argument so that it can explain how organizations representing very different union types achieved a common position vis-à-vis the Common Market of the South (MERCOSUR), or how positions have converged in opposition to the FTAA. In order to do so, it is important to understand how labor organizations became embedded in a new relational environment in the 1990s.

The Impacts of NAFTA and MERCOSUR

At the beginning of 1998, four years after NAFTA took effect, the AFL-CIO president made a historic trip to Mexico, the first visit by a U.S. labor federation president in seventy-four years. During that visit, John Sweeney talked to the whole spectrum of Mexican labor organizations, including independent ones, such as the Authentic Labor Front (FAT) and the then newly created National Union of Workers (UNT), thus officially ending the exclusive relationship the AFL-CIO had nurtured with the

---

[4] For example, Mark Anner argues that differences of industrial structure, state institutions and practices, and labor ideologies explain the variety in form and frequency of labor transnationalism in the Brazilian auto sector (Anner 2003).

Table 6.1. *Main National Labor Federations in the Trade Debates (2004)*

Labor federation	Brazil			Chile	Mexico			United States
	CUT	CGT	FS	CUT	FAT	CTM	UNT	AFL-CIO
International labor organization membership	ICFTU-ORIT* CCSCS**	ICFTU-ORIT CCSCS	ICFTU-ORIT CCSCS	ICFTU-ORIT CCSCS	ICFTU-ORIT	ICFTU-ORIT	ICFTU-ORIT	ICFTU-ORIT
Position in trade debates	Critical supporter of MERCOSUR, participated in the Campaign against the FTAA.	Critical supporter of MERCOSUR, but not active participant in the Campaign against the FTAA.	Critical supporter of MERCOSUR, but with no clear position on the FTAA.	Internal division during the U.S.-Chile FTA talks. Against the FTAA, but not active participant in the Campaign against the FTAA.	Early challenger of NAFTA; participated in the Campaign against the FTAA and joined the UNT in 1997.	In favor of NAFTA, changed its position to oppose the FTAA, but not an active participant in the Campaign against the FTAA.	Created after NAFTA (1997); against the FTAA, but not active participant in the Campaign against the FTAA.	Early challenger of NAFTA; participated in the Campaign against the FTAA.
Active participant in domestic trade coalitions	Yes	No	No	–	Yes	No	No	Yes
Active participant in the HSA ***	Yes	No	No	No	Yes	No	No	Yes

* International Confederation of Free Trade Unions – Inter-American Regional Organization of Workers; ** Coordination of Southern Cone Labor Federations; *** Hemispheric Social Alliance

Sources: Interviews with labor informants (see Appendix A).

CTM during the Cold War. What happened to lead to this change? Contentious debates among labor organizations from both countries about NAFTA's potential impacts are the key to understanding it.

Labor organizations in the Americas became more interested in debates about the impacts of trade agreements during the NAFTA and MERCOSUR negotiations in the early 1990s. As explained in Chapter 4, this temporal coincidence did not lead, however, to similarly coincidental goals or strategies in the two regions. What is common between these experiences is that both have been frustrating for labor organizations.[5] In South America, labor successfully guaranteed the participation of representatives in various regional integration fora, but, fifteen years later, Brazilian participants acknowledge that these efforts have produced little impact on integration policies (Jakobsen 1999; Portella de Castro 2007).

Neither NAFTA's Labor Side Agreement nor MERCOSUR's Social-Labor Declaration and Commission have led to concrete and measurable results in terms of better compliance with labor rights in these regions, notwithstanding the "sunshine effect" of the former (see, for example, Bognanno and Lu 2003) and the implementation of labor proposals, such as the regional public policy initiatives on unemployment in the Southern Cone (Portella de Castro 2007: 74). Through NAFTA and MERCOSUR, organizations learned that institutionalized participation in official negotiating fora and the inclusion of labor issues in treaties are important, but not sufficient to guarantee a better compliance with labor rights.

This learning process simultaneously *explains and is a product of* the embeddedness of labor actors in a new transnational environment of relationships, which has had an impact on how they see their roles in free trade negotiations, the demands sought, and their choice of pathways to transnationality. In particular, subregional experiences have helped generate important shifts in the relationships among labor organizations and between these and other civil society allies in the region. These shifts explain the answers given to the question about each organization's strongest allies, displayed as a network of the closest domestic and transnational ties in Figure 6.1.

It is interesting to note that the AFL-CIO's centrality in Figure 6.1 is due to the diversification of its relationships with Mexican organizations

---

[5] For a comparison of labor strategies in the two regions, see von Bülow (2003b).

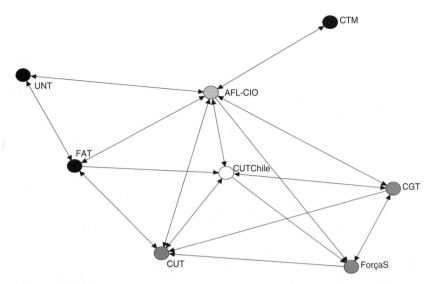

Figure 6.1. Closest Ties among Selected Labor Federations (Brazil, Chile, Mexico, and the United States).
Countries according to node colors: Chile (white), U.S. (light gray), Brazil (dark gray), Mexico (black).
Acronyms and abbreviations: CUT: Unified Workers' Federation – Brazil; ForçaS: Labor Force – Brazil; CGT: General Workers' Confederation – Brazil; FAT: Authentic Labor Front–Mexico; UNT: National Union of Workers–Mexico; CTM: Confederation of Mexican Workers – Mexico; AFL-CIO: American Federation of Labor–Congress of Industrial Organizations – United States; CUT-Chile: Unitary Workers' Central – Chile.
Sources: Interviews (see Appendix A).

and with new allies from other countries. Had the question *Who are your closest allies?* been asked before the mid-1990s, the figure would have shown a much more isolated AFL-CIO, as one official explains:

NAFTA was very significant in that the old Cold War definitions of trade union alliance – with whom we should work – were no longer viable. It put down a kind of practice dogma, if not an explicit dogma, that the only real partner in Mexico was the Confederation of Mexican Workers (CTM), and that even that partnership, the only way it could be maintained, was on a very superficial diplomatic basis. The challenge of NAFTA completely overturned that premise.[6]

In the case of MERCOSUR, the experience of almost two decades of joint attempts to influence the integration process significantly

---

[6] Interview with Stan Gacek, Assistant Director for International Affairs, AFL-CIO, Washington, D.C., October 2004.

broadened and strengthened labor organizations' ties in the region. This change has also happened among national federations within countries, at least in Brazil. The presence of the three largest Brazilian labor federations – CUT-Brazil, Labor Force (Força Sindical), and the General Workers' Confederation (CGT) – in the Coordination of Southern Cone Labor Federations (Coordinadora de Centrales Sindicales del Cono Sur – CCSCS) and in the MERCOSUR fora did not resolve their profound differences, but forced them to design common proposals and demands. CUT-Brazil did not reciprocate CGT's and the Labor Force's ties, as can be seen in Figure 6.1, but this is because of CUT's activism in the context of the Campaign against the FTAA, in which neither CGT nor the Labor Force participated actively (see Table 6.1). When the question about collaborative ties was limited to the debates about MERCOSUR, the CUT interviewee did mention the other two national labor federations as being among its closest allies.

The new relational embeddedness of labor organizations made it possible, in turn, to help change the role that the most important hemispheric labor organization – the Inter-American Regional Organization of Workers (ORIT) – had played until then in the debates about trade agreements and coalition building in the Americas.[7] As shown in Table 6.1, in 2004 all of the main labor actors in trade protests in the four countries studied were affiliated with the ORIT at the regional level, and with the International Confederation of Free Trade Unions (ICFTU) at the global level. Although the ICFTU was not the only global-level labor organization active in the region,[8] it emerged as the strongest one in the post–Cold War era (Myconos 2005: esp. ch. 5). Similarly, ORIT was not the only regional labor organization in this period,[9] but it had become by far the most representative and powerful, especially after the decision by several important previously nonaligned labor organizations, such as CUT-Brazil, to join (Costa 2005b: esp. 538–566; Wachendorfer 2007).

---

[7] One consequence of these internal shifts in ORIT was the change of its headquarters from the CTM building in Mexico City to Venezuela and, more recently, to São Paulo, Brazil.

[8] In November 2006 the ICFTU and the World Confederation of Labor joined forces to create the International Trade Union Confederation (ITUC).

[9] Another organization was the Latin American Workers' Confederation (Confederación Latinoamericana de Trabajadores – CLAT), but its membership was much smaller, and limited to Latin America. In March 2008, CLAT and ORIT joined forces and created the Trade Union Confederation of the Americas (TUCA).

This revitalized ORIT contributed significantly to strengthening the view among labor leaders that building sustained alliances with other civil society actors in the region was vital. Labor federations that had participated in efforts to create cross-sectoral trade coalitions at the domestic scale, such as the Canadian Labour Congress, and organizations that had historical ties to other civil society actors, such as CUT-Brazil, were key advocates of the so-called social alliances within ORIT.[10] An important event exemplifies this trend clearly. During the Workers of the Americas Forum, held in parallel to the Belo Horizonte FTAA Ministerial Meeting, in 1997, representatives of other kinds of CSOs were invited for the first time to participate in an ORIT-organized large-scale event (CUT 1997).[11] A final declaration, signed jointly by ORIT, NGOs, and social movement organizations, turned out to be the first step toward the creation of the Hemispheric Social Alliance (HSA) and the formulation of a broad agenda on trade negotiations. At this point, the lack of negotiating channels strengthened a common identity among labor organizations that were most opposed to the FTAA, and weakened those in the AFL-CIO and ORIT that advocated a less critical position (Smith and Korzeniewicz 2007).

The centrality of CUT-Brazil, the AFL-CIO, and the FAT in domestic and transnational networks of trade challengers is a result of their decision to seek links with other CSOs. However, these new links presupposed making changes in labor's particularistic agendas. Until the Belo Horizonte event, ORIT's demands had been specifically labor related: the creation of a Labor Forum and of a working group on social and labor issues (CUT 1997). These, however, had been ignored by the majority of negotiators, who argued that labor issues were under the purview of the International Labor Organization, and that civil society participation should be constrained to the national scale (Berrón 2007: 188).

When ORIT formally declared its opposition to the FTAA negotiations, in April 2001, its arguments were based on a wider set of issues, including those that were considered relevant by NGOs and social movement organizations affiliated with the HSA (Anner and Evans 2004: 41). Two of the most active AFL-CIO participants in this period justified the extension of

[10] Interview with Víctor Báez, Secretary General of ORIT, Belo Horizonte, December 2005, and with Rafael Freire, former International Relations Secretary, CUT-Brazil, São Paulo, March 2005.

[11] ORIT had organized previously two Labor Fora, in parallel to the FTAA Ministerial Meetings held in Denver (1995) and Cartagena (1996).

labor unions' agenda and coalition-building practices in terms of the need to enhance labor's moral credibility:

The weakness of labor unions in the trade debates is that everybody assumes that it is entirely self-interest that motivates you, so they can dismiss that. When you are working with religious organizations, the human rights organizations, it adds credibility....The labor movement in the U.S. is too small and too weak if it is isolated, and we recognize that.... We want people to understand that labor groups can play a progressive role in international trade discussions.[12]

We have focused more and more of our work on issues like investment, services, intellectual property, all these things that may not have a huge impact on the U.S., but do have a huge impact on developing countries. ... In Seattle [during the 1999 WTO Meeting], the press reported that what we were for was only focused on workers' rights, and they characterized it as sort of the anti-developmental agenda.[13] We realized that we needed to be more aggressive and more public about the fact that our critique is not just about labor standards.[14]

A FAT official in Mexico agreed, framing the issue in terms of the historical debates on labor's role as the vanguard of change within leftist circles: "Many labor unions still think that they are the main actors of revolutionary change. This is false.... We think that the specific labor agenda has to be converted in a public interest agenda, and we have not been able to do this."[15]

However, in practice not all labor organizations have accepted the argument that broader alliances and extended agendas are an imperative of new times. As Mark Anner and Peter Evans have pointed out, the level of engagement in the construction of the HSA, which presupposes acceptance of the need to collaborate with other types of organizations, varied widely among ORIT affiliates, and several important ones were not active participants (Anner and Evans 2004: 42; see Table 6.1). Indeed, debates about the scope of labor's alliances were a key source of contention in the 1990s and remained an unresolved issue in some cases:

---

[12] Interview with Thea Lee, Assistant Director for International Economic Policy, AFL-CIO, Washington, D.C., August 2004.

[13] Kenneth Gould and colleagues argue that, although labor provided the bulk of the funding for protests in Seattle, it primarily participated in labor rallies and labor marches, and its rhetoric was almost exclusively focused on wages, job loss, and other labor issues. See Gould et al. (2004: 93).

[14] Interview with Elizabeth Drake, Public Policy Analyst, AFL-CIO, Washington, D.C., August 2004.

[15] Interview with Antonio Villalba, National Coordinating Committee, FAT, Mexico City, August 2004.

We had to overcome a lot of resistance. There was a lot of confusion about the definition of civil society. Many argued that ... "what are social alliances worth, if NGOs are only the dog and its owner?" We had to fight that. The second obstacle was the fear that labor unions would lose their identity. The third was the attitude that social alliances are all right, provided that the labor movement led them. In 1998 was when we had most difficulties. Today, no ORIT affiliate questions the validity of social alliances. However, some do not put them in practice.[16]

The ORIT Secretary General mentioned the difficulties faced in 1998 because of another key event: the Summit of the Americas, which was held in Chile only one year after the Belo Horizonte meeting. While affiliates such as CUT-Brazil, the Canadian Labour Congress, and the AFL-CIO were, together with Chilean NGOs, trying to organize a joint Peoples' Summit in parallel to the official meeting, the local ORIT affiliate, CUT-Chile, rejected the idea. In the end, two events were organized simultaneously, the Labor and the Peoples' Summit: "It was very problematic for us in ORIT, because we were trying to forge a broader alliance, what became [known as] the 'social alliance.' We thought it was very important ... but it was difficult, because CUT was our main host."[17]

The different views on the breadth of coalition building are reflected in the answers given by representatives of labor federations when questioned about whom they would contact to get in touch with allies in order to plan parallel events to an FTAA Ministerial Meeting in another country (see the questionnaire in Appendix B). Although all respondents argued that they would use labor's diplomatic channels (either through ORIT or ORIT affiliates), the AFL-CIO, CUT-Brazil, and FAT also said that they would coordinate their actions with other kinds of CSOs through multisectoral trade coalitions.

Accommodations like these, however, present labor with a dilemma. The extension of issues and agendas allows willing labor organizations to collaborate with many heterogeneous actors at once, but often at the cost of simplification (or even suppression) of demands, diminished visibility of their own agenda, and greater complications in negotiating common actions. The provisional agreement reached among ORIT's affiliates and with their civil society allies was to sponsor an all-out opposition to the FTAA, to be maintained even if labor's particularistic demands were met during the negotiations. This rendered it possible that a broad group of

[16] Interview with Víctor Báez, Secretary General of ORIT, Belo Horizonte, December 2005.
[17] Anonymous interview with one of the AFL-CIO participants, October 2004.

CSOs presented a common front at the transnational scale, but at the same time created the potential for tensions when perceptions about domestic opportunities for negotiation changed.

In Brazil the election of Luis Inácio Lula da Silva as president in 2002 opened a fierce debate among members of the Brazilian Campaign against the FTAA about which tactics should be used in their mobilizations and how to frame their demands. In the United States, the division of the labor movement in the post-FTAA context has shed further light not only on domestic policy differences, but also on labor's choices of pathways to transnationality.[18] In the context of a new Democratic majority in the U.S. Congress, elected in 2006, the AFL-CIO changed its strategy. It went from a pathway of sustained transnationalization and efforts to build common projects with a broad set of allies from other countries, to temporarily focus on activism on the domestic scale.

These changes in light of dynamic political contexts were not unique to the case of labor organizations. As will be seen in detail in Chapter 10, a major challenge for all participants in trade agreement mobilizations has been to negotiate changes in pathways to transnationality through time.

"We Want Our Own Space": The Rise of Rural Transnationalism

On September 10, 2003, a group of farmers from around the world marched to protest the fifth World Trade Organization (WTO) Ministerial Meeting, which was opening that day in the tourist paradise of Cancun, Mexico. The Korean delegates led the March, among them the former president of the South Korean Federation of Farmers and Fishermen, Lee Kyung Hae. To the astonishment of most of the protestors, as the marchers clashed with the Mexican police, Hae took a knife out of his garments and killed himself, while holding a placard that read "The WTO Kills Farmers."

Mr. Lee's action dramatically symbolizes the relevance that the issue of international trade negotiations has gained among rural movements, and the radicalization of global protests against the WTO. The Cancun

---

[18] In 2005, seven unions separated from the AFL-CIO and created the Change to Win (CTW) coalition, among them important organizations in the trade debates, such as the International Brotherhood of Teamsters, the Service Employees International Union, and the United Farm Workers of America.

events also showed the heightened visibility that a group of rural organizations gained via the protests. These organizations represent mostly small farmers, who see trade negotiations as a threat to their survival, in developed and developing countries alike. The literature on rural movements has acknowledged the rise in transnational activism, pointing to the crisis sparked by the rapid liberalization of global agricultural trade in the 1980s as the main impetus for new cross-border organizing (Desmarais 2002; Edelman 2003, 2005). Precedents of transnational collective action exist, but early forms of collaboration were rarely long-lived or global in scale.[19] As a leader of the Brazilian Landless Rural Workers' Movement (MST) put it: "It is very striking that only now farmers are starting to achieve a degree of worldwide coordination, after 500 years of capitalist development" (Stédile 2002: 99).

The Cancun events also showed that, hand in hand with their increased capacity to organize and mobilize, many rural organizations resisted expanding their agendas and strategies in view of other CSOs' critiques of the WTO. Much like the position sustained by CUT-Chile during the 1998 Summit of the Americas, organizations affiliated with Via Campesina (VC), a global coalition of small farmers' groups created at the beginning of the 1990s, promoted an exclusive Forum – the International Farmers and Indigenous Forum – and a March that focused on its particular demands. Because VC affiliates in Mexico sent the largest contingent of protestors to Cancun, its leaders believed that they were entitled to occupy center stage,[20] as the Coordinator for North America explained: "In November 2002, we made a commitment: that for Cancun we would create a rural-indigenous space, and we would not work through

---

[19] For a review of antecedents of transnational alliance-building among peasant and small farmer organizations, see Borras et al. (2008, esp. 173–179). The International Union of Food, Agricultural, Hotel, Restaurant, Catering, Tobacco and Allied Workers' Association (IUF) was founded in 1920, merging three international trade secretariats that, in turn, had existed since before the First World War. However, until the 1960s its membership was mainly European (for the history of the IUF, see Rütters and Zimmermann 2003). The International Federation of Agricultural Producers (IFAP) has existed since 1946, but, once again, most of its membership and leadership came from developed countries. See http://www.ifap.org/about-ifap/history/en/, last accessed March 31, 2008. Specifically with respect to trade negotiations, as early as December 1980, an international farmers' protest was held at the GATT ministerial session in Brussels (Ritchie 1996: 499).

[20] As one of the members of an organization close to VC argued: "Vía Campesina does have mobilization capacity, it is not an NGO, and thus they have to be the main actors." Interview with Ana de Ita, CECCAM, Mexico City, August 2004.

the NGOs. We wanted our own space, open to everybody, not submitting ourselves to others."[21]

Since its foundation, the relationship between VC and NGOs has been extremely ambivalent: although NGOs helped to create the coalition and remain important sources of funding, there is a history of distrust fueled by what at least some rural movement leaders perceive as illegitimate attempts to speak on their behalf. As a consequence, VC sought to distance itself from "the paternalistic embrace of well-intentioned NGOs" (Desmarais 2003: 117).[22]

In spite of these tensions, VC affiliates were the most nominated rural organizations in the domestic networks of closest allies (see Figures 5.1–5.4): the MST in Brazil, the National Association of Rural and Indigenous Women (Asociación Nacional de Mujeres Rurales e Indígenas – ANAMURI) in Chile, the National Family Farm Coalition (NFFC) in the United States, and the National Union of Autonomous Regional Rural Organizations (Unión Nacional de Organizaciones Regionales Campesinas Autónomas – UNORCA) in Mexico. This centrality is a reflection both of the domestic importance of these organizations and of the early identification of multilateral trade negotiations as one of VC's priorities. At the global scale, its main demand has been the end of negotiations on the Agreement on Agriculture at the WTO, but it has also advocated changes in negotiations that touch on issues of biotechnology, biodiversity, and food safety.

In various multilateral arenas, VC has sought to promote a conceptual change in how agriculture is debated, from the "food security" framework to the "food sovereignty" one. Whereas "food security" refers to a situation in which all people at all times have access to adequate and nutritious food, "food sovereignty" is intended to be a broader concept, "which considers food a human right rather than primarily a commodity, prioritizes local production and peasant access to land, and upholds nations' rights to protect their producers from dumping and to implement supply management policies" (Edelman 2005: 339).

However, not all farmers' organizations agree with VC's positions. Many have moved away from its decision not to participate in any dialogue at the WTO, claiming that this position is neither sustainable

[21] Interview with Alberto Gómez Flores, National Executive Coordinator, UNORCA, Mexico City, August 2004.
[22] As Borras et al. explain, this "love-hate" relationship between rural movements and NGOs is not restricted to Via Campesina and its affiliates (Borras et al. 2008: 197–198).

nor effective. Thus, at the meeting in Cancun, the Brazilian National Confederation of Workers in Agriculture (Confederação Nacional dos Trabalhadores em Agricultura – CONTAG) and other IUF[23] affiliates supported the call made by the G-20 (a coalition of developing countries) for reduction in the use of subsidies by developed countries, while at the same time demanding special treatment for small-scale producers in the developing world.[24]

A few years earlier, the linkage between poverty reduction and trade, and more specifically the impacts of agricultural subsidies on world trade, had become matters of strong contention among CSOs and between them and governmental actors.[25] This debate was sparked by the release of Oxfam International's Report *Rigged Rules and Double Standards* (2002b). In one of its most debated passages, the Report stated:

International trade can act as a force for good, or for bad.... The real challenge is to make trade contribute to poverty reduction by changing the institutions, rules, and policies that marginalize the poor.... "Globaphobes" offer something radically different. Behind the banner of "national sovereignty" they propose a retreat from trade in favour of increased "self-reliance." Perhaps unsurprisingly, such thinking is more attractive to political constituencies of the rich world.[26"]

For VC, Oxfam International is wrong because trade subsidies are not the problem *per se*, neither for the developed nor for developing countries: "There is no debate about trade [within VC] because we share the same position. For us it is clear that countries have the right to subsidize their agriculture, but they also have the right to close their borders. The issue of market access is a trap."[27]

VC's affiliates have advocated this common position at the transnational scale, but their domestic agendas and frames vary significantly. For example, Brazil's MST prioritizes the issue of land property and agrarian reform, the NFFC in the United States prioritizes the issue of commodity prices, and both advocate in favor of domestic protections. The

---

[23] See note 19 above.

[24] Interview with Luís Facco, International Relations Secretariat, CONTAG, Brasilia, April 2005.

[25] For example, see the debates between Oxfam International and the Executive Director of the NGO Focus on the Global South (Bello 2002b, 2002c; Oxfam 2002a) and with the Indian activist Vandana Shiva (Shiva 2002; Twyford 2002).

[26] Oxfam (2002b: 24).

[27] Telephone interview with Víctor Quintana, Frente Democrático Campesino de Chihuahua, November 2005.

mix of different agendas at the domestic scale and suppression of issues at the transnational level leaves little room for cross-border coalition building with other types of organizations, or even with rural organizations or NGOs that have a different approach to the problem of agricultural subsidies.[28]

Rural Transnationalism in the Americas

To an even larger extent than in the case of labor, many of the collaborative ties among rural organizations uncovered in this study did not exist before the 1990s (see Figure 6.2). At the beginning of that decade, knowledge of the situation in other countries was scarce in the Americas (Brooks and Fox 2002: 42; Hernández Navarro 2002). Trade had already become an important issue for these actors, especially because of the trade rounds of the General Agreement on Tariffs and Trade (GATT) and unilateral liberalization processes, but it was not part of a cross-border agenda in the region. As one participant in Brazil's National Forum of Agrarian Reform and Rural Justice (Fórum Nacional da Reforma Agrária e Justiça no Campo) explained, when this coalition was created, in the mid-1990s, participants made no attempt to link domestic agrarian policies with what happened in international negotiations.[29]

A few exchanges among rural organizations from North America began during the NAFTA negotiations. In November 1991, rural and environmental organizations from Mexico, the United States, and Canada held the first Trinational Exchange on Agriculture, Environment, and NAFTA in Mexico City. Actors involved in these early collaboration efforts emphasize that it was the first time that organizations from the three countries collaborated on the basis of similar problems and sought common solutions (Lehman 2002: 169). The ties between Mexican and U.S. organizations shown in Figure 6.2 began to be nurtured at about that time. Other ties are even more recent, dating from the creation of VC and the collaboration around the FTAA and WTO negotiations, from the end of the 1990s onwards.

[28] For more details about the ideas sponsored by VC, see the document Via Campesina (2002), available at www.viacampesina.org.

[29] Interview with Edélcio Vigna, Advisor for Agrarian Reform and Food Sovereignty, INESC, Brasilia, February 2008.

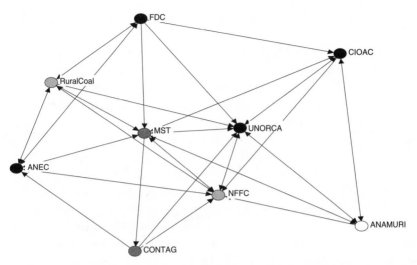

Figure 6.2. Closest Ties among Selected Rural Organizations (Brazil, Chile, Mexico, and the United States).
Countries according to node colors: Chile (white), U.S. (light gray), Brazil (dark gray), Mexico (black).
Acronyms and abbreviations: ANAMURI: National Association of Rural and Indigenous Women – Chile; ANEC: National Association of Rural Producers' Commercial Firms – Mexico; CIOAC: Independent Federation of Rural Workers – Mexico; CONTAG: National Confederation of Workers in Agriculture – Brazil; MST: Landless Rural Workers' Movement – Brazil; NFFC: National Family Farm Coalition – U.S.; UNORCA: National Union of Autonomous Regional Rural Organizations – Mexico; RuralCoal: Rural Coalition – U.S.
Sources: Interviews (see Appendix A).

The difficulties in achieving transnational collaboration, encountered by these actors as they began to mobilize with respect to trade negotiations, were similar to those discussed in the case of labor. There was no overall consensus to oppose the NAFTA negotiations. Most notably, the affiliation of Mexican organizations such as the National Peasants' Confederation (Confederación Nacional Campesina – CNC) to the Institutional Revolutionary Party (Partido Revolucionario Institucional – PRI), which was then in power, as well as the organizational fragmentation in both Mexico and the United States, limited the possibilities for transnational coalition building to stop negotiations or to try to meaningfully influence them (Hernández Navarro 2002: 153–154; Lehman 2002: 172). Unlike the case of labor, though, the absence of a prior history of ideological clashes made it easier for actors in the three countries to find their first counterparts with whom to share information when the negotiations began, even if this did not lead to sustained processes of regional coalition building.[30]

At the Southern end of the hemisphere, ties among rural organizations across national borders are even more recent. Although labor unions already had a regional organization when MERCOSUR negotiations began, rural organizations had to create one from scratch: the Coordinator of Family Farm Organizations of MERCOSUR (Coordinadora de Organizaciones de Productores Familiares del MERCOSUR – COPROFAM), founded in 1994. This small farmers' coalition brought together organizations from the MERCOSUR member countries (Argentina, Brazil, Paraguay, and Uruguay) and from Bolivia, Chile, and Peru. Its position has resembled labor's "critical support" of the integration process. The organization's goals have been to press for policies that help small farmers negatively affected by trade liberalization and to design common strategies to strengthen family-based agricultural production (see Table 6.2).[31]

The same year that COPROFAM was created, rural organizations also founded the Latin American Coordination of Rural Organizations (Coordinadora Latinoamericana de Organizaciones del Campo – CLOC). This initiative had less to do with regional trade negotiations than with the coming together of organizations during the 500 Years of Resistance Campaign, which culminated in 1992.[32] Only in its third Congress, in 2001, did CLOC present a clear position on the FTAA and bilateral free trade agreements (Berrón 2007: 109).

Thus, when FTAA talks began, there was a new albeit fragmented cross-border organizational picture, without a hemispheric coalition that brought together all the actors (VC, the International Federation

---

[30] One interesting exception is the transformation of a small farmers' coalition headquartered in the United States, the Rural Coalition, in a binational organization. In 1992, Rural Coalition organized its Assembly in El Paso, Mexico, with the goal of finding out more about Mexican reality and the possible impacts of NAFTA. Since then, Mexican and U.S. organizations have been part of its Board of Directors. Interview with Lorette Picciano, Executive Director, Rural Coalition, Washington, D.C., October 2004.

[31] In 2004, the MERCOSUR governments agreed to create a specific institutional space for the debate of small farmers' policies with participation of rural organizations – the Specialized Meeting on Family-Based Agriculture (Reunión Especializada de Agricultura Familiar – REAF).

[32] Interviews with Geraldo Fontes, MST International Relations Secretariat, São Paulo, March 2005, and with Francisca Rodríguez, International Relations Secretariat, ANAMURI, Santiago, Chile, May 2005. This Campaign was launched by a broad coalition of Latin American rural, indigenous, and faith-based organizations (among others), to protest the commemorations of the anniversary of the "discovery" of the Americas.

Table 6.2. *Rural Organizations' Participation in Trade Debates – Main Challengers from Brazil, Chile, Mexico, and the United States (2004)*

Rural Organization	Brazil		Chile		Mexico		United States	
	MST	CONTAG	ANAMURI	ANEC	UNORCA	CIOAC	NFFC	RC
International organization membership	VC* CLOC**	COPROFAM*** IUF****	VC CLOC	VC	VC	VC CLOC	VC	–
Position in trade debates	Active in Campaign against the FTAA.	Active in MERCOSUR and in Campaign against the FTAA.	Was against U.S.–Chile FTA, and the FTAA.	Was against NAFTA, less active against the FTAA than in demanding renegotiation of NAFTA.	Was against NAFTA, less active against the FTAA than in demanding renegotiation of NAFTA.	Was against NAFTA, less active against the FTAA than in demanding renegotiation of NAFTA.	Was against NAFTA and the FTAA.	Was against NAFTA and the FTAA.
Active participant in domestic trade coalitions	Yes	Yes	–	Yes	No	No	Yes	No
Active participant in the HSA*****	Yes	Yes	Yes	No	No	No	No	No

* Via Campesina; ** Latin American Coordinator of Rural Organizations; *** Coordinator of Family Farm Organizations of MERCOSUR; **** International Union of Food, Agricultural, Hotel, Restaurant, Catering, Tobacco and Allied Workers' Associations (IUF); ***** Hemispheric Social Alliance

Sources: Official web sites of the organizations and interviews (see Appendix A).

of Agricultural Producers [IFAP], and IUF functioned on the global scale, and COPROFAM and CLOC on the Latin American scale). The obstacles to unification reflected, in part, profound disagreements on how to move forward in trying to influence multilateral trade negotiations. These disagreements have been felt more strongly at the WTO than at the hemispheric scale, where challengers of trade negotiations affiliated with the various organizations came to share the decision to oppose the FTAA negotiations (see Table 6.2). As is also true in the case of labor, this broad consensus has allowed actors that would not normally work together to join hands in specific contexts.

Rural Organizations' Embeddedness in Social Networks and Political Contexts

The ties among organizations mapped in Figures 5.1–5.4 show the high profile of rural organizations, especially those affiliated with VC, in networks of challengers to trade agreements. As argued in the last chapter, the data also show differences between the domestic and transnational positions of these actors in the networks. At the transnational scale, rural organizations have the highest intragroup density: that is, they tend to have close ties to similar types of organizations, more than other types of organizations (see Table 5.5). Accordingly, when asked how they would contact organizations in other countries to organize their participation at an event parallel to a future FTAA Ministerial meeting, most informants answered that they would use transnational rural coalitions (such as VC), and not trade coalitions, as their privileged gateways.

At the domestic scale, however, density measures show that rural organizations do have important ties to other types of CSOs (see Table 5.3). In fact, their actions on trade often have been conducted in collaboration with others, through co-membership in national trade coalitions and campaigns, or in more informal ways. Some of these ties go back a long time, such as those linking rural organizations and faith-based groups in Brazil and in the United States.[33]

Thus, relationships between rural organizations and other challengers of trade agreements have been much more complicated and heterogeneous

---

[33] Sectors of the Brazilian Catholic Church have been involved in mobilizations for agrarian reform in Brazil for decades, and they played an important role in the creation of the MST. See, for example, Comparato (2001: esp. 114–115; Carter 2005).

than an account based solely on the Cancun protests might have suggested. Difficulties in coordinating action then were exacerbated by the interorganizational conflicts in Mexico and the lack of mobilization on the part of other actors (such as Mexican labor). This does not mean, however, that collaborative relationships between rural organizations and other types of organizations have been totally absent in Mexico.

The debates about the impacts of the liberalization of the trade in corn under NAFTA rules provide a good example of cross-sectoral collaboration. For many Mexican rural organizations, one of the key demands since the late 1990s has been to renegotiate the agrarian chapter of NAFTA and, more specifically, to take white corn and beans out of the trade liberalization calendar.[34] The negative impact of imports on small producers and the contamination of native species by U.S. genetically modified corn led to unprecedented collaborative efforts among rural, indigenous, and environmental organizations.[35] In 1999 these organizations launched a campaign against transgenetic contamination that linked the NAFTA provisions directly to the local impact on rural and indigenous communities in Mexico.

In the Mexican network (Figure 5.3) we can see that environmental organizations such as the Environmental Studies Group (Grupo de Estudios Ambientales – GEA) and Greenpeace and rural organizations such as UNORCA, the rural NGO Center for Studies for Rural Change in Mexico (Centro de Estudios para el Cambio en el Campo Mexicano – CECCAM), and the National Association of Rural Producers' Trading Firms (Asociación Nacional de Empresas Comercializadoras de Productores del Campo – ANEC) nominated each other as closest allies. Those ties reflect the collaboration on this campaign. On the one hand,

---

[34] The Movement El Campo no Aguanta Más (which would translate as something like "The Rural Sector Cannot Take It Any Longer") succeeded in temporarily unifying the broad range of rural workers' organizations in Mexico, around demands that included the renegotiation of the calendar of agricultural products liberalization under NAFTA and changes to Mexican rural policies. Not coincidentally, this initiative flourished in 2002, after the new Farm Bill was approved in the United States and a few months before the nine-year transition to liberalization in rice, soybeans, wheat, and various other products ended.

[35] Although corn was subject to a longer transition period (fourteen years) than other products, Mexico has issued import licenses that were not required under the NAFTA rules, and this has resulted in a dramatic increase of U.S. exports. With the full liberalization of corn trade in January 1, 2008, producers feared that U.S. exports to Mexico would increase even more. See the data on bilateral trade in corn in the report produced by the U.S. Department of Agriculture, in Zahniser and Coyle (2004).

this is an example of collective action that successfully linked the impacts of a multilateral trade agreement and local communities' environment and economic well-being. On the other hand, it highlighted the difficulties of taking broad-based domestic collaboration to the international scale.

When the Mexican allies petitioned the North American Commission for Environmental Cooperation (CEC) to investigate the contamination of maize fields, U.S. organizations did not join in. As the Director of Greenpeace-Mexico explained:

What happens in the U.S. is that the campaign against genetically modified organisms (GMOs) is very fragmented. The corporations are very strong and there are GMOs all over the place. I think it is very difficult to propose a transnational alliance as a strategy [on this issue]. Maybe some U.S. agricultural groups would agree, because of the problems they face to commercialize GMOs, but, even in this case, they would be weak allies.[36]

However, when actors do build cross-sectoral ties, their interaction may impact their visions of trade debates and lead to new approaches. The collaboration between Oxfam International and Oxfam America's offices and rural organizations is a good example. In this case, these relationships helped to transform Oxfam's vision of trade negotiations in the Americas and the strategies to be pursued:

When Oxfam first engaged on trade, the focus was on the WTO. From Europe, the FTAA was invisible. It was here in the Americas, and particularly in South America, I think, that civil society organizations that were engaged said: "you can't come to Latin America and talk about trade like that, we don't know the WTO, but we know the FTAA, and it doesn't represent a potential for us. Quite the contrary: it's a threat." That was a battle that was waged, because Oxfam didn't want a negative message [about trade]. It wanted a positive message that trade can be an engine for poverty reduction. That was a struggle that was waged from the bottom-up internally in Oxfam, but certainly pushed by allies.[37]

As a result, although Oxfam International and VC clashed regularly at WTO meetings, Oxfam offices in Latin America and in the United States worked closely with VC affiliates in opposition to agreements such as the FTAA, CAFTA, and others. However, similarly to the case of labor, this

---

[36] Interview with Alejandro Calvillo, Director of Greenpeace-Mexico, Mexico City, August 2004. It is also interesting to note that, although Greenpeace-Mexico was very active in this campaign, Greenpeace in the United States did not have a campaign against GMOs.

[37] Interview with Stephanie Weinberg, Oxfam America's Trade Policy Advisor, Washington, D.C., February 2008.

common position did not erase perennial disagreements over strategies and key issues. In particular, the topic of U.S. agricultural subsidies remains a source of contention. At the same time that some of the organizations that have challenged trade negotiations criticize them, the NFFC argues that it is the depression of prices that is really the root of the problem, making subsidies necessary for the survival of U.S. farmers.[38] Also, tensions between the demands for fair prices for farmers versus cheap food for urban people or cheap raw materials for food and fiber manufacturers have not been solved (Edelman 2003: 215).

In sum, rural organizations have increasingly occupied spaces in trade debates by creating new transnational organizations, and by rallying actors from developed and developing countries around the idea of food sovereignty and opposition to further trade liberalization. Challengers of trade agreements, however, remained divided between those affiliated with VC and those that were not, which reflected important differences in pathways to transnationality. At both global and hemispheric scales, discussions about the use of agricultural subsidies and the role of the WTO remained extremely divisive, and were suppressed intermittently, in efforts to build common agendas that tended to be more successful in the context of single-issue campaigns.

More specifically, the suppression of differences and the minimalist consensus to work jointly against the FTAA allowed many of these actors to work together, while tensions reemerged periodically. At the domestic scale, broader alliances were possible around specific issue-based campaigns, such as the one concerning corn in Mexico. At the transnational scale, rural organizations affiliated with VC engaged less than labor organizations in the construction of broad coalitions to challenge trade negotiations, as the analysis of organizational pathways to transnationality will show.

The Potential Brokerage Roles of NGOs

Besides labor and rural organizations, the third most frequently nominated group of actors in the networks mapped in Brazil, Chile, Mexico, and the United States was a set of NGOs. These actors share a key characteristic: all have participated in trade debates from a multi-issue

---

[38] Interview with Katherine Ozer, NFFC Task Force on Trade, Washington, D.C., October 2004.

perspective. This distinguishes them from NGOs that take a specialized look at trade agreements.[39] Furthermore, they are well-established, domestically rooted organizations: in Brazil, the Federation of Organisms for Social and Educational Assistance (Federação de Órgãos para Assistência Social e Educacional – FASE), the Institute of Socio-Economic Studies (Instituto de Estudos Socioeconômicos – INESC), and Alternative Policies for the Southern Cone (Políticas Alternativas para o Cone Sul – PACS); in Mexico, the Peoples' Team (Equipo Pueblo – DECA-EP); in Chile, the Chilean Alliance for a Just and Responsible Trade (Alianza Chilena por un Comercio Justo y Responsable – ACJR) and the Center of National Studies on Alternative Development (Centro de Estudios Nacionales de Desarrollo Alternativo – CENDA); in the United States, Public Citizen, the Development Group for Alternative Policies (D-GAP), and the Institute for Policy Studies (IPS) (see Table 6.3 and Figures 5.1–5.4).

It is precisely because these actors have a broad approach to trade agreements that they can develop close ties with a variety of types of organizations. These links are not automatic, though. They have been the result of these actors' decision to invest in building the capacity to participate in policy debates from a variety of entry points. Given the specific characteristics of trade negotiations, which are highly technical arenas that extend over many issue areas, the effects of which are hard to evaluate fully, these NGOs' analytical skills can be powerful tools in networks of challengers to trade agreements.

On the other hand, the centrality of these NGOs is an interesting puzzle if one considers that, in comparison with labor and rural organizations, they have very little mobilization capacity and no consistent history of participation in trade debates. They do not represent specific constituencies affected by trade agreements, nor do they seek to do so. Furthermore, as seen above, in spite of recent initiatives, many member-based organizations still resist sharing visibility and resources with NGOs,[40] and the reverse is also true: many NGOs are wary of collaborating

---

[39] For example, Doctors Without Borders has worked specifically on the impacts of trade agreements on access to medicines, and Human Rights Watch has focused on the interface between labor rights violations and trade agreements.

[40] This resistance was clear, for example, when the Brazilian chapter of the HSA discussed whether to send a representative to follow global trade negotiations in Geneva, and unions opposed sending someone from the NGO that had made the proposal. In the end, the compromise reached was to send two representatives: one from a labor union (CUT's Steelworkers Confederation) and another from the NGO INESC (interview with Fernando Lopes, Secretary-General of CNM/CUT, São Paulo, March 2005). On

Table 6.3. *Selected Multi-Issue NGOs in Trade Challengers' Networks (2004)*

NGO	Brazil			Chile		Mexico	United States		
	FASE	INESC	PACS	CENDA	ACJR	DECA-EP	D-GAP	IPS	Public Citizen
Position in trade debates	Active in Campaign against the FTAA.	Active in Campaign against the FTAA and in debates about MERCOSUR.	Active in Campaign against the FTAA.	Active in Campaign against U.S.-Chile FTA.	Active in Campaign against U.S.-Chile FTA and Campaign against the FTAA.	Active in Campaign against NAFTA and Against the FTAA.	Active in Campaign against NAFTA and Against the FTAA.	Active in Campaign against NAFTA and Against the FTAA.	Active in Campaign against NAFTA and athe FTAA.
Active participant in domestic trade coalitions	Yes	Yes	Yes	–	–	Yes	Yes	Yes	Yes
Active participant in the HSA	Yes	Yes	No	No	Yes	Yes	Yes	Yes	No

Source: Interviews with representatives of multi-issue NGOs in charge of trade issues (see Appendix A).

with unions and rural workers' organizations. Finally, not all of the most central NGOs in the networks sponsored the same pathways to transnationality. Although some moved toward sustained transnationalization as they became involved in trade debates, others entered the international arena only periodically, and still others preferred to internalize debates, focusing on national targets and issues.

NGOs as Newcomers to Trade Debates

Most NGOs began to pay closer attention to trade negotiations only in the 1990s, and many not until the end of that decade.[41] Many U.S. and Mexican NGOs became active during the NAFTA debates, but, in the Southern Cone, the regional integration process did not have the same appeal. For some, MERCOSUR was a "neoliberal project" that would benefit only corporations.[42] For others, it was yet another attempt at Latin American integration that was doomed to fail. Furthermore, NGOs resented the fact that channels for civil society involvement had a "capital-labor corporativist logic"[43] that prioritized the participation of labor and business organizations in negotiating arenas.

However, there were a few precedents of NGO participation in the Southern Cone in the pre-FTAA period: in 1993 and 1995 the Brazilian NGO INESC organized seminars that brought together parliamentarians, negotiators, and CSOs to debate the potentially negative impacts of MERCOSUR on small farmers.[44] Throughout the decade, there were other attempts to participate in discussions about regional integration, led by consumers, women, and environmental NGOs, but these were not sustained and did not have important impacts on MERCOSUR negotiations (von Bülow 2003a: esp. 99–100; Hochstetler 2003).

the often hostile relationships between labor organizations and NGOs, and how these may be overcome, see the contributions in Eade and Leather (2005). On how similar tensions were also present during the process that led to the creation of the Pro-Canada Network in the mid-1980s, see Huyer (2005).

[41] There are a few exceptions, however. The Brazilian NGOs PACS and IBASE, for example, began following the GATT negotiations as early as the mid-1980s. As mentioned in Chapter 3, some U.S. and Canadian NGOs also began to pay attention to global trade negotiations around that time.

[42] Interview with Marcos Arruda (General Coordinator) and Sandra Quintela (Programs Coordinator), PACS, Rio de Janeiro, March 2005.

[43] Interview with Iara Pietricovsky, Executive Board, INESC, Brasilia, April 2005.

[44] Interview with Edélcio Vigna, Advisor for Agrarian Reform and Food Sovereignty, INESC, Brasilia, February 2008.

Most importantly, though, NGOs were *not* newcomers to debates on macroeconomic issues and global governance. Since the 1980s, many had been working jointly with social movement organizations on issues such as foreign debt and the impacts of policies promoted by international institutions, most notably the World Bank and the International Monetary Fund. These ties were both domestic and transnational.[45] In addition, previous linkages, created over other issues and in other international arenas – such as United Nations conferences or the activism on human rights during Latin America's military dictatorships (Keck and Sikkink 1998; Friedman et al. 2005) – were in part available to be reactivated when trade became a relevant issue to these organizations.

In the NAFTA countries, a much larger set of NGOs played a key role in the debates about the trade agreement and in building the coalitions to challenge it. However, there were differences with respect to the kinds of NGOs that became involved and their pathways to transnationality. For example, the Canadian women's movement was actively involved in the trade debates (MacDonald 2005); this was not true to the same extent either in the United States or in Mexico. In the United States, environmental NGOs were key actors during the NAFTA debates, but the interface between environment and trade had a much lower profile in the other two countries. Roles differed too. Some NGOs became key mediators across different types of organizations and national borders, while others gained influence due to their analytical and organizational skills but focused their activism on the domestic scale.

Multi-Issue NGOs as Transnational Brokers?

Brokers have been defined in the social network analysis literature as actors that are in a position to link groups that were previously disconnected (see, for example, Marsden 1982: 202; Gould and Fernández 1989). More recently, Doug McAdam, Sidney Tarrow, and Charles Tilly defined brokerage as "the linking of two or more previously unconnected social sites by a unit that mediates their relations with one another and/or with yet other sites" (McAdam et al. 2001: 26). The understanding of brokerage in this book broadens the definition by extending the role of brokers to situations of remoteness among actors that are not necessarily disconnected.

---

[45] For example, the relationship between FASE in Brazil and D-GAP in the United States originated in the context of debates about structural adjustment policies.

As Ann Mische has argued, "the existence of completely disconnected clusters is only a limiting case in relation to more commonly occurring partial forms of intersections and disjunction" (Mische 2008: 49).

Thus, I propose to define brokerage in broad terms, as bridging initiatives that link actors (individuals, organizations, or sectors) that are separated by geographical distance, lack of trust, or lack of resources, or simply because they are unaware of each others' existence. In this sense, brokerage is not simply reaching out to connect actors. It involves negotiating differences and developing common meanings, even if provisional ones (Mische 2008: 50, 138–139). This is particularly true in the analysis of transnational collective action among heterogeneous actors that often have multiple ties linking them, through their co-participation in many different campaigns, events, or coalitions. Such an understanding of brokerage moves from a focus on static positions of actors in social networks to the study of the processes by which brokers arrive at and sustain these positions (or not) (Diani 2003b).

A few NGOs have attempted to play such brokerage roles in the networks under discussion here, and only in some cases have they been successful. The history of domestic relationships among CSOs plays an important part in explaining these outcomes. For example, some of the Brazilian NGOs that occupy central positions in the domestic network (Figure 5.1) became aware of trade debates through their historical connections to labor organizations. Before the Belo Horizonte FTAA meeting of 1997, CUT's Secretary of International Affairs contacted FASE (an old ally that in the beginning of the 1980s had helped to build the labor federation) to discuss the creation of a domestic coalition of organizations focused on trade, one that would function as the counterpart of other domestic trade coalitions and as the national chapter of the HSA.[46] The Secretariat of the Brazilian Network for the Integration of the Peoples (Rede Brasileira pela Integração dos Povos – REBRIP) has been headquartered at FASE since that time. Before 1997 this NGO had not had a prominent role in trade debates.

The Washington-based NGO D-GAP, which served as headquarters for the Secretariat of the U.S. Alliance for Responsible Trade (ART) between the founding of the coalition and until 2006, is a similar case of successful brokerage. Both D-GAP and FASE are well-established NGOs

---

[46] Interview with Fátima Mello, International Relations Coordinator of FASE and Executive Secretariat of REBRIP, Rio de Janeiro, March 2005.

with previous relationships with various types of CSOs in their countries and abroad, working on a wide range of issues, related to development, poverty, and democratization of international organizations.

The relatively low profile that D-GAP and FASE have kept in trade debates helps to explain the fact that they are not the organizations with the highest in-degree in domestic networks, and, in spite of their brokerage roles across scales, that they are even less central in the transnational one. As the person in charge of REBRIP at FASE explained, the ability to play brokerage roles in such heterogeneous organizational environments entails accepting holding such a low profile:

We don't do anything [that is trade-related] as FASE.... There is a group of NGOs in Brazil that knows its roles and limits, and that does not want to represent or to take the place of social movements. I think that after decades of working together, we now have the maturity to recognize each organization's role. This is FASE's prime commitment in terms of its relationships with others: we privilege the participation of social movements in all we do. We are against exclusive articulations among NGOs.[47]

When asked how they would contact challengers of the FTAA in other countries, almost all multi-issue NGOs included in this study would use trade coalitions as their gateways to organize a transnational mobilization. Only one – the Chilean CENDA – would use other channels, but, as will be seen in the next chapter, Chile's case is different because it became the only one of the four countries without a domestic trade coalition.

In sum, NGOs seem to be more likely to successfully play brokerage roles among trade challengers when (1) they approach trade from a multi-issue perspective; (2) they are willing to coordinate collective action, while at the same time not attempting to speak for others, or to occupy center stage; (3) they have good previous relationships with the main member-based organizations in the country; and (4) they have good relationships with key actors in other countries, or are actively pursuing them. Not all multi-issue NGOs have wanted to play brokerage roles, though.

"It's Not about Trade"

The growing number of issues that are currently seen as being "trade-related" reflects not only the push by government officials to broaden the agenda, but also the increased involvement by NGOs that are capable of

[47] Ibid.

linking trade agreement negotiations to a great variety of topics, and of providing a unifying rhetoric. In this sense, these actors are the main boosters of the mechanism of "extension" of agendas in domestic and transnational trade coalitions. Debates about investment rules, public services, food safety, and intellectual property, for example, have become more relevant, and have shown great potential for organizing across different types of organizations. This extended agenda also allowed NGOs and their allies to eschew the label of "protectionists" while mobilizing against free trade agreements, because, after all, *it's not about trade* (Wallach 2004).

Public Citizen, Equipo Pueblo, PACS, and CENDA are examples of this expanded agenda-setting role in the United States, Mexico, Brazil, and Chile. Unlike D-GAP and FASE, these NGOs have participated in the trade debates by prioritizing their particular demands and strategies. Their network centrality is explained better by the specific skills they bring to the field, than to brokerage roles played in trade coalitions, although they also have built strong linkages with other actors.

Global Trade Watch was created in 1995 as one of Public Citizen's six internal divisions, thus establishing trade as one of the organization's priority areas of action. With a eleven-person staff dedicated to trade negotiations in 2008,[48] Public Citizen stood out as one of the organizations that had invested most heavily in hiring specialized human resources.[49] Most of these resources have focused on lobbying the U.S. Congress. Since the Legislative branch has significant influence over trade policies (see the discussion about trade policy making in Chapter 10), lobbying legislators is a key activity for U.S. trade agreement challengers. The marriage of expertise in various trade-related issue areas and previous knowledge about the workings of Congress explain why Public Citizen was one of the most nominated actors in the field of trade challengers, in the United States as well as at the hemispheric scale. Out of 123 organizations in the four countries studied, 41 (almost 34 percent) mentioned Public Citizen as a close ally. As one union leader explained: "If I wanted to know some specific question of the more minute detail of NAFTA or WTO or the FTAA, I would call Lori [Lori Wallach, the Director of Global Trade

---

[48] See www.citizen.org/trade, last accessed April 1, 2008.

[49] In 2004, ORIT, for example, a much larger organization, only had five staff members following trade negotiations. Interview with Víctor Báez, ORIT Secretary General, Belo Horizonte, December 2004.

Watch] and she would be able to answer the question. It's an incredible resource to have."[50]

Interestingly, Public Citizen's centrality in the networks does not mean agreement with its strategies. Many of those who said that Public Citizen was one of their organization's closest allies also stated that they strongly disagreed with many of the positions it had sponsored since NAFTA went into force. In part, these tensions were a matter of personal differences among individuals, but they were also a reflection of disagreements over pathways to transnationality. These disagreements were made more explicit given Public Citizen's strategy of domestication of trade issues, best seen in its pragmatic emphasis on winning the battles in the U.S. Congress. As one of the interviewees explained:

During one of the fast track debates, Public Citizen did focus groups, which showed that the issues to focus on were food safety, drugs, and trucking. We [in the Alliance for Responsible Trade] totally disagreed with that approach. I understood that these were issues that resonated with a lot of Americans, and I think that they were very cautious in the way they worded their statements, but ... a step loose from them, those arguments became pretty anti-Mexican.[51]

Accordingly, when asked what was the greatest difficulty in the relationships with organizations in the South, Public Citizen's then-coordinator for the FTAA answered that it was to explain the strategies that have to be implemented in order to win votes in Congress, or to stop negotiations.[52] The case of the campaign against the entrance of Mexican trucks into the United States after passage of NAFTA is a good example that shows that not only labor, but also NGOs, may fall in "national traps":

The Mexican trucks problem is a nightmare for us. Our position has been that it has to do with environmental laws.... If you are letting trucks in without making Mexican standards as high as U.S. standards, that means that the U.S. environmental law is being trumped by a trade treaty. But the way the Mexicans view it, is that it's a very xenophobic, racist initiative, that we don't want Mexicans in the U.S.[53]

---

[50] Interview with Christopher Townsend, Political Action Director and International Representative, United Electrical Radio and Machine Workers (UE), Arlington, VA, October 2005.

[51] Anonymous interview, Washington, D.C., September 2005.

[52] Interview with Timi Gerson, Public Citizen's FTAA Coordinator, Washington, D.C., May 2004.

[53] Ibid.

For Public Citizen, their choice of allies and frames has to do with the differences between short-term goals while lobbying in Congress, and long-term goals when building transnational coalitions and common projects: "I think a lot of organizations in terms of frame one and frame two. Frame one is ... winning the specific Congress battles. But frame two is your global perspective, what you want the world to look like. Frame one is who would you fight the battle with, versus who you want to win the war with."[54] With over fifteen years' experience in following trade negotiations, Public Citizen has made changes in its activities and attitudes that were at least in part a result of interactions with allies in Latin America. During the FTAA debates, it invested in hiring Spanish-speaking staff to be able to find allies in the region and to better communicate its choice of strategies.[55] However, the continuous disagreements remain a good example of the difficulties in trying to implement a pathway of sustained internalization and simultaneously build collaborative relationships overseas.

The Strength of Missing Ties

The combination of social network data and qualitative information shows that challengers of trade agreements became embedded in a new relational environment through their participation in collective action on trade. Had the same mapping of relationships been done in the mid-1990s, the resulting networks would have been very different. Many of the core organizations simply would not have been there. A good example of these changes is provided by looking at the transnational ties between U.S. and Latin American CSOs. We can be confident that CUT-Brazil would not have identified the AFL-CIO as a close ally before the mid-1990s, nor would so many organizations in Brazil, Chile, and Mexico have nominated D-GAP or Public Citizen. In the first case, because of the ideological clashes of the Cold War period; in the second case, because these relationships were limited to a few organizations or did not exist. Perhaps even more importantly, the analysis showed the relevance of South–South ties, and the increasingly important presence of Latin American organizations in mobilizations related to trade agreement negotiations.

---

[54] Ibid.
[55] Ibid.

This new relational environment has not been an automatic outcome of the changes in the global governance of trade, or the result of the end of the Cold War. It has been the consequence of a dynamic, continuous, and contentious process of negotiation and learning among actors. Good examples of this process, analyzed in this chapter, are the transformation of the attitudes and positions of Oxfam's offices in the Americas, the suppression of clear references to the problem of agricultural subsidies in statements signed by coalitions, and the extension of labor federations' rhetoric to include other CSOs' issues, such as environmental concerns, at the domestic and transnational scales.

The networks mapped not only provide enlightening information on challengers' collective action through existing ties, but also through the missing ties. In spite of important differences among the cases of Brazil, Chile, Mexico, and the United States, in general terms three sets of CSOs are either totally missing from the networks of closest allies, or have been pushed to the periphery of these networks through time: local organizations from outside the most populated urban areas, reformist actors that demanded specific changes in trade agreements, and grassroots organizations. In terms of issues, missing from the networks are indigenous organizations, organizations that focus on racial equality, and youth groups.

These missing nodes and links are, to a certain extent, a result of the lack of financial resources to incorporate actors situated geographically far away from each other. They are also, however, a product of political disagreements. In the case of the United States, for example, organizations from outside the Washington, D.C. "Beltway" have criticized some of the most prominent actors in trade debates, such as the AFL-CIO and Public Citizen, for prioritizing lobbying activities, and for concentrating too many campaign resources in their hands. In Mexico, local CSOs have also complained about their lack of access to decision-making processes about the strategies to be followed, the distribution of funding, and the definition of goals and targets. In Brazil, the national chapter of the HSA had difficulties incorporating the grassroots organizations that participated actively in the Campaign against the FTAA in that country after 2004. In Chile, the critiques of those who felt blocked from decision-making processes eventually led to the disappearance of the national coalition created during the U.S.-Chile free trade negotiations.

The strength of these missing ties is part of the analysis presented in the following part of this book, which discusses the organizational pathways to transnationality taken by challengers of trade agreements. More specifically, it offers an analysis of how different coalition-building choices have been able (or not) to respond to the critiques of those who have felt excluded.

Organizational Pathways
to Transnationality

7

The Creation and Demise of Transnational Coalitions

As an increasingly wide spectrum of civil society organizations (CSOs) began to debate how they could coordinate actions to challenge free trade agreements, there was a glaring lack of blueprints available for coalition building across groups, sectors, and national boundaries. Previous transnational arrangements in the Americas were in the main specific to categories or types of organizations, such as international labor or religious organizations, with few intersections among them. These initiatives were institutionalized in hierarchical and territorial terms, as national organizations became affiliated with international bodies.

Trade-related coalition-building efforts in the Americas led to the emergence of a new repertoire, which built upon but extrapolated from preexisting initiatives, bringing about a constellation of new and old *organizational pathways to transnationality*. As noted in Chapter 2, the process of coalition building is not linear. Organizations do not necessarily become more international through time. Furthermore, there is no deterministic trend leading CSOs from intermittent participation to adhering to more sustained organizational pathways.

To capture these dynamics, this chapter analyzes the process that led to the creation of hemispheric coalitions on trade. Chapter 8 complements this analysis by focusing on the creation of trade coalitions in Brazil, Chile, Mexico, and the United States. The main argument is that actors have built organizational arrangements that are influenced by previous social networks and coalitions, but that these have been rearranged through the creation of new ties and efforts to balance power relations, the diffusion of successful experiences and their adaptation in new environments, and the creation of brokerage roles that link the national and transnational scales.

In spite of the dearth of ready-made recipes for coalition building, actors do have visions of what kinds of alternatives are unacceptable to them. The literature on transnationalism has highlighted the mounting rejection by actors of hierarchical and centralized organizations. Accordingly, it has placed a positive emphasis on the tendency for transnational collective action to be organized loosely, preferably around campaigns that have a limited lifespan, and in which agreements are narrowly targeted and temporary (Anheier and Themudo 2002; Tarrow and della Porta 2005). However, little has been written about how actors choose among different possibilities and, more specifically, about the creation of coalitions that are not loose campaigns but, at the same time, are also not simply the reproduction of hierarchical and centralized forms of transnational coalition building. We still need to analyze the different balances between past organizational forms and the creation of new ones that are represented by current organizational pathways to transnationality, and how actors move among the various options that are available to them.

Campaign and Affiliation Coalition-Building Modes

Trade challengers' coalitions have coexisted with a variety of other transnational coalitions, many of which proliferated after the 1980s.[1] The goal has not been to replace preexisting coalitions, nor to compete with them, but to create intersecting spaces for coordinating collective action. Thus, in 2005, a national labor federation such as the AFL-CIO discussed trade-related goals and strategies simultaneously within the Hemispheric Social Alliance (HSA), the Continental Campaign against the Free Trade Area of the Americas (FTAA), the Stop CAFTA Coalition (a coalition against the U.S.–Central America Free Trade Agreement), and in the international labor arenas. Similarly, many gender and human rights nongovernmental organizations (NGOs) participated in various trade coalitions, and this did not call in question their participation in other domestic, regional, and global initiatives.

---

[1] In their research on Latin American regional organizations (which they called "regional networks"), Patricio Korzeniewicz and Bill Smith identified nearly three hundred (see Korzeniewicz and Smith 2003a: 13). This number would be even higher if it was extended to the entire hemisphere.

This pluralism is evidence of the rejection of forms of organization with rigid membership rules that characterized much of transnational collective action in the past. As one of the Chilean founders of the HSA explained, there was general agreement among participants on the need to define rules of coexistence that would allow for plural transnational collective action: "We had in common this critique, that is related to the construction of a new subject, that we needed to work in an efficient way, linking the international with local impacts, but without these false, modernist representations of large conglomerates, and [the creation of] representations that are often fictitious."[2]

However, this common rejection did not translate into a common organizational pathway. The variety of available coalition-building forms reflects different visions of what actors thought transnational collective action should look like, what their role should be, and with whom they wished to be allied. More specifically, organizational arrangements proposed different balances between the seemingly contradictory organizing principles of equality and effectiveness. These ranged from coalition building that granted great autonomy to members through less hierarchical structures that were not sustained through time – the *campaign mode* on which the transnational collective action literature has focused most of its attention – to more ambitious projects of creation of long-term *affiliation-based* coalitions, with clearer membership boundaries and internal division of labor rules.

These different options have been built by trade challengers in the Americas since the second half of the 1990s, at the domestic as well as at the transnational scale (see Figure 7.1). Initiatives such as the Continental Campaign against the FTAA and the Stop CAFTA Coalition are good examples of the campaign mode, and the HSA and the International Gender and Trade Network (IGTN) best exemplify the affiliation mode (see Figure 7.2).

These coalition modes are themselves internally heterogeneous in terms of governance rules. For example, affiliation-based coalitions range from the traditional forms of hierarchical organization linking the local to the global level, as in the case of international labor organizations, to more flexible and multisectoral alliances such as the IGTN and the

---

[2] Interview with Coral Pey, then Executive Director of the Chilean Alliance for a Just and Responsible Trade (ACJR), Santiago de Chile, June 2005.

DOMESTIC	YEAR	TRANSNATIONAL
	1986→	Creation of the **Coordination of Southern Cone Labor Centrals** (CCSCS)
Creation of Pro-Canada Network, later renamed **Action Canada Network** (ACN)	←1987	
Creation of **Common Frontiers**, Canada	←1988	
Creation of the **Mexican Action Network on Free Trade** (RMALC), the Quebec Coalition on Trilateral Negotiations, later renamed **Quebec Network on Continental Integration** (RQIC), and the U.S. Mobilization on Development, Trade, Labor and the Environment, later renamed **Alliance for Responsible Trade** (ART)	←1991	
Creation of U.S. **Citizens' Trade Campaign** (CTC)	←1992	
Creation of the Chilean Network for Peoples' Integration (RECHIP), later renamed **Chilean Alliance for a Just and Responsible Trade**	←1994	
	1997→	Launching of the idea of creation of the **Hemispheric Social Alliance** (HSA) during FTAA Ministerial Meeting
Creation of the **Brazilian Network for the Integration of the Peoples** (REBRIP)	←1998→	First Peoples' Summit in Santiago
	1999→	First meeting of the Hemispheric Coordination of the HSA; launching of the **International Gender and Trade Network (IGTN)**
	2001→	Second Peoples' Summit in Québec; I Hemispheric Meeting against the FTAA in Havana.
Launching of **national chapters of the Campaign against the FTAA** in Argentina, Brazil, Mexico, Bolivia, Colombia, Ecuador, Uruguay, and other countries	←2002→	Launching of the **Continental Campaign against the FTAA**; II Hemispheric Meeting against the FTAA in Havana; Launching of **Stop CAFTA Campaign**.
	2004→	III Hemispheric Meeting against the FTAA in Havana
	2005→	IV Hemispheric Meeting against the FTAA in Havana; Third Peoples' Summit in Mar del Plata
	2006→	V Hemispheric Meeting against the FTAA

Figure 7.1. Two Decades of Coalition Building on Trade in the Americas, 1986–2006.

HSA. Both of these coalitions were created in the context of mobilizations around trade in the 1990s. However, whereas the IGTN brings together groups, activists, and intellectuals concerned with highlighting the interface between gender relations and trade negotiations, the HSA promotes

		ENDURANCE	
		−	+
INTERNATIONALIZATION	−	Domestic chapters of the campaign against the FTAA; other domestic coalitions	HSA domestic chapters; other domestic coalitions
	+	Continental Campaign against the FTAA; other transnational campaigns	Hemispheric Social Alliance; International Gender and Trade Network

Figure 7.2. Organizational Pathways to Transnationality on Trade in the Americas.

a broader space for dialogue among different civil society sectors, which includes the IGTN and other women's movement groups.

With respect to the endurance of organizational pathways on trade in the Americas, coalitions built around campaigns tended to last as long as a specific agreement was under negotiation, whereas affiliation-based initiatives such as the IGTN and the HSA have lasted longer. In terms of degree of internationalization, participation in campaigns and/ or affiliation-modes of coalition building does not necessarily entail a domestication or a transnationalization of strategies and discourses. For example, CSOs that became involved in the Campaign against the FTAA could limit their participation to only being part of the domestic chapter, or they could also play active roles in international events, such as the hemispheric encounters held periodically by the Campaign in Cuba (see Figure 7.1).

Among this plurality of initiatives, the case of the HSA is an especially interesting one, because its members sought to create what transnational collective action scholars have deemed hardest: long-term collaboration, based on consensual rules for coordination and representation among a broad variety of actors. However, HSA founders have been only partially successful in their goal to create an open and horizontal hemispheric coalition.

The Creation of the Hemispheric Social Alliance

During the Belo Horizonte FTAA Ministerial Meeting, held in 1997, CSOs from five countries approved the idea of creating a new hemispheric

121

coalition. Participants from coalitions and NGOs from Brazil, Canada, Chile, Mexico, and the United States, together with the Inter-American Regional Organization of Workers (ORIT), proposed that it should be a permanent space that would bring together the same variety of types of CSOs that had been crucial in mobilizing Canadian, Mexican, and U.S. constituencies during the North American Free Trade Agreement (NAFTA) negotiations.

Throughout the following decade, the HSA underwent four phases, from the definition of the coalition's goals and internal governance rules, to direction setting, implementing the tasks agreed upon, and, finally, revising the goals and relationships among members.[3] Between 1997 and the first Coordination Meeting, held in March 1999, members discussed how the HSA would function, engaged in affiliating more organizations from different countries, and put together the main demands presented to national governments (mostly related to the FTAA negotiations). Between 1999 and January 2002 there was a period of consolidation, which ended with the launching of the Continental Campaign against the FTAA. This was also a period of revising the group's direction, during which the coalition went from formulating broad demands that changed the agenda and contents of negotiations, to reaching a clearer stance for opposing the hemispheric negotiations.[4]

The third phase went from 2002 to the Miami Ministerial Meeting, at the end of 2003. During those two years, the FTAA remained the main topic in the coalition's agenda, and members mobilized together with the Continental Campaign in opposition to the agreement. Finally, since 2004, as the FTAA negotiations became stalled, the coalition entered a new phase, progressively broadening its agenda to focus on global-level negotiations and other regional agreements, while at the same time linking these negotiations to issues such as foreign debt and militarization. This has also been a period of intense debates about the future of the coalition in a post-FTAA era, and of changes in its internal organization.

---

[3] For a discussion of phases in coalition building, see Brown and Fox (1998: 449–450).

[4] Before 2001, the HSA demanded greater access to the decision-making process and to information on the progress of negotiations, and a broadening of the scope of these negotiations to include a social and environmental agenda. See, for example, the Belo Horizonte joint declaration by unions and NGOs (ORIT et al. 1997). At the Québec Summit of the Americas, held in 2001, the HSA launched its new catchphrase: "The HSA says NO to the FTAA; other Americas are Possible" (see Berrón 2007: 34–35; Smith and Korzeniewicz 2007: 160–164).

The HSA did not unite the whole universe of CSOs that sought to challenge trade negotiations, but it did bring together some of the main actors in this multi-organizational field (see Figure 7.3).[5] Most of its members were located somewhere on the center-to-left of the ideological spectrum, united by a common critique of free trade policies and a negative assessment of the consequences of trade agreements. Although it is true that conservative sectors that challenged trade agreements could be found in the various countries, these maintained only informal relationships with the HSA and its national chapters and engaged intermittently in short-term collaborative efforts. Furthermore, as the coalition moved toward a more oppositional stance on the FTAA negotiations, this led it farther from business organizations that wanted to change specific topics of the negotiation and to be guaranteed a greater presence in the negotiating table.[6]

The hemispheric – not only Latin American – character of the HSA was, in itself, a novelty in terms of coalition building in the region. As one of the participants argued: "There is a rupture with the Latin Americanist vision that we cannot make an alliance with Northern movements, and this is very important, it is a contribution of the Hemispheric Social Alliance. … We are in a different era, it is not anymore 'the ones in the South fight, those in the North show solidarity.'"[7]

Although there have been many instances in the past of North–South collaboration in the Americas, the HSA innovated as an organization that sought to be a sustained coalition based on common goals and principles sustained by a wide variety of CSOs. As can be seen in Figure 7.3, members of the Hemispheric Council included national chapters and regional organizations. Many of these predated the HSA's creation.

Because of its broad membership, reaching across various civil society sectoral domains as well as the North–South divide, the HSA has

---

[5] As will be seen below, important exceptions were those organizations that participated in the Continental Campaign against the FTAA but were not members of the HSA, such as Public Citizen in the United States, or various ecumenical organizations in Brazil, and the conservative organizations that challenged free trade negotiations but did not participate in either of these initiatives.

[6] Shortly before the Belo Horizonte meeting, in 1997, unions in the Southern Cone signed a joint declaration with business organizations within the MERCOSUR Social and Economic Forum, in which they called for more transparent negotiations and the opening of channels of dialogue (FCES 1997). Some of these unions went on to participate in the HSA.

[7] Interview with Héctor de la Cueva, Director, CILAS, Mexico City, August 2004.

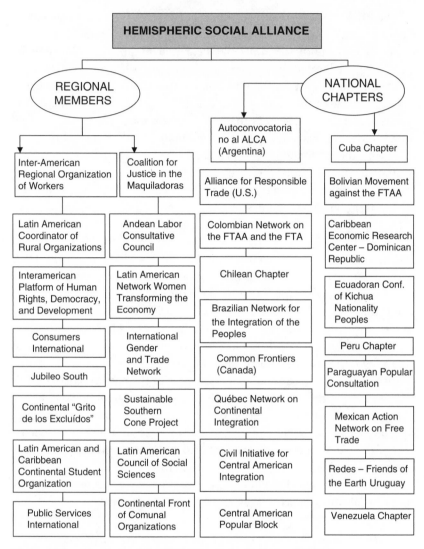

Figure 7.3. Members of the HSA Hemispheric Council (2006).

been considered an example of "the possibility of broader alliances built around the larger issue of democratising economic governance" (Anner and Evans 2004: 40). It is defined by its members as an "open space," a "forum of progressive social movements and organizations of the Americas, created to exchange information, define strategies and promote common actions, directed at finding an alternative and democratic development model."[8]

In terms of its organizational structure, the Alliance did not conceive itself "as an organization with structures and hierarchies of any type, but as an ongoing process under construction," but it admitted the creation of "minimum and flexible coordination instances at the hemispheric, regional, national, local, sectoral levels."[9] It did not have its own office spaces, nor permanent staff. It did have a rotating Secretariat, a Coordinating Group, thematic working groups, and a Hemispheric Council in which all affiliated organizations could participate (see Figure 7.3).[10] Its decision making was by consensus. It did not collect fees from its members, but, instead, raised funds from international foundations and NGOs to pay for its small organizational structure, meetings, and publications.[11] On the one hand, this avoided criticism of bureaucratization and diminished the dependency on members that had more access to financial resources. On the other hand, it limited the amount of activities that the HSA Secretariat could perform[12] and created dependency on resources from actors from outside the coalition.

In spite of the emphasis on horizontality and consensus, the HSA cannot be characterized as an "open space" accessible to all. Its dual affiliation entrance (through regional coalitions or national chapters) generated greater flexibility than most affiliation-based coalitions, but it did separate those who could become members from those who could not. Individuals and autonomous organizations could not apply directly for membership, and thus actors that were not members of regional coalitions, and/or did not wish to become members of national chapters, were in practice excluded.

At the time of the interviews done for this research with informants from 123 CSOs in Brazil, Chile, Mexico, and the United States (see

---

[8] See http://www.asc-hsa.org, accessed March 1, 2006.

[9] Ibid.

[10] Initially, the intention was to create a more sophisticated organization, with hemispheric-wide thematic working groups, but only two were active up to 2005: the group in charge of monitoring the FTAA negotiations, and the Gender Committee. Interview with Gonzalo Berrón, HSA Secretariat, São Paulo, April 2005.

[11] For example, the publication of various versions of the HSA document "Alternatives for the Americas," in Spanish, Portuguese, and English, was funded by the John D. and Catherine T. MacArthur Foundation, the Rockefeller Foundation, and the Solidago Foundation.

[12] For this criticism by Canadian participants in the HSA, see Koo (2001: 44).

Appendix A), fifty-five – almost 45 percent of the total – did not participate in the HSA. Although this is not a representative sample, it does indicate that an important segment of the networks of trade challengers remained outside this coalition. Furthermore, as argued previously, even in the case of those who were members of national chapters and/or regional organizations affiliated to the HSA, the level of commitment to transnational coalition building varied considerably.

Throughout the period studied, there were still open debates about rules for participation. As one participant explained:

> There are questions which will come up about the legitimacy of certain participants. We have had some of that discussion with regard to the Cuban Workers' Central, about whether it should be a part or not of the HSA. In my own opinion, I don't think that the inclusion of the more officialist organizations from Cuba has been that much of a detriment to the process, but of course the big question becomes: will officialist organizations in Cuba be as critical of the FTAA once the embargo is lifted and Cuba is included in the FTAA?[13]

This question never had to be answered, but it points to key ongoing debates about rules for participation in transnational coalitions. In fact, since its creation, members of the HSA made conscious efforts at expanding participation and diminishing internal power asymmetries. In its first phase, the "NAFTA 'Veterans,'" as John Foster calls the Canadian, Mexican, and U.S. national chapters, were at the core of the Alliance's activities (Foster 2005: 221). In the composition of the Coordinating Group created in 1999, however, there was a balance between North and South, and between national chapters and regional organizations.[14] The Secretariat was headquartered at the Mexican national chapter, then it moved to Brazil, and finally to Colombia, in 2007. This turn toward the South helped mitigate the mistrust of some Latin American organizations toward organizations from the North, which added to the tensions among participants during the first phase of the Alliance (Saguier 2007: 256–257).

However, the HSA has also been criticized for not being "as hemispheric as the name suggests" (Massicotte 2003: 121). Spanish became

---

[13] Anonymous interview, Washington, D.C., October 2004.

[14] The members of HSA's Coordinating Group were Common Frontiers (Canada), the Quebec Network on Hemispheric Integration (RQIC), the Alliance for Responsible Trade (U.S.), the Mexican Action Network on Free Trade (RMALC), the Brazilian Network for the Integration of the Peoples (REBRIP), the Civil Initiative for Central American Integration (ICIC), the Inter-American Regional Organization of Workers (ORIT), and the Latin American Coordination of Rural Organizations (CLOC).

the organization's de facto language, which guaranteed that Spanish-speaking Latin American participants would not have to face the language barrier. On the other hand, for the region's Portuguese, English, and French speakers, this could be an exclusionary factor. It is somewhat less of a problem for those Brazilians who have grown accustomed to participating in MERCOSUR arenas, but it is certainly a greater problem in English- and French-speaking countries, as well as in the case of indigenous peoples' organizations.[15] Although some U.S. CSOs hired staff that spoke Spanish and/or Portuguese, many others did not, and that effectively limited their participation in meetings and phone conferences, as a U.S. representative in the HSA argued: "All HSA meetings are in Spanish, so English-speakers don't even think about going. . . . Yes, language was a big issue."[16] In practice, the result was a tendency for the same limited pool of individuals, those who had the language skills and/or came from the most resourceful organizations, to attend meetings and participate in conference calls.

The freezing of the hemispheric negotiations and the launching of a series of bilateral and regional negotiations involving the United States and Latin American countries had a double negative effect on the HSA. The unifying element – the opposition to the FTAA – ceased to exist. On top of that, the various free trade agreements led to a fragmentation of initiatives and agendas in the region. Nevertheless, the HSA still survived. In 2007 its members reaffirmed the status of the Alliance as a "permanent space of articulation for action" that "develops its own campaigns and supports and participates in those promoted by other movements and organizations" (HSA 2007a). One of the main challenges identified by actors in this context was to further broaden its membership base, especially by including those who had participated in the Continental Campaign against the FTAA, which entailed expanding the issues debated and revising its organizational structure (HSA 2007b).

---

[15] For example, Canadian participants raised the problem of exclusion of indigenous peoples because of language obstacles (see Koo 2001: 58).
[16] Interview with Karen Hansen-Kuhn, ART Secretariat and D-GAP, Washington, D.C., September 2005. At the beginning of 2008, the ART Secretariat had to find voluntaries to translate the HSA bulletin, which was issued only in Spanish, a language that most members did not understand and that limited the possibility of using these materials as effective tools of information diffusion and mobilization of English-speaking grassroots organizations.

The Continental Campaign against the FTAA

The launching of the Continental Campaign against the FTAA, at the beginning of 2002, was an opportunity for those who could not – or *would not* – participate in the HSA to become part of the networks of challengers of trade agreements through a different organizational pathway. The Campaign differed from the HSA in terms of the level of commitment asked of participants, the mobilization tactics, and the establishment of internal rules and brokers. It also had a narrower goal: to stop the FTAA negotiations. In spite of the fact that the idea of the Campaign was forged within the HSA, it progressively became larger than the Alliance and gained a life of its own. In Brazil, Mexico, Peru, and other countries, the Campaign led to a temporary organizational bifurcation between the HSA and the Campaign's national chapters. In Canada, Chile, the United States, Venezuela, and other countries, this division did not occur, because the Campaign never formed a separate chapter (Berrón 2007: 150–151).

Two overlapping groups of CSOs participated in the Campaign, but not in the HSA: those with previous grievances with key founding members of the Alliance,[17] and those that did not wish to commit to the creation of an affiliation-based transnational coalition. Many (but not all) of the organizations in the latter group privileged the participation in the domestic chapters of the Campaign, rather than the creation of sustained transnational relationships with challengers from other countries. As a key participant in these coalition-building efforts argued, sectors such as the rural workers and indigenous movements felt more at ease and participated more actively in a looser coalition with a narrower agenda, than in the HSA (Berrón 2007: 36).

The Campaign welcomed the participation of CSOs, members of political parties, parliamentarians, and individuals in general that shared the common goal of stopping the FTAA negotiations. It created a loose structure that included a Coordinating Group, a Secretariat, and national chapters, but with more flexible participation rules than the HSA. The Continental Coordinating Group was composed of two representatives of movements, committees, chapters or platforms per country, and two from

---

[17] When the decision to launch the Campaign was made, in 2001, there was resistance by some actors in Latin America to participate in the HSA because of the presence of ORIT as one of the key founding organizations. Interview with Gonzalo Berrón, HSA Secretariat, São Paulo, April 2005. See also the discussion about internal tensions in the coalition in Saguier (2007).

each continental or regional network (Continental Campaign against the FTAA 2002). Participation in local, national, and hemispheric meetings was open to all.

Between 2001 and 2005, the Campaign's most important transnational assembling spaces were the hemispheric meetings organized in Cuba, the first of which happened before the Campaign's official launching (see Figure 7.1). The Porto Alegre World Social Forums that were held in 2002, 2004, and 2005, as well as the Americas Social Forums, also were important venues for the Campaign to recruit new members, promote meetings, and present its demands (Midlej e Silva 2008: 23). Not by chance, the official launching of the Campaign occurred in Porto Alegre in 2002.

The Campaign's most significant decision was to organize public consultations about the FTAA in every country, in which people would vote with ballots, or would sign declarations, against the agreement. Brazilian activists, who had the experience of organizing a consultation on the national public debt a few years earlier, presented this idea. Promoted by a broad coalition, under the organizational umbrella of the Jubilee South Campaign, that consultation had gathered six million votes against the payment of the debt.[18] The consultation on the FTAA would serve similar goals, the most important of which were to raise popular awareness about the impacts of the agreement, to mobilize grassroots organizations, and to put pressure on national governments to hold an official consultation and/or to stop negotiating (Continental Campaign against the FTAA 2002). Each national chapter of the Continental Campaign had autonomy to decide in which way it would organize the consultation.

In spite of the focus on popular education and grassroots mobilization, this type of coalition cannot be characterized as an "open space" either. It faced many of the same challenges as the HSA, namely, the language obstacles and the lack of resources to finance local grassroots participation in international meetings. Furthermore, although for some the location of the annual hemispheric meetings in Cuba was a way of motivating activists, because of its importance as the "Mecca"[19] for activists who come from leftist traditions, for others it represented an additional obstacle. For example, many U.S. CSOs have not been to Cuba, as one of the U.S. organizations that did send representatives explained:

[18] See www.jubileubrasil.org.br, accessed November 19, 2006.
[19] Interview with Gonzalo Berrón, HSA Secretariat, São Paulo, April 2005.

129

Having these meetings in Cuba means it is incredibly hard to get the high-level figures from the groups that have political capacity in the U.S. I am talking about the million-number unions and main progressive environmental and farm groups. I think that a lot of these groups might be reticent to go to these meetings just given the travel stunts you have to pull to avoid getting hit by the U.S. travel laws.[20]

The Campaign's main demand was never met – official consultations on the FTAA never happened in any country of the Americas – and, after 2004, the stalling of negotiations led to a decline in mobilization levels across the hemisphere.[21] The greatest source of fragility of this coalition-building mode is its narrow focus on a single agreement: the FTAA. However, as will be seen in the next chapter, the impacts of the Campaign and of the HSA differed sharply across countries.

---

[20] Interview with Lori Wallach, Executive Director, Global Trade Watch, Public Citizen, Washington, D.C., September 2005.

[21] In the first hemispheric meeting held in Cuba, in 2001, there were about 800 participants. This number grew in the following editions, but declined after 2004.

8

Diffusion and Differentiation of National Coalitions

The creation of domestic trade coalitions in the Americas is an interesting example of transnational diffusion of new organizational formulas that sought to provide answers to problems of coordination, representation, mobilization, and knowledge production. In spite of the important differences among civil societies in the hemisphere, similar initiatives were diffused across national boundaries. The Mexican and the U.S. trade coalitions founded at the beginning of the 1990s were mirror images of the Action Canada Network that had been created earlier (see Figure 7.1). These, in turn, influenced the coalitions later created in the South of the hemisphere. For example, when debates about the need to create the national chapter of the Hemispheric Social Alliance (HSA) began in Brazil at the end of that decade, the way in which those involved in initial discussions framed their goal was "to create a Brazilian RMALC" (the Mexican Action Network on Free Trade).[1] The experience of coalition building in the only developing country in the North American Free Trade Agreement (NAFTA) region was a key reference for the founders of the HSA chapter in Brazil, more so than the geographically closer experience of the Common Market of the South (MERCOSUR), which, as explained in the last chapter, had not generated sustained coordination across different civil society sectors in the 1990s.

These first trade coalitions were created with very specific goals in mind: to fill the need for coordination in collective action on trade within civil society, to be political spaces for interaction across ideational, sectoral, and national boundaries, and to translate the technical language of trade agreements to civil society actors and the population in general.

---

[1] Interview with Fátima Mello, REBRIP Secretariat, Rio de Janeiro, March 2005.

These initiatives were not meant to be simply spaces for convergence of movements, such as the World Social Forums, nor did they aim to be only arenas for the organization of short-term gatherings, such as the event coalitions that came together around Counter Summits. At the same time, participants did not wish to impose a rigid and hierarchical decision-making structure that limited the autonomy of members (REBRIP 2007).

In trying to strike a balance between institutionalization and autonomy, the coalitions' main common organizational characteristics were (1) they were affiliation based (civil society organizations [CSOs] and civil society coalitions became members, although in some cases individuals also were allowed to participate); (2) they were multisectoral; (3) decision making was by consensus; (4) there was an internal division of labor, whereby specific individuals and/or member organizations were in charge of internal coordination and external representation functions; and, of course, (5) they focused primarily on trade agreement negotiations.

The challenges these coalitions faced were similar, such as the balancing of power to avoid allowing the members with the most resources to dominate the coalition, and having to deal with the tensions arising from the need to provide resources for the coalition, while at the same time ensuring the survival and autonomy of member organizations.[2] Faced with similar challenges, however, actors reacted in different ways. The cases of the affiliation-based coalitions that functioned in the four countries studied – listed in Table 8.1 – show two different outcomes of coalition-building efforts up to 2006: crisis and attempts to rebuild on a different basis (the cases of Chile and Mexico) and domestic divisions (the cases of Brazil and the United States).

Table 8.2 lists the coalitions that were among those most named as closest allies in trade-related activities by the informants interviewed in Brazil, Chile, Mexico, and the United States. The data suggest that RMALC and the Chilean Alliance for a Just and Responsible Trade (Alianza Chilena por un Comercio Justo y Responsable – ACJR) remained important references to challengers of trade negotiations in other countries. The fact that a Mexican coalition was the organization most identified as a closest ally at the transnational level underscores the point made in the previous

---

[2] There is a large literature on coalition building that raises these challenges. See, for example, Staggenborg (1986: 384–385).

Table 8.1. *Main Affiliation-Based Trade Coalitions in Brazil, Chile, Mexico, and the United States*

Country	Trade coalition	Period of activity	Number of members in 2006*	Affiliated with the HSA
Brazil	REBRIP – Brazilian Network for the Integration of the Peoples	1999–	38	Yes
Chile	ACJR – Chilean Alliance for a Just and Responsible Trade	1995–2006	Not membership-based after 2004	Yes
Mexico	RMALC – Mexican Action Network on Free Trade	1991–	16	Yes
United States	ART – Alliance for Responsible Trade	1991–	32	Yes
	CTC – Citizens' Trade Campaign	1992–	19 (plus affiliated state coalitions)	No

* These are approximate numbers, based on estimations made by the secretariats of the coalitions themselves. The numbers of members fluctuated through time, and often some of those listed as members were not active participants.

Sources: Official coalitions' web sites, last accessed October 31, 2006: www.citizenstrade. org; www.art-us.org; www.rmalc.org.mx; www.rebrip.org.br; www.comerciojusto.cl.

chapter about the importance of South–South ties and the visibility of Southern organizations in trade debates. However, to further understand the meaning of these ties, it is necessary to complement this information with a qualitative analysis of the processes of coalition building. The next sections of this chapter focus first on the Mexican and Chilean coalitions, and then on the cases of coalition building in the United States and in Brazil.

The Cases of RMALC in Mexico and the ACJR in Chile

The Mexican Action Network on Free Trade (RMALC) was created in 1991 as a meeting space with a life span that was linked to that of the

Table 8.2. *Coalitions Most Often Named as Closest Allies in Brazil, Chile, Mexico, and the United States (by In-Degree, Country, and Type of Organization)*

Organization	Country	In-degree (%)*	Type of organization and trade-related affiliations
RMALC (Mexican Action Network on Free Trade)	Mexico	29	Trade coalition; national chapter of the HSA
ACJR (Chilean Alliance for a Just and Responsible Trade)	Chile	19	Former Chilean Trade Coalition; national chapter of HSA up to 2006
REBRIP (Brazilian Network for the Integration of the Peoples)	Brazil	15.9	Trade coalition; national chapter of the HSA
ART (Alliance for Responsible Trade)	United States	14.6	Trade coalition; national chapter of the HSA
Jubilee South Campaign	Brazil	11.7	National Secretariat of the Jubilee South Campaign; Secretariat of the National Campaign against the FTAA; co-secretariat of the Continental Campaign against the FTAA

* Percentage of the total possible number of nominations.
Sources: Interviews (see Appendix A).

debates over the NAFTA negotiations.[3] Fifteen years later RMALC still existed. By then, however, it had a very different organizational and political profile. Although during its early history RMALC was administered by volunteers and temporarily occupied part of the space of the offices of the Authentic Labor Front (FAT), in 2005 the coalition had six paid staff[4] and occupied a larger portion of the FAT building in Mexico City, on a permanent basis. In spite of this greater organizational capacity, RMALC became progressively less powerful than it was in the beginning of the

---

[3] Interview with Bertha Luján, former Executive Coordinator of RMALC, Mexico City, August 2005.

[4] Interview with Maria Atilano, Executive Coordinator of RMALC, Mexico City, August 2004. Only in 1995 was RMALC able to get its first fax and computer, hire its own secretary, and diminish its financial dependence on the FAT. See Massicotte (2004: 255).

1990s, in terms of its ability to bring together a broad spectrum of actors across Mexican civil society. It had fewer active members,[5] and fewer of those were member-based organizations. Furthermore, important trade-related mobilizations held in Mexico, such as the multitudinous protests of agricultural workers and family farmers against the liberalization of trade under NAFTA, were not organized through RMALC, nor did RMALC have an important role in them.[6]

The first Chilean trade coalition created was the Chile Action Network for Peoples' Initiative (Red Chile de Acción por una Iniciativa de los Pueblos – RECHIP), which helped organize the 1998 Peoples' Summit. It did not survive long, however, because of strong disagreements among Chilean CSOs. As argued in Chapter 6, in Chile was where there were some of the sharpest tensions between member-based organizations and nongovernmental organizations (NGOs). The national labor federation and rural workers' organizations did not want to collaborate with NGOs that they saw as not sufficiently representative (Jakobsen 2007: 5). Furthermore, even among the participants in RECHIP there were important political differences, as one of the actors at the time summarizes:

From the Peoples' Summit emerged three challenges: the first was the definition of a coalition-building politics. If we wanted to work on the FTAA we would have to work with key actors from the North, with [actors such as] ORIT [Inter-American Regional Organization of Workers]. We had to go beyond the Cold War [politics of alliances]. The second was to work simultaneously at the national and international levels, something that sounds obvious now, but we had difficulties with this for a long time.... And the third was to define a politics of influence vis-à-vis the state.... I think that RECHIP should have dealt with those challenges before the Summit, but I also think that the rupture was positive, we learned that we had incompatible viewpoints [on these challenges].[7]

Neither RECHIP nor its successor, the Chilean Alliance for a Just and Responsible Trade (ACJR), were able to find a sustainable consensus on these issues. As a result, they never had as many members or as much international visibility as RMALC. However, the ACJR was the only space that brought together Chilean CSOs that criticized the U.S.–Chile

---

[5] It started with forty-two affiliated organizations; this number grew during the NAFTA debates to over 100 and in 2006 was close to sixteen.

[6] A coalition of rural workers' organizations organized various protests in Mexico City and on the border between Mexico and the United States between 2003 and 2006. See the analysis of rural workers' movements in Chapter 6 of this book.

[7] Interview with Coral Pey, then Executive Director of the ACJR, Santiago de Chile, June 2005.

Free Trade Agreement and other negotiations, and it played a key role in the first stages of the creation of the HSA.

It is because of their leading roles in Latin American debates about trade, up to the end of the 1990s, that the Mexican and Chilean coalitions were the two most nominated by organizations interviewed in the four countries (see Table 8.2). In spite of their centrality in this transnational network, however, by the turn of the century, both coalitions seemed doomed to disappear. The accusations aimed at them were similar: both had to face criticism from domestic CSOs over lack of transparency and accountability in decision making and complaints of issue ownership. Fierce internal power struggles led to an increasing lack of participation by members, fueled by accusations that coalitions were becoming controlled by a few individuals who did not have the legitimacy to assume coordination or representation roles.

After a contentious process of discussions, in 2004 the ACJR ceased to exist as a coalition but kept the same name and was refounded by a small group of individuals as an NGO. Given the absence of a national chapter of the Continental Campaign against the Free Trade Area of the Americas (FTAA), it remained the only Chilean organization that maintained trade debates at the top of its agenda, that regularly monitored trade negotiations, and that produced analytical documents on a consistent basis.

The decision to give up on trying to build an affiliation-based coalition was not an easy one. The coalition members who supported it argued that it was the only way to work in a "real" way, without depending on the member organizations to contribute to maintain the coalition.[8] Others warned that the new organization would be weaker than a coalition, because it would not be able to count on the institutional and political support of members, or to profit from their embeddedness in international networks.[9] In fact, after a couple of years, the ACJR closed its doors because of lack of funding for its projects.[10]

Although the option of transforming the coalition into an NGO was also raised as a possible solution to RMALC's crisis, its remaining members preferred to promote a negotiated restructuration, aimed at reestablishing its political role as an affiliation-based coalition of organizations. The

[8] Ibid.
[9] Interview with Bernardo Reyes, Instituto de Ecología Política (IEP), Santiago de Chile, June 2005.
[10] E-mail communication with the former Executive Director of the ACJR, Coral Pey, June 2008.

main challenges were to broaden participation and to maintain high levels of activism by member-based organizations.

In spite of the important differences in state–civil society relationships in the two countries, in both cases the close ties between key CSOs and the political parties in power affected coalition-building attempts negatively.[11] As noted in Chapter 6, some of the largest labor and rural organizations preferred to use their direct channels with government officials to negotiate specific sectoral demands and often refrained from openly criticizing trade agreement negotiations. In general terms, RMALC and the ACJR had difficulties in sustaining the participation of member-based organizations and were most successful in attracting NGOs and researchers, most of them from the capital cities, Santiago de Chile and Mexico City.

It is also true that few CSOs in both countries had staff dedicated to following trade agreements, in contrast with better financed organizations in the United States. Their challenges amounted to more, however, than a matter of scarcity of resources. For most CSOs, after NAFTA and the U.S.–Chile FTA passed, trade became a marginal issue on their agendas. Thus, neither in Mexico nor in Chile did the Continental Campaign against the FTAA mobilize as many individuals and CSOs as in Brazil. Critics of RMALC and the ACJR argue, however, that lack of participation was not simply due to lack of interest or resources, but rather to a centralization of activities in a handful of individuals who decided and spoke in the name of others.

Those Mexican and Chilean organizations who still thought of RMALC and the ACJR as strategic political spaces in the 2000s saw their greatest strength not so much as gateways to transnational coalition building or as coordinators of collective action, but as domestic sites of knowledge production. They remained the most important intellectual references for CSOs looking for a critical analysis of trade agreements and their impacts, one that translated issues in terms that their members could easily understand.[12] However, both coalitions were largely unable to

---

[11] In the case of Mexico I am referring to the close ties between most of the labor unions and rural organizations and the Institutional Revolutionary Party (Partido Revolucionario Institucional – PRI), in power at the federal level until 2000. In the case of Chile, I am referring to the ties linking CSOs and the political parties of the coalition "Concertación de Partidos por la Democracia," which held the Presidency of the country between 1990 and 2010.

[12] Several of the Mexican and Chilean interviewees highlighted the importance of RMALC and the ACJR in knowledge production. Since it was founded, RMALC played a key role

sustain the coordination, articulation, and representation roles that they were supposed to play. Their knowledge production skills contributed to solidifying their profiles as NGOs or research institutions in the eyes of other CSOs, and not as relevant political actors.

Ironically, as one of RMALC's most active participants explains, the weakening of these coalitions happened at the same time that the trade-related agenda broadened and became even more complex: "RMALC functions less and less as a network of organizations. ... At the same time that its agenda has broadened and its prestige has increased, there is a phenomenon of diminished participation of RMALC members directly as RMALC, which has created an ever smaller working team that is more and more overwhelmed by too ambitious an agenda."[13]

Differences among participants became more explicit when there was a representational role that needed to be fulfilled at the transnational level. Tensions were enhanced with the creation of the HSA, because national chapters such as RMALC and the ACJR were expected to be able to represent their members in international meetings. For example, when the HSA Hemispheric Council met in São Paulo in 2005, it had resources to pay for only one representative of each national chapter to attend. In Mexico, the question was: Who should travel to Brazil, someone who had been following the debates on the agenda of that specific meeting most closely, or someone new, who would go to learn? Those who argued the first option were criticized for claiming issue ownership; those who argued the latter were, in turn, criticized for creating efficiency problems. As one of the Mexican participants in this debate argued: "We were sent an e-mail from someone who thought [he or she] was the adequate representative, because [he or she] was following that specific issue. I was very critical of it, because there are other organizations that have been following the issue as well, and we are not stupid."[14]

This example relates to the difficulties in expanding participation in the coalition, a challenge that has been acknowledged, by participants and

in diffusion of information about trade negotiations and in making critical analysis of trade agreements accessible to CSOs, in Mexico as well as in other countries. Between 1991 and 2003, RMALC published or co-edited twenty-three publications, in addition to numerous popular education materials and bulletins (Massicotte 2004: 289).

[13] Interview with Héctor de la Cueva, Director, Center for Labor Investigation and Consulting (CILAS), Mexico City, August 2004.

[14] Interview with an anonymous member of a Mexican CSO, Mexico City, August 2005.

critics alike, since RMALC was founded.[15] One strategy designed to deal with this challenge was the creation of parallel spaces for coordination, oriented toward specific issues or events, such as the Mexican Committee of the Continental Campaign against the FTAA, the Committee of Mexican Citizens on the European Union–Mexico Agreement, and the Coordination of the Peoples' Forum, in preparation for the World Trade Organization (WTO) protests in Cancun. However, these spaces were provisional, and thus unable to generate the kind of sustained affiliation-based coalition building that the national chapters of the HSA were supposed to be based upon. Tensions also were felt between groups located in Mexico City and those outside of the capital, the latter of which complained about lack of accountability and access to decision-making processes.[16]

The inability to decentralize power, in spite of numerous complaints and initiatives in the last two decades, led to great skepticism about RMALC's capacity to change, even though in 2004 a new, broader provisional committee was created to oversee its restructuring. As one of the participants of the provisional expanded committee explained, the risk of reproducing previous mistakes remained: "They [the core leadership of RMALC] are called the 'Four Fantastic.' … We [the individuals participating in the expanded provisional coordination] have to be careful that we do not become the 'Eight Fantastic.' I have talked to people that say: 'there has been talk for a long time about opening and democratizing RMALC, and nothing ever changes.'"[17]

Brokerage across Scales of Activism

To capture the ability of RMALC and ACJR to play a brokerage role between the domestic and the transnational scales, CSOs were asked how they would reach out to U.S. organizations in the case of a trade event being organized in that country.[18] Almost half of the Mexican CSOs

---

[15] For a description and analysis of the various attempts to improve RMALC's functioning, see Massicotte (2004: esp. 316–332).

[16] Telephone interview with Víctor Quintana, advisor, Frente Democrático Campesino de Chihuahua, November 2005.

[17] Interview with one of the participants of the expanded RMALC committee, Mexico City, August 2005.

[18] The question was: "Suppose the next Ministerial Meeting of the FTAA will be held in the United States and you need to discuss a strategy for participating in it with U.S. organizations. Do you: a) get in touch with them directly; b) get in touch with them

that answered said they would contact counterparts through RMALC. However, only one of them would use RMALC as the exclusive gateway. Most would directly contact specific U.S. counterparts, and/or use other brokers, such as the HSA Secretariat, regional-level sectoral organizations, and other Mexican organizations (see Figure 8.1). As two of RMALC's members explained, there has been a multiplication of transnational ties and a diminished dependence on RMALC as the single gateway through which to reach out to organizations in other countries:

At first maybe the door was RMALC, but now we have a series of relationships that have been built.... The process has spilled over to other issues, people became specialized, bilateral contacts were made. Now there are other levels of relationship.[19]

RMALC has contacts and a considerable weight at the international level, but does not really bridge the national and global levels. They make the contacts, but the information is not shared.... Thus we do not feel represented by it, and do not consider it useful. You begin to build ties by yourself."[20]

Although this fragmentation represents a challenge for RMALC (and the HSA), it also indicates a vitality of the field of trade that did not exist before in Mexico. As one of the founders of RMALC explains:

There is a positive side to this, which is that the range of organizations involved in trade issues has broadened. It is still far from ideal ... the most important national movements react to the local and national agendas, very rarely do they react to the international agenda, or make the connection between the national and the international agenda. ... In spite of this, though, there has been a growth of what was before something that was very centralized in the RMALC, and that now incorporates many other organizations.[21]

When asked the same question, the majority of Chilean CSOs answered that they would contact U.S. counterparts not through the ACJR, and not directly, but through other brokers, such as regional sectoral organizations or other Chilean organizations (see Figure 8.2). In Mexico the weakening of RMALC was cause and consequence of a multiplication of ties, but, at least in part, this has been a positive

through coalitions such as RMALC/ACJR; c) get in touch through other Mexican/ Chilean organizations; d) get in touch through regional coalition; e) don't know." Respondents could choose more than one option. See the questionnaire in Appendix B.
[19] Interview with Brisa Maya, National Center for Social Communication (CENCOS), Mexico City, August 2005.
[20] Interview with an anonymous participant, Mexico City, August 2005.
[21] Interview with Héctor de la Cueva, CILAS, Mexico City, August 2004.

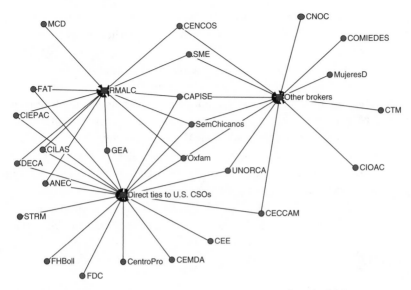

Figure 8.1. Gateways Used by Mexican CSOs to Reach U.S. CSOs.
• Civil society organizations.
□ gateways used to contact allies in the United States before an FTAA meeting.
Source: Interviews with representatives of CSOs (see Appendix A and the list of main abbreviations used).

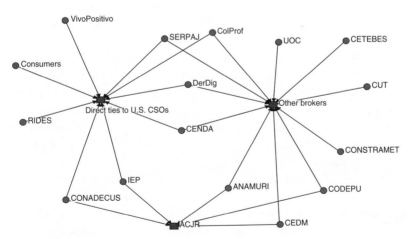

Figure 8.2. Gateways Used by Chilean CSOs to Reach U.S. CSOs.
• Civil society organizations.
□ gateways used to contact allies in the United States before an FTAA meeting.
Source: Interviews with representatives of CSOs (see Appendix A and the list of main abbreviations used).

process of creation of new direct transnational ties. In Chile, however, the tendency was for the ACJR to be replaced by other brokers, and not by direct ties.

In sum, RMALC and the ACJR remained influential in terms of their capacity to produce and diffuse knowledge and information about trade negotiations. The expertise of individuals who had been following trade negotiations closely for many years was a source of legitimacy and respect. They also profited from their status as the national chapters of the HSA. However, their capacity to play the brokerage roles of representative at the transnational level and of mediator between the transnational and domestic scales became greatly weakened in the period studied. The gap between the perceived roles of RMALC and the ACJR domestically and in other countries was acknowledged by Mexican and Chilean CSOs, who felt that these coalitions moved from being gateways to becoming gate-keepers of international contacts (and, as a consequence, of information and funding).

Coalition Building in the United States and Brazil: Different Pathways within the Same Country

When U.S. challengers of NAFTA began to meet at the beginning of the 1990s, they divided themselves in three main groups, which eventually became the Alliance for Responsible Trade (ART), Citizens' Trade Campaign (CTC), and a looser group of civil society organizations that supported the agreement after Bill Clinton assumed the presidency in 1993. Although there have always been overlaps between ART's and CTC's memberships and agendas, they represent two fundamentally different pathways to transnationality.

ART has been a heterogeneous coalition of groups that brings together the AFL-CIO, church groups, development NGOs, family-farm organizations, women's groups, and environmental NGOs. CTC has a similar membership profile, bringing together important labor unions, such as the United Steelworkers of the Americas, environmental organizations, and some grassroots organizations, but with much less of a presence of faith-based groups. The main differences between the two relate to their chosen strategies, which, in turn, reflect different visions of what collective action on trade agreements should be. Whereas ART invested much of its resources in building ties with organizations in Latin America, and presented itself as advocating "a consciously internationalist position on trade,"[22] CTC focused on coordinating efforts to change trade policies by lobbying U.S. decision makers.

Because of these differences, CTC has criticized ART for not being sufficiently pragmatic (or "strategic," as the word is used by CTC members), and thus inefficient, while ART has criticized CTC for having a narrow, short-term view of change, one that often alienates international partners. ART was one of the founders of the HSA and has been the U.S. national chapter of the coalition since it was created. As a consequence of its internationalism, ART became much better known among its Brazilian, Chilean, and Mexican counterparts than CTC (hence the absence of the latter from Table 8.2). On the other hand, CTC was better known in the U.S. Congress and among government officials at the federal, state, and local levels than ART. For CTC, building transnational ties simply was not a priority. These were left for members to do by themselves,[23] and/ or for ART to do, as the head of Public Citizen's Global Trade Watch explains:

When I start saying to my union friends: "The folks in Costa Rica want to know why they don't know your name," they say: "Isn't there someone who does that? There are all these church groups that are doing all that, right?" So there is a bit of a disconnect between the U.S. domestic work and the transnational work done regarding hemispheric trade issues by CTC and by ART which sometimes confuses our Latin American allies, who don't realize who does what. ... For instance, when I am at a World Social Forum meeting in Brazil, someone from Central America might ask what I think of a particular document – which I don't know about because it is a broad statement being created as part of the solidarity process. I send that person to someone from ART.[24]

When U.S. organizations were asked how they would contact Mexican CSOs if an important FTAA negotiation meeting was being held in Mexico, from the total of twenty-eight organizations that answered, half responded that they would use ART and/or CTC to coordinate contacts; the other half chose to sidestep national coalitions and directly contact Mexican organizations and/or to contact them through other brokers, such as other U.S. organizations (see Figure 8.3). Not surprisingly, among those who said they would rely on national trade coalitions, there was a clear preference for ART over CTC.

---

[22] http://www.art-us.org/about_art, accessed November 14, 2006.
[23] Telephone interview with Larry Weiss, Executive Director of CTC, September 2005.
[24] Interview with Lori Wallach, Global Trade Watch, Public Citizen, Washington D.C., September 2005.

Even though ART has not faced a crisis such as the one that impacted coalitions in Mexico and Chile, it is not the exclusive gateway between the national and the transnational scales. As can be seen in Figure 8.3, only four of the twenty-eight CSOs answered that they would use this coalition as their only gateway to coordinate international contacts. This is the result of the increased collaboration among organizations across borders, of the division between coalitions, and of the dissatisfaction of a group of CSOs that felt that both ART and CTC excluded them from decision-making processes. Since the NAFTA negotiations at the beginning of the 1990s, organizations that characterized themselves as "grassroots, base-building organizations," located outside the District of Columbia, have consistently complained about being "neglected and undervalued by the other major sectors involved in trade campaigns" (Grassroots Global Justice 2005: 1).

In part, this is a matter of availability of resources. When there are funds, representatives of organizations are able to travel to Washington, D.C. (or to Mexico City) and participate in meetings, or, on the contrary, organizations based in Washington are able to reach out to organizations located elsewhere.[25] However, by itself, lack of resources does not explain the absence of many of these organizations from the coalitions. As in the cases of Mexico and Chile, exclusion is fundamentally a matter of power struggles, in terms of who had access to resources, and who got to define goals and strategies, as is argued in a document produced by the U.S. coalition Grassroots Global Justice, which is worth quoting at length:

Some of our challenges arise from disagreements about who should drive the strategies and tactics of a campaign – the D.C. organizations that are counting votes on Capitol Hill or the grassroots organizations that work year-round to hold their elected officials accountable. While it is helpful for NGOs to communicate with grassroots organizations about specific targets and key districts, grassroots organizations should then be given the resources and political space to assess what are the best strategies and tactics to move their elected officials. This has not been the case, instead we have seen NGOs enter our communities with resources and their own plan.... There is also a perceived lack of respect for the day-to-day base-building work of permanent grassroots organizations that create infrastructure for a short-term campaign on a specific issue, which the NGOs can then take advantage of." (Grassroots Global Justice 2005: 6)

---

[25] For example, ART hired a "grassroots coordinator" who operated out of Chicago, but this initiative ended because of lack of funds. Interview with Karen Hansen-Kuhn, ART Secretariat, Washington D.C., September 2005.

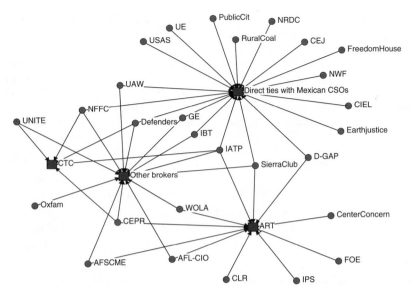

Figure 8.3 Gateways Used by U.S. CSOs to Reach Mexican CSOs
• Civil society organizations.
□ gateways used to contact allies in the United States before an FTAA meeting.
Source: Interviews with representatives of CSOs (see Appendix A and the list of main abbreviations used).

It is true, however, that for local grassroots organizations it is very difficult to sustain action on trade when it is not high on the local or national political agendas, due to lack of time and resources in general, as well as due to a different understanding of what mobilizations related to trade are trying to accomplish. For these organizations, trade agreements are part of a broader agenda and broader goals, and should not be treated separately from them. Thus, when ART tried to incorporate these organizations in its Steering Committee, "some joined and then were not terribly active."[26] Mobilizations have been reactive, so when there is an agreement in Congress to be voted on, collective action escalates.

For the HSA, the division between ART and CTC, and the absence of important civil society groups from both, were crucial challenges. The fact that key organizations represented in CTC, such as the Sierra Club and Public Citizen, were not part of the HSA represented an important

[26] Ibid.

gap, which was filled partially by the participation of some of these actors in the Continental Campaign against the FTAA:

For instance, when we hear from our partners: "Why aren't the Teamsters and Public Citizen members of the HSA?" [I answer that] "There are no individual memberships to HSA, only country-based coalitions are members, and there are different coalitions in this country, and the one you have [as the HSA national chapter] is not the one that has those groups." The Continental Campaign has made it easier, it is broader, and has a different, more campaign-oriented model, and that was a useful thing, because it gave us a place, a space, to talk about common strategy in the hemisphere.[27]

In contrast with the other three countries, in Brazil collective action on trade became an important part of CSOs' agendas only after the FTAA negotiations had begun, in the second half of the 1990s. A domestic trade coalition, the Brazilian Network for the Integration of the Peoples (REBRIP), was created formally only in 2001.[28] In spite of being late-comers, Brazilian CSOs quickly acquired centrality in the transnational network of trade challengers, especially in the context of anti-FTAA protests (see Table 5.4 and Figure 5.5). This would have been unthinkable if the data had been collected before 2001. The rapid rise of Brazilian organizations also meant increasing complexity in the transnational field of trade challengers, as one participant explained:

You had the international "Jet Set," [of trade negotiation critics] which included Lori Wallach, Walden Bello, Martin Khor, Vandana Shiva, Oxfam, and Action Aid.... This Jet Set was very functional, few people, it works well, even if they have their disagreements. But when you have a Brazilian network that has roots, a connection with the base, and an organization such as CONTAG [the National Confederation of Agricultural Workers] that says "listen, my dear, I represent nine million workers and have three thousand unions in my base," well, things change.... I think that people feel bad when they see the capacity of a Southern network, that is not a one-person organization.... They are not used to the contradictions typical of a big network. Within Public Citizen it is easy to be coherent. If two people agree, you have done it. Now, you go and try to reach an agreement within REBRIP![29]

Although REBRIP was thought of in its beginnings an emulation of RMALC, as explained above, it was created in a very different context

---

27   Interview with Lori Wallach, Global Trade Watch, Public Citizen, Washington, D.C., September 2005.
28   Interview with Fátima Mello, REBRIP Secretariat, Rio de Janeiro, March 2005.
29   Interview with an anonymous participant, Rio de Janeiro, April 2005.

than its Mexican counterpart. First, its creation was parallel to that of the HSA, and thus it was born as part of a hemispheric-wide debate about collective action on trade agreements, a mediating space of negotiation and coordination of meanings and positions not only at the domestic level, but also between the domestic and the transnational levels. Second, by the time REBRIP effectively became active, it was clear that the RMALC experience could not and should not be replicated in Brazil, but that it had to be adapted. This was so not only because the Mexican context was different from the Brazilian, but also because, by then, Brazilians had become aware of its diminished participation and legitimacy problems.

REBRIP's participants sought to avoid these problems by creating an affiliation-based structure that relied less on the role of intellectuals formulating trade analyses, and more on opening channels for the incorporation of key CSOs. Although RMALC's attempt at creating internal working groups was not sustainable, in REBRIP's case thematic working groups were important to secure the participation of some of the country's most important CSOs. The example of the Working Group in Agriculture is a good one, because it brought together key member-based organizations that would not normally collaborate among themselves (such as the MST and CONTAG) with international NGOs (such as Oxfam and Action Aid). REBRIP's members were also aware of the need for internal balancing of power, if the coalition was going to avoid the problems that plagued its Mexican and Chilean counterparts. As one CUT participant explained, it was not easy to find equilibrium between large membership-based organizations and NGOs:

There is the risk of REBRIP being transformed into an NGO, given the strength of the NGOs in it, but it depends a lot on the participation of the social movements. For example, if we [CUT] participate with a low profile, there is a greater risk of a more NGO-face; if we participate with too high a profile, the alliance explodes.[30]

Of the four HSA national chapters analyzed here, in the first years of the 2000s REBRIP had become the one with greatest capacity to bring together CSOs. It was not, however, the single meeting space for trade challengers in Brazil, and it did not unite all actors. The launching of the National Campaign against the FTAA, in 2002, brought together an even

---

[30] Interview with Rafael Freire, CUT-Brazil's International Relations Secretariat, São Paulo, May 2005.

broader group of actors around the goal of defeating the agreement, which met in National Assemblies and in a myriad of local "popular committees" organized in all twenty-seven states. These local committees could be created on the initiative of any individual, with or without an organizational affiliation, and had substantial autonomy to organize activities (Midlej e Silva 2008: 90–91). Among those actors, some did not participate actively in REBRIP, such as church groups, individuals without affiliations, and members of political parties.

A common characteristic of REBRIP and the Brazilian Campaign against the FTAA was that both avoided creating organizations with their own offices and staff. Instead, these coalitions relied on previously existing organizations. Thus, REBRIP's Secretariat was located in a long-standing Brazilian NGO (the Federation of Organisms for Social and Educational Assistance), and the Campaign's Secretariat was located in the Jubilee South Campaign headquarters.

The Brazilian chapter of the Campaign is an especially good illustration of the relevance of taking into account the overlap between previous social networks and trade protest ones. The Jubilee South Campaign was created at the beginning of the 1990s to mobilize for the cancellation of the foreign debts of developing countries. In Brazil, this Campaign is an early example of the construction of a multisectoral, campaign-based coalition. The consultation on the foreign debt, held in 2000, was a key precedent to the launching of a similar initiative on the FTAA. In 2002 members of the Jubilee South incorporated the fight against the FTAA negotiations in their agenda, treating it as a continuation of previous efforts.

In September 2002, approximately ten million people voted in a consultation that aimed to show the strength of popular opposition to the FTAA negotiations.[31] Brazil was, by far, the country in the hemisphere that was able to mobilize most people. In this, the ability of sectors of the Catholic Church that enthusiastically embraced the Campaign to reach all across the country was extremely important (Midlej e Silva 2008: 101). Consultations were also held in Canada, the United States, Mexico, El Salvador, Colombia, Paraguay, and Argentina. It was in Argentina that

---

[31] According to the Jubilee South Campaign, 10,149,542 people voted in 41,758 poll locations scattered around the country, and more than 95 percent voted in favor of Brazil's leaving the negotiating table. See www.jubileubrasil.org.br, accessed on November 19, 2006, and, for a detailed analysis of the Brazilian Campaign against the FTAA, see Midlej e Silva (2008).

the second best result was achieved, with 2.5 million votes (Berrón 2007: 37).

However, the mobilization process also highlighted differences among participants of the Campaign, especially between the most important national labor federation (CUT), other national-level CSOs, and political parties that were engaged in the presidential campaign of Luis Inácio Lula da Silva, on the one hand, and organizations such as the Landless Rural Workers' Movement (MST), progressive Catholic groups, and some left-wing parties, on the other. The organization of the consultation only one month before the presidential elections led to disagreements between those who were afraid that the radical opposition to the FTAA would "contaminate" and negatively influence Lula's candidacy, and those who wanted to take the opportunity to pressure Lula to make a clear commitment to excluding Brazil from the FTAA negotiations if elected.[32]

When asked how they would reach allies in the case of an FTAA meeting held in the United States, Brazilian organizations were divided. As illustrated in Figure 8.4, few (only four out of twenty-seven CSOs that answered the question) would contact U.S. organizations directly, but only two would make contact exclusively through REBRIP, without also going through either the National Campaign against the FTAA and/ or other brokers. Similar results were obtained when Brazilian CSOs were asked about the gateways used to reach out to Chilean and Mexican organizations.

These results suggest that, as in the other countries, Brazilian challengers of trade agreements reject trade coalitions as their single gateway and tend to also rely on direct ties, or on the direct ties used by other allies. However, in the case of Brazil there is a greater tendency than in the other countries for different gateways to be used *in addition to* trade coalitions, and not instead of them.

National Coalitions: From Gateways to Gatekeepers?

When the FTAA negotiations stopped, collective action on trade progressively waned, and coalitions found it harder and harder to deal with the tendency for dispersion and diminished interest, as CSOs focused

---

[32] The exclusion of Brazil from the negotiations was not a part of Lula's campaign promises, although the candidate's discourses maintained a critical tone with respect to the agreement.

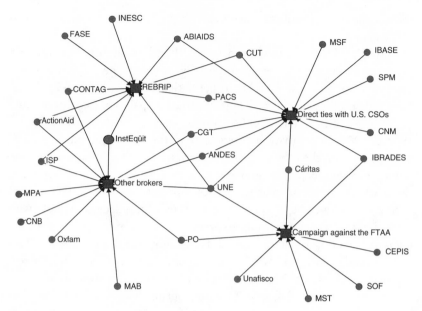

Figure 8.4. Gateways Used by Brazilian CSOs to Reach U.S. CSOs.
• Civil society organizations.
□ gateways used to contact allies in the United States before an FTAA meeting.
Source: Interviews with representatives of CSOs (see Appendix A and the list of main abbreviations used).

their attention on more pressing issues on their agendas. In this context, the challenge for the national chapters of the HSA has been to reinvent themselves on the basis of other targets and strategies. Meanwhile, the Continental Campaign against the FTAA disappeared.

The privileged focus of the transnationalism literature on short-term campaigns or events was very important to understand the new dynamics of cross-border collective action emerging in the 1990s. Because of this emphasis on episodic collective action, however, it provided few clues as to how these emerging forms overlapped, or intersected, with previously existing organizational pathways. The efforts at coalition building analyzed in this chapter underscore the relevance of adopting a longer-term perspective, if we are to understand the different prospects of success of these initiatives.

In spite of the different coalition-building dynamics in the four countries, there are similar patterns and challenges worth highlighting. In terms of the scope of participants, in all countries one finds actors that complain about their exclusion from existing affiliation and campaign-based coalitions. In Mexico and Chile this has led to a profound crisis of domestic affiliation-based coalitions, but the same problem has been raised by actors in Brazil, in the United States, and in hemispheric initiatives.[33] An unsolved question is how to provide effective channels for the participation of organizations from outside the major urban areas, especially local organizations with small budgets. Although this problem has not been ignored by coalition builders, no good solutions have been found yet. This is acknowledged by the literature as a general coalition-building challenge, but it is even harder to address when multiscale collective action around a complicated issue is involved, as in the case of trade in the Americas. Most organizations in the networks mapped in the trade challengers' networks are headquartered in large urban areas, and they are the ones that have greater access to funding, information, links to allies in other countries, links to trade negotiators, and to legislative authorities.

A different – but related – challenge is that, through time, fewer organizations have come to rely exclusively on domestic trade coalitions when planning transnational collective action. As seen in Chapter 6, labor, rural, and environmental organizations tended to reach out to their institutional equivalents in the other country and/or to international organizations, such as the Inter-American Regional Organization of Workers' or Via Campesina. This chapter showed that linkage specialization is a broader tendency, which affects many actors in the transnational field of trade. To the extent that trade coalitions are replaced by other brokers, this tendency puts into question not only the potential survival of these coalitions, but also the whole structure of multisectoral coalition building across the local, national, and hemispheric scales that had been set in place. It also indicates a tendency for actors to shy away from sustained transnational coalition building on trade. However, if other gateways are used in addition to trade coalitions, this suggests a positive process of multiplication of ties.

Furthermore, there is a general tendency for collective action to remain reactive, following the cycles and agendas of official negotiations, despite the efforts at building coalitions that aim at establishing long-term

---

[33] In the Argentinian case, similar complaints were made by CSOs located outside the Buenos Aires area (see Herkenrath 2006).

collaboration. Across the countries, maintaining high levels of mobilization between trade negotiations has been a challenge.

Finally, in all four countries the relationships between CSOs and the political forces in power affected coalition-building processes, although in different ways (see the discussion in Chapter 10). CSOs were divided with respect to how they should relate to government officials, and these divisions became even starker in contexts of political change.

The next chapter takes a closer look at the ability of actors to present alternative proposals to the free trade policies they are challenging. In the post-FTAA context, it was a consensus among challengers of trade agreements that the slogan "Just Say No" had become insufficient.

PART FIVE

The Search for Ideational Pathways

9

Alternatives for the Americas

Parliamentarians, government officials, the media, and civil society organizations (CSOs) often haven confronted challengers of trade agreements with the question: *What do you propose instead?* The pressure to present alternatives during negotiations is felt in domestic as well as in international fora. As this chapter will show, challengers of trade agreements have struggled to design proposals, but have done so through very different ideational pathways. Given the ideological heterogeneity and the organizational fragmentation among challengers of trade agreements, analyzed in the previous chapters, this is not surprising. Furthermore, considering that since the beginning of the 1990s debates about international trade policy making in the Americas have tended to become more and more polarized, with shrinking ground for agreement between supporters and challengers of new free trade negotiations, it has been easier for CSOs to coalesce around the opposition to specific negotiations.

At the beginning of the 1990s, CSOs that challenged the North American Free Trade Agreement (NAFTA) did make an effort to present a variety of alternative proposals. The founders of the Mexican Action Network on Free Trade (RMALC) carefully named the coalition to avoid presenting itself simply as anti-trade or anti-NAFTA. Instead, they called for the opening of channels of dialogue and denounced the lack of transparency in the negotiations. They organized numerous events to debate alternatives and proposals.[1] However, these initiatives had very limited

---

[1] See, for example, the results of the trinational forum on citizens' alternatives to NAFTA, held in Mexico City (RMALC 1992), and the 1993 evaluation of activities prepared by RMALC, in which it argued that developing an alternative proposal to free trade negotiations should be a top priority for the coalition (RMALC 1993).

impact. Similarly, in Chile the Chilean Alliance for a Just and Responsible Trade (ACJR) presented various proposals that aimed at including new clauses in trade agreements relating to gender equality, labor rights, and intellectual property, among other issues.

In the United States, most attempts at influencing domestic negotiators focused on a limited set of issues, such as the contents of the environmental and labor side agreements to NAFTA. Similarly, in the Southern Cone, the Coordinator of Labor Federations demanded, at the beginning of the 1990s, the approval of a regional charter of fundamental labor rights (CCSCS 1993).

During the Free Trade Area of the Americas (FTAA) mobilizations, groups of challengers of trade agreements tried to go beyond denouncing agreements or making specific claims at the domestic level, to create a common understanding of what a more general alternative to free trade agreements should look like at the hemispheric level. This chapter presents an analysis of one such attempt. The document produced by members of the Hemispheric Social Alliance (HSA), entitled "Alternatives for the Americas" (henceforth "Alternatives"), is a unique[2] effort by a diverse range of CSOs to craft a hemispheric platform that sought to build collective identity within this heterogeneous coalition, and to foster challengers' credibility with negotiators and other civil society actors.[3] In its first version, the authors defined it as "more than an economic doctrine. ... It brings together proposals that were considered viable and on which there was a broad consensus. The priority was the establishment of the basis of an inclusive alliance" (HSA 1998: 6, 10).

The demands presented in "Alternatives" are not anticapitalist.[4] It is not an antitrade nor an anti-globalization platform. In all its editions, the authors emphasized that their goal was not to reestablish protectionist barriers, even though the protection of specific sectors is proposed, and calls

[2] As characterized by Doucet (2005).

[3] For example, during a meeting between CSOs and official negotiators, held in Miami in parallel to the 2003 FTAA Ministerial Meeting, government officials criticized protestors for not presenting alternative proposals. In response, one of the members of the Mexican Action Network on Free Trade (RMALC) argued that since the beginning of the 1990s civil society challengers of free trade agreements had been working on alternative proposals, which were consolidated in the document "Alternatives for the Americas."

[4] For example, on the issue of foreign investment, all versions of the document argue that "investment regulation should not mean imposing excessive controls on investors or establishing protections for inefficient industries. Rather, it should involve orienting investment and creating conditions to enable investment to serve national development goals while obtaining reasonable returns" (see Table 9.1).

for a more interventionist state are made.[5] This is, however, a revolutionary document, in the sense that, based on its critique of free trade policies, it presented a nonnegotiable denial of neoliberal policies and proposed the creation of "a new society." This upwards "generality shifting"[6] provided a broader justification for the continuing existence of the HSA than the one offered by the cycles of free trade agreement negotiations. In its 2005 version, the move toward a longer-term and broader agenda, in which neoliberalism became the central target, was made more explicit: "The HSA rejects any agreement based on the neoliberal model. ... At the same time, we see the defeat of trade agreements as being only the first step. ... The ultimate goal is a new non neoliberal society" (HSA 2005: 5, author's translation).

Although it is unclear what would replace the "neoliberal society," the different versions of the document consistently demand a rebalancing between regulations (domestic and international) and private initiatives, with a strong emphasis on the role of national states as the main actors in international relations, and national populations as the ultimate guarantors of popular sovereignty through participatory democracy:

The goal should not be protectionism, but building a state accountable to society that can implement a democratically established national development plan. This may involve the protection of certain sectors considered strategic within a country's plan, but, more importantly, it means promoting forward-looking development. Regulation does not imply inhibiting private initiative. On the contrary, it means establishing clear rules balancing rights and obligations.[7]

By framing the challenge of creating a new template for trade negotiations as part of a broader crusade against neoliberalism, the authors of "Alternatives" presented their ideas as going beyond specific trade agreement negotiations. In terms of their targets, those that engaged in this effort aimed at building a long-term project of change oriented not at a single government, but at the whole hemisphere. Such an effort represents one ideational pathway to transnationality among others. It

---

[5] For example, its fourth edition stated that "The issue for us, therefore, is not one of free trade vs. protection or integration vs. isolation, but whose rules will prevail and who will benefit from those rules" (HSA 2002: 2).

[6] Generality shifting is defined by Mische as a mechanism by which "speakers slide up or down levels of abstraction in regards to the generality or inclusiveness of identity categories" (Mische 2003: 271).

[7] HSA (2001: 42).

was not the one taken by all – or even most – challengers of trade agreements in the Americas.

Mechanisms and Ideational Pathways

Members of the HSA produced five successive editions of "Alternatives for the Americas" between 1998 and 2005. A comparison of these editions offers a good illustration of the relational mechanisms by which the authors attempted to construct agreements through time: extension, diffusion, suppression, and transformation of the contents of the document (see Table 9.1).

Although the authors initially focused on topics that were on the agenda of official negotiations, the last editions added issues that were considered important to challengers of agreements themselves. Most notably, "Alternatives" incorporated new chapters on education, communications, gender, and services (see Table 9.1). Furthermore, within the various chapters were also found changes that led to a broader approach and a longer list of demands. These changes reflect the increased plurality of trade challengers' networks, which, throughout the 1990s, had become increasingly heterogeneous (as seen in Chapter 3). Initially, "Alternatives" was a document written mostly by what had been called the "NAFTA Veterans" and reflected the debates these actors considered most relevant.[8]

An example that illustrates the extension of topics is the greater emphasis given to the debate about immigration. This issue was, of course, raised by Mexican CSOs and by Latino organizations in the United States since the NAFTA negotiations, but occupied a more visible space in "Alternatives" only in its final editions.

Extension is directly related to another mechanism: diffusion. Perhaps the best example of the diffusion (from the North to the South) is the issue of investment. This was not a prioritary topic on the agenda of CSOs outside the NAFTA region, but it was quickly diffused, especially after the first compensation demands made by investors under the investor-to-state dispute resolution system created by the agreement. Criticism of NAFTA's rules on investment was quickly incorporated in the discourses of challengers of trade agreements throughout the hemisphere. Diffusion

---

[8] Interview with Alejandro Villamar, member of the Mexican Action Network on Free Trade (RMALC), Mexico City, May 2001.

from the South to the North also occurred, later in the 1990s, as more Southern organizations became active in the process of thinking about alternatives within the HSA. For example, the 2005 edition of the environment chapter included the issue of genetically modified organisms, which, as argued in Chapter 6, had become an important issue in the agendas of many Latin American CSOs.

The five editions of "Alternatives" are as interesting for what is written in them as for what is suppressed. Absent, for example, is a common position on existing South–South processes of integration. In spite of the critical support given by labor federations of the Southern Cone to the Common Market of the South (MERCOSUR), some of which were active participants in the HSA, this integration process is not mentioned. Suppression, in this case, is the outcome of insurmountable disagreements among members. Thus, CUT-Brazil refused to open a debate within the coalition that might question labor's long-held position on this issue.[9] Also absent are references to more recently launched South–South initiatives, such as the creation of a South American Community of Nations, the Peoples' Trade Agreements, and the Bolivarian Alternative for the Americas (ALBA) proposed by the governments of Cuba and Venezuela in December 2004. These were received with varying degrees of sympathy and suspicion by HSA members. Suppression from the agenda allowed actors to "agree to disagree" on how to react to these initiatives.

Finally, the contents of demands and proposals have been transformed through time. A good example is the issue of so-called labor clauses. The proposal put forward in the 2005 version of "Alternatives" (see Table 9.1) was the result of a contentious debate among challenges of trade agreements, labor and nonlabor, over the extent to which it is really advisable to introduce labor clauses with trade sanctions for violators. Given the fear of many CSOs that these clauses would harm workers in the South and benefit Northern actors, the temporary consensus reached shows the transformation of positions, toward a proposed arrangement in which labor clauses would be targeted primarily at businesses (and not at countries, as in the case of NAFTA's labor side agreement), and would be triggered only when expressly requested by organizations representing the workers whose rights had been violated.

In spite of the dedication of members of the HSA to the development of "Alternatives," not all challengers of trade agreements viewed this initiative

---

[9] Interview with CUT leaders, São Paulo, April 2005.

		ENDURANCE	
		−	+
	−	Domestic claims: National chapters of the FTAA Campaign	Domestic projects: CTC
INTERNATIONALIZATION			
	+	International claims: Continental FTAA Campaign	International projects: Hemispheric Social Alliance

Figure 9.1. Ideational Pathways to Transnationality on Trade in the Americas.

favorably. For some, the lack of consensus on key issues, the internal contradictions of the document, and the inconsistencies found in the text rendered it useless as a practical negotiation tool.[10] Although the need to have alternative proposals was not questioned, for some the exercise of preparing various editions of "Alternatives" was a waste of time, because it did not provide guidelines for change in the short term. For others, the issue of the target was also important. A document that is acceptable to all countries could not possibly be suited to lobbying domestic political actors.

The debates about alternatives are thus linked to debates about which strategies are most effective in different political settings. For organizations such as the Washington-based nongovernmental organization (NGO) Public Citizen, resources are best spent by making demands and presenting grievances specifically designed to address U.S. legislators' concerns.[11] This implies focusing on sensitive electoral issues such as the threats to American jobs, the environment, and food safety, instead of framing concerns in terms of neoliberalism as a whole.

The different approaches to the challenge of thinking about proposals and how to frame them allow us to divide trade challengers roughly into four groups (see Figure 9.1). The first group sponsored a pragmatic approach to alternatives, which focused on specific claims directed at the domestic arena. *Periodic internalization* was the pathway used by CSOs that prioritized influencing decision-making processes by presenting demands related to specific agreements to domestic actors. The national

[10] Members of CSOs that are not part of the HSA made these critiques during interviews.
[11] Interview with Lori Wallach, Global Trade Watch, Public Citizen, Washington, D.C., September 2005.

chapters of the Campaign against the FTAA offer the best example of this ideational pathway. A second group sponsored a longer-term project, but one that was also directed primarily to the domestic scale. The U.S. coalition Citizens' Trade Campaign (CTC) is a good example of this *sustained internalization* pathway, because, although it is very much focused on changes at the domestic level, it sponsored a longer-term project of change in trade policy making that went beyond specific free trade agreement negotiations.

Two other ideational pathways are represented by those actors that engaged in efforts to negotiate common frames with allies from other countries. The *periodic transnationalization* is best exemplified by the actions of the Continental Campaign against the FTAA. Its hemispheric meetings were attempts to find agreement with actors from the various national chapters. Finally, *sustained transnationalization* refers to the route taken by members of the HSA, especially those that saw the international arena not just as an intermittent option to further their immediate goals, but as a long-term site of political action. They were the ones who wrote the successive editions of "Alternatives for the Americas."

Although this typology of ideational pathways to transnationality allows us to understand better the different priorities of CSOs, it is too simplistic, for three main reasons. First, the boundaries that separate them are fuzzy. Often actors engaged simultaneously in claims and project making at both the domestic and international scales. Second, as will be argued in greater detail in the next chapter, actors' pathways shifted according to changes in the political context. Furthermore, all the groups mentioned shared a central point: the emphasis on the threats to national sovereignty posed by trade negotiations. Consequently, the need to reinstate local and national power to implement public policies became a unifying theme across ideational pathways.

The Sovereignty Dilemma

The focus of activists' discourses on threats to national sovereignty crossed North–South boundaries, as well as the left–right divide in the ideological spectrum. However, the identification of the sources of these threats, and the understanding of what should be the most appropriate responses to them, varied considerably along these two axes. In the United States, some of the most vociferous critics of trade negotiations throughout the 1990s and the first years of the twenty-first century were conservative groups that understood these negotiations as undermining the national interest. For these actors, the United States should participate in the multilateral trade system only under its own rules. As a research fellow at the United States Business and Industrial Council (USBIC) Educational Foundation argued:

> We certainly are not opposed to liberal laws on trade where it serves U.S. nationalism, but we do not believe that they always serve U.S. national interests. I want the American government to set the terms of doing business with the United States unilaterally.... I don't believe in a rules-based trade system.... The WTO has become an anti-American "kangaroo court." The highest priority of its members is to keep the U.S. markets much more open to their imports than their markets are open for U.S. exports.[12]

The conservative groups' arguments emphasize the dangers of the growing U.S. trade deficit that result from free trade negotiations, the costs of creating new international organizations and bureaucracies, and the negative impacts of pressures toward the cutting of production costs, with the consequent loss of jobs to other countries.[13] Other conservative strands of U.S. politics focused on the alleged transfer of power from national to international institutions enhanced by trade agreements, and the potential for increased flows of migrants to the United States. As one article published in *The New American* argued, "the internationalist architects of the FTAA intend to transform the nation-states of the Western Hemisphere – including the United States – into mere administrative units of the supranational FTAA" (Jasper 2002).

The partial overlaps of the arguments presented by those groups and the ones sponsored by more progressive trade agreement challengers led to controversial short-term alliances during the NAFTA debates. As Michael Dreiling explains, at times center-to-left CSOs had difficulties differentiating their approach from the conservative nationalist opposition to the agreement, a problem that led to internal fissures in the U.S. trade coalitions and to tensions with their Mexican counterparts (Dreiling 2001: esp. 77–85). In the years that followed, most of the interaction across the ideological spectrum was limited to nonpublic exchanges of information, with occasional strategy meetings on lobbying

---

[12] Interview with Alan Tonelson, Research Fellow, United States Business and Industrial Council Educational Foundation (USBIC), Washington, D.C., February 2005.

[13] For a more thorough exposition of these arguments, see, for example, Tonelson (2000).

policy makers, and the signing of broadly worded joint letters addressed to trade negotiators.[14]

Differences between these groups of trade challengers in the United States were clearest when proposals about how to deal with threats to national sovereignty were debated. Although the center-to-right groups sustained their position strictly from within national borders and a national interest discourse, this research has shown how at least a part of center-to-left trade challengers took more internationalist pathways. As argued before, however, all trade challengers, irrespective of ideology, often found themselves squeezed between pressures to act according to "national interests" and the building of transnational agreements and solidarity. One participant, from the U.S. Catholic Conference of Bishops, explained this dilemma clearly:

> It gets a little crazy. [We have to answer] why are the U.S. bishops supporting people in other countries, who are not the negotiators, over and against the United States? ... We would say that [it is about] commutative justice, that the bargain itself should be just, that the U.S. has the responsibility to look at not whether the deal will be good for the U.S. or the U.S. people, but whether it is going to be good for the people that the bishops are concerned about in this [other] country. That's a very complicated political argument [to make] when people ask whether we are for or against a trade agreement.[15]

Other organizations dealt with this issue by maintaining an internal division of labor between staff that followed trade negotiations at the domestic level and staff in charge of international relations. Whereas the first focused on local and national agendas, the latter presented a broader rhetoric. That was the case of several U.S. labor unions, which had an office in charge of legislative relations and another in charge of international relations.[16] Both dealt with trade-related issues, but did not always coordinate their actions. This separation of domestic and transnational discourses and strategies can lead to tensions and misunderstandings with allies, as in the case of the U.S. steelworkers' successful lobby in Congress

---

[14] For example, on November 7, 2001, a total of 170 CSOs, including the United States Business and Industrial Council Educational Foundation (USBIC) and various labor unions, NGOs, and rural organizations, sent a letter to the Speaker of the House of Representatives in opposition to the "fast track" bill that was being debated.

[15] Interview with Rev. Andrew Small, Policy Advisor, U.S. Conference of Catholic Bishops, Washington, D.C., January 2006.

[16] It was the case, for example, of the USWA, UNITE, and UE during the debates about the FTAA.

for protections against imports: "We did not communicate with the unions [in other countries] that would be most affected by the new bill. That mistake will not happen again, that was a lesson that we learned."[17]

From a Southern perspective, claims that free trade agreements threaten U.S. national sovereignty have been difficult to understand and accept, because actors in developing countries tend to see these initiatives as tools that promote – not threaten – U.S. national interests and U.S. imperialism in the region. As one of the most prominent activists building transnational ties from within Mexico at the time of the NAFTA mobilizations explained, the Southern view of sovereignty threats was one-sided: "The sovereignty problem in Mexico is directly related to the development level and the economic model that presupposed an economy subordinated to the U.S. The treaty was seen as one more mechanism of sovereignty loss. … In the U.S. and Canada, given their level of development and their normativity, they had legal, economic, even political protections [that we did not have in Mexico]."[18]

The motto of the Brazilian Campaign against the Free Trade Area of the Americas – *Sovereignty, yes! The FTAA, no!* – illustrates the way in which the process of multilateral negotiation was domesticated through a national sovereignty frame. In this case, it went hand-in-hand with an anti-imperialist narrative typical of the political left. Although Brazilian organizations were not troubled by the choice of framing in their campaign,[19] these appeals could also be a potential obstacle to building common ground transnationally. As a representative from the AFL-CIO explained, when asked about relationships with Latin American allies: "it is very hard to explain that [anti-imperialist] sentiment to U.S. workers. You show them: 'Here's a great picture of an anti-FTAA demonstration in Brazil, see how we are unified against this agreement?' And someone asks: 'Why is that American flag burning?!' Trying to explain that is very difficult."[20]

The interaction among actors over the years did not work out fully the tensions derived from nationalist framings, but at least some CSOs

---

[17] Interview with Jerry Fernández, international corporate campaigner, United Steelworkers of America (USWA), Brasilia, April 2005.

[18] Interview with Bertha Luján, former member of FAT and RMALC's Coordinating Group, Mexico City, August 2005.

[19] A specific question was asked about this of the person in charge of the Secretariat of the Campaign against the FTAA, who answered that the issue of whether or not a sovereignty-based frame was appropriate was never raised by participating organizations. Interview with Rosilene Wansetto, São Paulo, April 2005.

[20] Interview with a representative of the AFL-CIO, Washington, D.C., August 2004.

became more knowledgeable about how to avoid them. For example, when Latin American activists were brought to talk with U.S. legislators in the post-NAFTA years, anti-imperialist claims were downplayed: "When we talked to our partners coming up, we tried and helped them think through how to make their arguments in a way that they get listened to. You know, talking about U.S. imperialism probably wouldn't be helpful with most members of Congress."[21]

In the last editions of "Alternatives for the Americas," HSA members assumed that the issue of national sovereignty was a key one for all countries. Four main elements composed the shared view of the authors on this: first, national sovereignty is considered a fundamental right and should be preserved; second, it is the nation-states' responsibility to ensure that national sovereignty is protected; third, the ultimate guarantors of sovereignty are the citizens, and thus sovereignty should be understood as "popular sovereignty"; and fourth, national sovereignty is not in contradiction with the establishment of international regulations, as long as these are democratically arrived at, with the explicit consensus of the citizens of each country.

The 2002 version of "Alternatives" further clarified the understanding of national sovereignty: "National sovereignty should not be understood as autarchy, isolationism or as a pretext for disguised violations of universal human rights. Sovereignty continues to be a right of nations and a basis for legal equality of states within the universe of nations" (HSA 2002: 53–54). Thus, sovereignty claims represent political arguments about the right to self-determination, rather than economic arguments against trade liberalization. In spite of this common understanding, actors remained caught between the emphasis on national capabilities and self-determination, and the presentation of alternatives that in fact led to *more* international regulation and *less* self-determination.

Caught between the Inside/Outside in Global Governance Debates

The sections of "Alternatives" (2005) on enforcement and dispute resolution, labor rights, environmental protection, and human rights illustrate the ambiguous positions taken often by challengers of trade agreements

---

[21] Interview with Karen Hansen-Kuhn, ART Secretariat, Washington, D.C., September 2005.

in global governance debates.[22] For example, authors defend the preeminence of international environmental agreements over free trade treaties, at the same time that they demand national sovereignty over the right to restrict investments that have negative environmental impacts. This is not an "anti-globalization" position, but it is an approach that admits that global rules can be simultaneously the problem *and* the solution. In fact, environmental organizations have often been willing to impose limits to national sovereignty in exchange for higher standards of protection, as one U.S. participant explains:

There is a central conflict of framing and thinking within the environmental world. We have a strong belief that communities should have a strong right to protect their way of life and their environment. The problem is that if you deal with global scale problems, like global warming, you have to deal with them at a global level. In a sense, you are going to diminish the individual rights of people and communities. It's a fundamental tension which we don't talk about very much.[23]

The position in favor of more global governance is even stronger in the sections on human rights and labor. Not only did authors demand the ratification of international human rights conventions, but they also favored the inclusion of their content in trade agreements. In the case of labor, the two key demands were the incorporation of a labor clause and the progressive upwards harmonization of working laws and conditions among signatories of trade agreements. It would be hard to find any HSA member opposed to these demands, but they presuppose a vision of global governance that was not necessarily shared by all, one that accepted international regulations that placed a limit to national sovereignty. Although the authors of "Alternatives" demanded that trade agreements not force lower standards upon developed nations, they have not fully assessed whether they really want a global institution to uphold domestic norms internationally, and which institution should do so (Aaronson 2001: 176–178).

It was when actors debated possible sanctions and enforcement rules that consensus were hardest to achieve, as the authors of "Alternatives" themselves admitted:

---

[22] Doucet (2005) approaches this tension through a discussion of territorial forms of democracy in "Alternatives."

[23] Interview with Jacob Scherr, Director, International Program, National Resources Defense Council (NRDC), Washington, D.C., October 2004.

We must acknowledge at the outset the particular challenge of developing agreement on an enforcement process. It is relatively easy to reach agreement on a concept of substantive rights.... But adding the issue of enforcement to the mix raises the important question of "enforcement at whose expense?" During the numerous groups' discussions that led to the creation of this document, it was the issue of enforcement that brought out sentiments of nationalism, regional factions, and concerns about protectionism. The proposal for a living wage in the context of an enforcement process can variously be interpreted to be a plan to force low wage countries to lose their comparative advantage of cheap labor, a protectionist ploy by high wage countries to curb job losses to low wage countries, or an unrealistic economic theory that will destroy 'natural' wage differentials set by the free market.... The proposals herein reflect an emerging consensus.[24]

Not surprisingly, then, this is one of the sections that most changed in the comparison between the first and the fifth editions of "Alternatives" presented in Table 9.1. The 2005 version put a stronger emphasis on incentives, instead of coercion. As in the case of labor rights, the perpetrators of violations (and not the countries) should be the ones made accountable for them. It accepted the idea of supranational tribunals to investigate cases and decide on enforcement, but demanded the participation of representatives of those affected by decisions in the process (see Table 9.1). Similarly to the cases of the sections on labor, environment, and human rights, it provided an ambiguous balance between the creation of (and compliance with) international rules and institutions and respect for national sovereignty.

The different emphasis in the approaches to global governance did not divide actors neatly between groups that sponsor "internationalist" versus "nationalist" ideational pathways. Rather, the same actors adopted proposals that led to more or less global governance ambiguously, depending on the issue, the context, and the results of negotiated interactions with allies. Although there were many other disagreements within the field of trade challengers, the ones derived from the emphasis on one or the other of these forces constituted the most important obstacle to be faced by actors when thinking about common alternatives.

Throughout the years of mobilizations against the FTAA, HSA members avoided facing these unresolved issues by keeping "Alternatives for the Americas" as a "living document" that could be changed in its next version. Still, actors had to deal with a well-known dilemma in their

---

[24] HSA (2001: 74; 2002: 95).

Table 9.1. *"Alternatives for the Americas": Main Topics and Proposals in Two Versions (1998, 2005)*

Main Topics	Main Proposals and Demands	
	1998 (1st version)	2005 (5th version)
Human rights	• Common agenda on human rights to be included in every agreement; • Ratification of key international conventions; • Inclusion of a "democracy clause" in FTAs; • Reform and strengthening of the Inter-American System of Human Rights.	• *Human rights as the legal and normative framework;* • Ratification of key international conventions *and the inclusion of their content in trade agreements;* • Inclusion of a "democracy clause" in FTAs; • Reform of the Inter-American System, *which should monitor the impacts of trade agreements on human rights.*
Environment	• Preeminence of international environmental agreements over FTAs, rules should be guided by the "precautionary principle"; • Reorientation of investments toward alternative energy projects; • National sovereignty over the right to restrict investment that aggravates social or environmental problems.	• Preeminence of international environmental agreements over FTAs; rules should be guided by the "precautionary principle"; • Reorientation of investments toward alternative energy projects; • National sovereignty over the right to restrict investment that aggravates social or environmental problems; • *Rejection of the development of genetically modified organisms;* • *Moratorium on mining exploitation in culturally and ecologically significant areas;* • *Stronger regulation of the use of insecticides, toxic waste, and procedures for registration of emissions and transfer of pollutants.*
Sustainability	(Part of the Forests and Sustainable Energetic Development Section) • Greater incentive for investments in energy renovation and efficiency;	• *Inclusion in trade agreements of mechanisms to favor domestic production of goods necessary to provide for basic needs;* • *Progressive reduction of exports of goods intensive in natural resources and energy;*

	• Eliminate policies that stimulate the rise in demand of fossil fuels; • Creation of a Consortium of Efficient and Renewable Energy Technologies.	• *Establishment of mechanisms to impede the deterioration of prices of raw materials;* • *Joint management of common environmental resources in the hemisphere.*
Labor	• Incorporation of a labor clause (the commitment to respect basic workers' rights with an enforcement mechanism delegated to the International Labor Organization [ILO] with the possibility of trade sanctions targeted at governments or businesses), and a safety net for workers that lost their jobs; • Progressive upwards harmonization of working rights and conditions.	• *Incorporation of a labor clause (with the possibility of trade sanctions targeted primarily at businesses, and only initiated when expressly requested by organizations representing the workers whose rights have been violated), and a safety net for workers that lost their jobs;* • *Progressive upwards harmonization of working rights and conditions;* • *Access of migrants, women, and informal workers to labor rights.*
Mining	• Moratorium on mining exploitation in culturally and ecologically significant areas.	(Became part of the environment section)
Immigration	• Greater protection of immigrants' rights; • Inclusion in FTAs of development initiatives in zones that are major exporters of labor.	• *Inclusion in FTAs of development initiatives;* • *Elimination of obstacles to the free movement of labor in the MERCOSUR and the Andean Pact regions;* • *Inclusion of the immigration issue in the FTAA negotiations;* • *Amnesty for undocumented workers;* • *Ratification of a hemispheric convention on immigrants' rights.*

(continued)

Table 9.1 (continued)

Main Topics	Main Proposals and Demands	
	1998 (1st version)	2005 (5th version)
Role of the State	• No limitation on popular sovereignty and on states' capacity to meet the economic and social demands of its citizens; • Recognition that strategic sectors need special treatment; government procurement policies should include preferences for domestic suppliers and marginalized groups.	• No limitation on popular sovereignty and on states' capacity to meet the economic and social demands of their citizens; • Recognition that strategic sectors need special treatment; government procurement policies should include preferences for domestic suppliers and marginalized groups; • *Exclusion of education and health from trade agreement negotiations;* • *Submission of binding international agreements to popular ratification.*
Foreign investment	• Tougher regulation of foreign investment; • Multilateral regulations to prevent unfair competition and a race to the bottom; • Internationally recognized human, labor, and environmental rights should take precedence over investors' rights; • Introduction of performance requirements.	• Tougher regulation of foreign investment; • Multilateral regulations to prevent unfair competition and a race to the bottom; • Internationally recognized human, labor, and environmental rights should take precedence over investors' rights; • Introduction of performance requirements; • *Removal of investor-state dispute mechanisms from FTAs.*
International finance	• Total restructuring of the World Bank and the International Monetary Fund, or their substitution for new institutions; • Tougher regulation of speculative capital flows and institution of the "Tobin tax"; • Abandonment of structural adjustment conditions;	• *Replacement of Bretton Woods institutions for others, including a Global Central Bank and an International Insolvency Court;* • Tougher regulation of speculative capital flows and institution of the "Tobin tax"; • Abandonment of structural adjustment conditions; • *Foreign debt audits and cancellation of the debts of low-income countries;*

	• Inclusion in FTAs of the issue of renegotiation of foreign debts.	• *Recognition of the existence of an ecological debt by the North.*
Market access and rules of origin	• Nonreciprocal and preferential treatment for less developed nations; • Negotiations should deal with non-tariff barriers that are used for protectionist purposes, while accepting restrictions to protect public health and the environment; • Tariff reductions should be decided through a participatory process and accompanied by support for local industries during the transition; • Harmonization and modernization of customs procedures; • Countries should be able to establish national content rules.	• Non-reciprocal and preferential treatment for less developed nations; • Negotiations should deal with non-tariff barriers to trade that are used for protectionist purposes, while accepting restrictions to protect public health and the environment; • Tariff reductions should be decided through a participatory process and accompanied by support for local industries during the transition; • Harmonization and modernization of customs procedures; • Countries should be able to establish national content rules.
Intellectual property rights	(Part of Author Rights' section) • Rejection of the patenting of life forms and protection of the collective rights of local communities to the conservation of species; • The Cartagena Convention on Biodiversity should take precedence over trade agreements;	• *Countries should remain free to establish intellectual property systems that reflect their level of development;* • *Respect for the right to invoke safeguards for compulsory licensing, parallel importing, and public noncommercial use provisions;* • *Protection periods for patents should not be longer than ten years, and for authors' rights no longer than twenty years;*

(continued)

Table 9.1 (continued)

Main Topics	Main Proposals and Demands	
	1998 (1st version)	2005 (5th version)
	• Obligatory licensing to producers of generic medicines.	• *Exclusion of intellectual property issues from trade negotiations;* • No patenting of life forms and *defense of indigenous peoples' rights;* • *Primacy of the rules of the Cartagena Protocol on Biodiversity on genetically engineered organisms over FTAs;* • *Guarantee that copyright laws will benefit cultural workers;* • *Primacy of international human rights conventions over intellectual property rights.*
Agriculture	• Special treatment for agriculture in trade and investment agreements; • Countries should ensure food security, including the right to exclude strategic products from agreements; • Agrarian reform to redistribute land; • Incentives to the development of sustainable agriculture and foresting; • Support for family agriculture; • Upwards harmonization of subsidy policies, to achieve equal percentages of the GDP.	• *Respect for the principle of food sovereignty in all FTAs;* • Countries should ensure food security, including the right to exclude strategic products from agreements; • *Prohibition of the use of patents of seeds and plants;* • Agrarian reform to redistribute land; • Incentives to the development of sustainable agriculture and foresting; support for small producers, and payment *of fair prices;* • *Subsidies based on the needs of the majority of producers and financed through indirect taxes to large producers that engage in dumping.*

172

Enforcement and dispute resolution	• Mechanisms of enforcement and dispute resolution should focus on the reduction of inequalities; labor issues, human rights, and environmental issues should be an integral part of trade agreements; • Review of the laws and practices of the countries before they become members of an agreement; • Continuous audits of businesses and the creation of a mechanism to receive complaints about the behavior of firms in each country; • Transparency through public reports and an appeals mechanism open to governments and civil society organizations; • Compensatory mechanisms and regional funds to help countries comply with rules.	• *Social standards provisions should form the core of FTA;* • *Enforcement system based on incentives, so that affirmative enforcement of standards should be an unusual and extreme occurrence. In violation cases, emphasis should shift from government entities to the companies that are failing to comply with laws. Enforcement process should be transparent and public; reports on compliance made by neutral experts and civil society partners, and the development of plans to bring countries into compliance. Enforcement should utilize national law. Tribunal should be formed by experts and representatives of the affected sector, with a clear appeals process and civil society participation. Penalties should focus on correcting the violation and withholding benefits under the FTA;* • *Social audits of companies operating in two or more countries within the area of an FTA, monitored by independent local organizations.*
Services	—	• *Standards that regulate trade in services should be different than those applied to goods;* • *Preservation of states' ability to maintain publicly owned companies as the exclusive providers of vital services, and inclusion of special and differential treatment for developing countries;*

(continued)

173

Table 9.1 (*continued*)

Main Topics	Main Proposals and Demands	
	1998 (1st version)	2005 (5th version)
Gender	—	• *Countries have the right to exclude essential services from negotiations, or to introduce temporary safeguard measures;* • *Consumer protection laws take precedence over FTAs.* • *Inclusion of women's groups in decision-making processes;* • *Gender impact assessment of trade policy and the integration of gender concerns in the renegotiation of agreements.*
Education	—	• *Education should be excluded from negotiations, at the hemispheric and global levels;* • *Funding for public education should be equivalent to at least 8 percent of GDP;* • *Equal and free access to all levels of education, with special attention given to girls and women.*
Communications	—	• *Respect for the right to communicate as a universal human right;* • *Public broadcasting should be exempted from the FTAA provisions, and community and independent media sectors should receive special treatment;* • *Sovereignty of states to regulate communications issues.*

efforts to build a joint programmatic framework. The development of a progressively more sophisticated and detailed set of demands and proposals limited the array of interpretations of what trade agreements and their impacts are, and risked transforming the Alliance into what its creators rejected since the beginning: a new "International" for the twenty-first century. Ultimately, in order to remain members of the HSA, actors may have to lose their ability to use different pathways to transnationality. The next chapter analyzes the relevance of this problem of compatibility among pathways when civil society actors perceive that new opportunities for action have opened for them.

10

Transnational Collective Action in Dynamic Political Contexts

In December 2007, the U.S. Congress approved the free trade agreement between Peru and the United States. This agreement did not have large economic impacts in the region, nor did it open the way to the resuscitation of hemispheric talks. What makes it an interesting story, though, is that it passed by a large bipartisan vote, in spite of rising skepticism about free trade agreements in the last few years and the recent election of a new majority of Democratic legislators. In 2001 the Trade Promotion Authority (TPA) bill had passed by only one House vote. In 2006 the U.S.–Central America Free Trade Agreement (CAFTA) passed by just two votes. However, U.S. civil society organizations (CSOs) that had fought adamantly these previous initiatives were divided on how to respond to the Peru free trade initiative. For the first time since the North American Free Trade Agreement (NAFTA) was approved, the American Federation of Labor–Congress of Industrial Organizations (AFL-CIO) decided not to oppose a new trade deal negotiated in the Americas. This position can be understood only in light of the changes in the political environment in the United States.

The Democratic Party won the majority of seats in Congress in the 2006 elections, in which many of the contenders gained votes by criticizing NAFTA-like agreements in local campaigns (Destler 2007: 1). In this context, challengers of the U.S. free trade policy thought they had a new opportunity for action that would go beyond saying "no" to every new free trade initiative. However, as a group of CSOs were preparing to present the Democratic leadership with a proposed template that changed significantly the contents of future negotiations, in May 2007 a group of Democrats and Republicans announced a new bipartisan compromise.[1]

---

[1] Interview with Todd Tucker, Research Director, Global Trade Watch, Public Citizen, Washington, D.C., March 2008.

Although the majority of Democrats voted against the U.S.–Peru free trade agreement in the House of Representatives, the bipartisan deal secured its passage.[2] On the eve of the vote, Speaker Nancy Pelosi explained the Democratic Party's willingness to negotiate: "I don't want this party to be viewed as an anti-trade party." The compromise, reached without broad consultation with CSOs, proposed a limited set of reforms in the language of free trade agreements that centered on the issue of labor rights.[3]

By promoting some of the changes that U.S. labor unions had demanded for more than a decade, such as the introduction of a binding commitment prohibiting countries that signed the agreement from lowering labor standards, the Democratic leadership was able to apply pressure on the AFL-CIO not to oppose the agreement.[4] The historical relationship between the AFL-CIO and the Democratic Party helps to explain why this pressure was so effective. After the 1995 ascension of a new leadership to the AFL-CIO, this federation strengthened its already existing ties to the Democratic Party, by mobilizing more people and resources in order to elect pro-union politicians (Francia 2006). After twelve years of a Republican majority in Congress, labor leaders did not want to burn their bridges with Democrats who were willing to fight for their agenda, if not so much on trade, certainly on other issues.[5] The fact that the agreement would not lead to extensive job losses in the United States also helped make it a more palatable deal to trade unions.

However, the neutral position assumed by the AFL-CIO vis-à-vis the U.S.–Peru free trade agreement was by no means consensual among labor unions. The debates before its vote in Congress displayed clear disagreements among the AFL-CIO's own affiliates,[6] and between the AFL-CIO

---

[2] In the House of Representatives, 116 Democrats voted "nay," 109 voted "aye," and 8 abstained from the vote. In the Senate, Democrats remained divided, but the majority (29) voted for the agreement.

[3] Interview with Todd Tucker, Research Director, Global Trade Watch, Public Citizen, Washington, D.C., March 2008.

[4] For an analysis of the language on labor rights in FTAs negotiated by the United States and the deal reached between Democrats and Republicans in 2007, see Elliott (2007).

[5] See the analysis in Roof (2008), about the Democrats' support of labor's legislative agenda.

[6] For example, although the United Auto Workers (UAW) agreed to support the agreement, the International Association of Machinists and Aerospace Workers (IAM), another key AFL-CIO affiliate, maintained its opposition. For the former, it was a way of strengthening its opposition to other free trade agreements that were perceived as more harmful, such as the one under negotiation with South Korea (interview with anonymous

leadership and unions affiliated with the newly created Change to Win Coalition (CTW). When the CTW unions separated from the AFL-CIO in 2005, one of their main critiques was that the AFL-CIO leadership spent too many resources on trying to elect friendly Democrats, with poor results, instead of supporting badly needed organizing drives (Chaison 2007). After the bipartisan deal was publicized, CTW leaders took the opportunity to distance themselves further from the AFL-CIO by maintaining their opposition to the deal. Beyond the labor movement, there were also strong disagreements between the AFL-CIO and some of its closest civil society allies in previous mobilizations. In fact, the contentious debates almost led to a serious rupture within the Alliance for Responsible Trade (ART), one of the coalitions that rallied opposition to free trade agreements in the United States.[7]

The AFL-CIO's Peruvian allies did not share the AFL-CIO's position either. It speaks to the importance of transnational ties that the U.S. labor federation made a point of telling the Peruvian Unitary Workers' Central (CUT-Peru) of its decision and explaining the reasons for changing positions.[8] However, it is also relevant to note that the opposition to the agreement was not very strong in Peru, where challengers were divided between a group opposed to the deal and another that wanted to negotiate changes in its contents. Furthermore, the transnational network of U.S. and Peruvian CSOs was not as dense as the ones that linked challengers of trade agreements in the United States and other Latin American countries, such as Brazil or Mexico. As a result, and in contrast to what happened within the United States, the AFL-CIO's internal divisions and its neutrality position were neither well publicized nor criticized in that country.[9]

The literature on social movements long ago taught us that in order to understand the origins and development of mobilization, it is important

---

AFL-CIO representative, Washington, D.C., March 2008). For the latter, changes in labor provisions still fell short of their demands. In addition, the machinists also argued that they had concerns regarding the procurement, investment, and service chapters of the deal. See the arguments put forward in a letter by IAM's International President to the U.S. Congress (Buffenbarger 2007).

[7] Interviews with members of ART, Washington, D.C., March 2008.

[8] Interview with anonymous AFL-CIO representative, and with Julio César Bazán, President, Unitarian Workers' Federation (CUT-Peru), Lima, Peru, July 2008.

[9] Interviews with Juan José Gorriti, General Secretary, General Workers' Confederation of Peru (CGTP-Peru), and Julio César Bazán, President, Unitary Workers' Central (CUT-Peru), Lima, Peru, July 2008.

to consider the threats and opportunities offered by the specific political context in which action takes place (see, for example, Tilly 1978). Latin American scholars also contributed to this literature by analyzing the historically complex and dynamic relationships among states, political parties, and social movements in the region.[10] As transnational collective action became a more relevant phenomenon, the literature has emphasized the need for an analytical approach that considers perceptions of political opportunities across domestic and international scales (Sikkink 2005; Smith and Korzeniewicz 2007).

This chapter seeks to contribute to this literature. It focuses specifically on one aspect of the dynamic interactions across domestic and international scales: the impacts that changes in domestic political contexts may have in transnational collective action. It analyzes variations in CSOs' expectations of success and strategies as potential allies acquired greater political power in their own countries and/or elsewhere. To understand these variations, it is important to recognize the relevance of actors' political embeddedness.

Transnational Collective Action and Political Systems

The story of the U.S.–Peru free trade agreement lends credence to the idea that actors' expectations of political opportunities vary according to their political embeddedness and are a key component of any explanation about the dynamics of transnational collective action. It confirms that an analysis of motivations of action based on the static interests of whole categories, for example, "labor in the United States," is insufficient. Instead of assuming that labor will form a unified front to defend its constituents' interests, that rural organizations will defend rural workers' interests, and that Brazilians will defend Brazil's interests, what CSOs perceive as self-interest varies even among those belonging to the same sectors and sharing the same nationalities.

Furthermore, these visions of self-interest change through time. As the literature on the role of ideas has emphasized, in situations of uncertainty, such as the period of ideological turmoil that followed the end of the Cold War, the way actors perceive their interests, and how to achieve

---

[10] There is a large literature on state corporatism that analyzes the historical ties among state, labor, and business. For comparisons across Latin American countries, see, for example, Murillo (2001) and Bensusán and von Bülow (1997).

them, are more amenable to change.[11] This is not an argument about the end of ideologies. It is an argument about how previous responses to the impacts of trade liberalization, from demands for protection of specific industrial sectors to going back to state-led developmentalism, became largely inadequate in the political and economic context of the 1990s (see, for example, Murillo 2001; Panfichi 2002; Dagnino 2002). This crisis of protectionist models as viable alternatives created an ideological gap that represented a challenge for CSOs across the hemisphere that looked for alternatives. The differences in each country's specific trade policy-making rules help to explain the variety of ways in which actors faced this challenge.

Institutions and Trade Policy Making

Part of the scholarship on trade policy making understands its outcomes through the lenses of Putnam's two-level game, according to which domestic groups pressure governments at the national level to adopt favorable policies, and, in turn, national governments seek to maximize their ability to satisfy domestic pressures at the international level (Putnam 1988).[12] This is certainly an important part of the story, but the literature on transnational collective action has shown that it implies a limited access of nonstate actors to the international system that is not true in many issue areas (Keck and Sikkink 1998: 4; Sikkink 2005: 153–154). Trade is undoubtedly one of them. The ties built between nonstate and state actors in the last two decades of trade debates show a much more complicated dynamic of interaction across scales than the one we are able to see through a two-level game model.

Almost all the 123 CSOs included in this research had some kind of trade-related relationship to actors in the domestic political system, ranging from informal dialogue to institutionalized forms of participation in decision-making processes.[13] A smaller but growing number of organizations also had links to legislators and government officials in other

[11] For example, see Blyth (2002: esp. chs. 1 and 2) for an analysis of the impact of ideas in the context of "Knightian uncertainty."

[12] For examples of the application of this framework to hemispheric trade negotiations see Ostry (2002) and Sáez (2005).

[13] Of the 123 CSOs, only sixteen answered that they did not have trade-related activities vis-à-vis the Legislative arena, and only eighteen did not engage in any kind of trade-related dialogue with government officials.

countries.[14] The ways in which these relationships were constructed or activated within and across countries were a constant source of disagreements among challengers of trade agreements, which varied significantly in terms of their ties to political parties and government officials. These debates gained specific contours according to the different trade policy-making rules in place in each country.

In Brazil, Chile, and Mexico, the negotiation of international trade agreements is under the exclusive jurisdiction of the Executive branch. These are then submitted to national Congresses for a "yes" or "no" vote, without the possibility of revisions or amendments. Thus, the main actors in the negotiations have been the ministerial bureaucracies, although the specific agencies that are responsible for carrying out negotiations vary.[15]

The United States stands apart from the Latin American countries because its Constitution grants Congress the primary power over trade policy making. Since 1974, it has been part of the legislators' attributions to approve periodically a Trade Promotion Authority Act (TPA, best known as "fast track" legislation), which grants temporary authority to the President to negotiate with other countries, at the same time that it limits the role of Congress to approving or rejecting the treaties within ninety days, without the possibility of amending them. Although restrictions on the role of Congress have sparked criticism by challengers of free trade negotiations, U.S. legislators still have considerably more power than their Latin American counterparts. Through the TPA, legislators can specify objectives that they expect negotiators to pursue, and they can introduce criteria that must be met in order for agreements to be subsequently approved. For CSOs, the need to periodically pass the TPA provides them with opportunities to debate the costs and advantages of the proposed trade policy. Finally, the President has to notify Congress before

---

[14] Many Latin American organizations have participated in hearings and meetings in the U.S. Congress related to the debates about trade agreements since NAFTA; most of these are not direct ties, however, but are short-term relationships brokered by U.S. CSOs. Likewise, U.S. CSOs have traveled to Latin America and met with negotiators and parliamentarians, often through arrangements made by local allies.

[15] In Brazil, a key negotiating actor is the Ministry of Foreign Affairs, but others are also involved, especially the Ministry of Development, Industry and Foreign Trade, and the Ministry of Agriculture. In Chile, trade negotiations are similarly centralized in the Ministry of Foreign Affairs, and especially in the General Direction of Economic International Relations (Direcon). In Mexico, the most important negotiating role is played by the Ministry of Economic Affairs.

entering into an agreement and is required to consult with Congressional Committees during the negotiations.

These different policy-making rules present challengers with various logics in terms of their targets, the need to present alternatives, the contents of these alternatives, and the ways opportunities for action can be constructed. In the United States, efforts at influencing trade policy making are divided between lobbying Congress – especially during "fast track" and trade agreement votes – and the Executive agency in charge of negotiations, the U.S. Trade Representative (USTR) – especially during trade agreement negotiations. In Latin America, on the other hand, most of trade challengers' efforts at influencing negotiations are directed at the Executive agencies in charge of negotiations. Thus, changes in the power held by different political forces in the Legislative branch have greater impact in trade policies and CSOs' strategies in the United States than in Latin America. The election of new Presidents, on the other hand, may lead to more important changes in Latin America.

"Boomerang" and "Monkeywrenching" in Dynamic Political Environments

During the NAFTA negotiations, the strategy developed jointly by Mexican and U.S. challengers of the agreement was an exemplary case of what Margaret Keck and Kathryn Sikkink called the "boomerang effect" (Keck and Sikkink 1998), and that Thomas Risse and Kathryn Sikkink later expanded into the "spiral model" (Risse and Sikkink 1999). At the time of negotiations, Mexico had a highly centralized political system, with a powerful presidency that overshadowed Congress and a state corporatism that linked the largest labor and business organizations to the then ruling party. Faced with repression and the absence of communication and negotiation channels within their own country, a group of independent Mexican CSOs, with the help of U.S. allies, took their grievances directly to the U.S. Congress.[16] Simultaneously, U.S. and Canadian organizations fed Mexican allies information on the progress of negotiations to which they would not otherwise have had access.

---

[16] Mexican CSO leaders participated in various types of activities: public hearings, debates, press conferences, and meetings with U.S. legislators and their staff in the U.S. Congress.

182

In spite of important differences between the Chilean and the Mexican political systems, a similar North-to-South dynamic was reproduced during the U.S.–Chile free trade agreement negotiations. The first draft of the agreement was made available to Chilean CSOs by ART, who sent it to the Chilean Alliance for a Just and Responsible Trade.[17]

During the Free Trade Area of the Americas (FTAA) negotiations, boomerang-type interactions have occurred, but instead of Southern organizations looking toward the North for information and influence in decision making, there was a much more balanced interaction between North and South, and even, at specific moments, an inversion of the direction of the previous "boomerangs."[18] In contrast to the political situation in Mexico during the NAFTA negotiations, countries such as Argentina, Brazil, and Chile had gone farther in consolidating their democracies in the mid-1990s. Particularly after the election of Luis Inácio Lula da Silva in Brazil (in 2001), Nestor Kirchner in Argentina (in 2002), and Hugo Chávez in Venezuela (in 1998), challengers of free trade agreements in these countries often had better access to policy makers than U.S. challengers under a Republican administration. These new Latin American administrations viewed the potential gains of the FTAA with more skeptical eyes than had previous administrations.

In this new political environment, CSOs in the United States sought to build ties to potentially sympathetic governmental officials overseas, using civil society allies in those countries as informal brokers. For example, Brazilian CSO representatives that had the chance to be members of official delegations[19] became a source of information for challengers from other countries, much in the same way that U.S. and Canadian CSOs had been sources of information for Mexican and Chilean CSOs during the NAFTA, Canada-Chile, and U.S.–Chile free trade agreement negotiations. As one of the U.S. informants explained: "The NGO [nongovernmental organization] access to negotiators has diminished greatly [during President Bush's administration], and what access we do have is

---

[17] Interview with Coral Pey, then Executive Director of the ACJR, Santiago de Chile, June 2005.

[18] The inversion of the direction of the boomerang goes counter to the idea that this type of tactic is most successful when sent from the South toward the North. For a critique of this narrow understanding of the boomerang as a typically Southern tactic, see Keck (2006).

[19] Representatives of Brazilian CSOs participated as part of official delegations at the 2003 FTAA Ministerial Meeting, held in Miami, at the WTO Meetings held in Cancun (2003) and in Hong Kong (2005), and at various meetings among FTAA negotiators.

more of a public relations event than it is any real debate. ... When we need information on the FTAA we go to the Brazilian or Venezuelan negotiating teams, because we have so little access to U.S. negotiators."[20]

Through these exchanges of information, U.S. CSOs hoped to have a direct and disrupting impact on negotiations. For example, a U.S. participant during the 2003 FTAA Ministerial Meeting used access to U.S. negotiators to feed information to the Brazilian delegation that he thought would be disruptive to the negotiations: "There was collaboration with the Brazilian negotiators. I actually funneled information [to the Brazilian negotiators] because I was at some meetings of U.S. negotiators, and they were saying some over the top unthinkable stuff about Brazil."[21]

These disrupting or, as some actors call them, "monkeywrenching" tactics were taken to another level by the Washington-based NGO Public Citizen, in attempts to exploit existing tensions among negotiators by sending them different messages:

Here we are, saying fast track is going to be horrible [for U.S. national interests], that the U.S. will give up everything, and Congress will have no check on anything. And here's what the memo [we wrote] to Brazilian negotiators said: "Guess what? In the fast track, Congress has constrained USTR [U.S. trade representative], and USTR can no longer give you agricultural concessions."[22]

Neither the "boomerang" nor the "monkeywrenching" tactics are new. The use of leverage with other actors is well known in the repertoire of collective action,[23] as is the adaptation of frames according to the targets. However, neither of these tactics can be subsumed within a two-level game model that presupposes that nonstate actors limit their actions fundamentally to the domestic scale. They are part of a repertoire of action that is best understood through a fuller interactive look at collective action across scales. Furthermore, the shift in the origins of the flow of information from the North toward the South means that countries in the South no longer were merely places where impacts of decisions taken in the North were felt, but were perceived instead as decision-making sites.

[20] Interview with Alexandra Spieldoch, at the time Senior Program Associate, Center of Concern, Washington, D.C., May 2004.
[21] Interview with an anonymous U.S. participant, Washington, D.C., July 2004.
[22] Interview with Timi Gerson, FTAA Coordinator, Public Citizen, Washington, D.C., May 2004.
[23] For an earlier description of cross-national strategies similar to the "boomerang," see Singer (1969: 25–26).

Other types of ties to the political system are the ones between CSO activists and political parties. Coalitions such as the Hemispheric Social Alliance (HSA) have not admitted the formal presence of representatives of political parties, but many of the activists that participated were affiliated with political parties, giving the latter at least an informal presence in the coalition.[24] Within the national chapters of the Campaign against the FTAA, political parties' participation was commonly found. In the Brazilian case, various leftist political parties participated actively in the Campaign at the national and local scales, but they were denied any formal role in the organization of the plebiscite (Midlej e Silva 2008: 95, note 42). The Cuban Communist Party was a key actor in the Campaign, especially during the Hemispheric Encounters held in that country.

In general terms, however, in Latin America neither political parties nor legislators were prominent actors in the FTAA debates. In fact, one of the challengers' strategies in Brazil, Chile, and Mexico was to try to push national legislators and political parties to participate more actively, but these initiatives had limited success. An exception was the Brazilian Trotskyst Unified Workers' Socialist Party (Partido Socialista dos Trabalhadores Unificado – PSTU), which not only participated in the Brazilian Campaign against the FTAA, but also made the rejection of the agreement the main platform plank of its Presidential candidate in the 2002 elections (Midlej e Silva 2008: 86). However, this is a small party that accounted for less than 0.5 percent of the total valid votes in 2002.[25]

In spite of the tendency for politicization of trade agreements, and the fact that trade agreements have dealt progressively with highly sensitive domestic policy issues, Latin American legislators have tended to be mere spectators of negotiations. Most Congresses in the region have assumed a passive stand, in the sense that they intervene only when results are submitted for their consideration, after negotiations have concluded (Sáez 2005: 12–13). In Brazil, CSOs pressured for the creation of a parliamentary commission to follow the FTAA negotiations in the Chamber of Deputies. However, this arena was never very active, and, after negotiations stalled, it disappeared.[26] Even in the case of the Common Market of

---

[24] Interview with Gonzalo Berrón, Advisor, Trade Union Confederation of the Americas, São Paulo, February 2008.

[25] http://www.tse.gov.br/internet/eleicoes/2002/quad_part_cargo_blank.htm.

[26] Interview with anonymous Brazilian legislative staff, House of Representatives, Brasilia, December 2004. See also Midlej e Silva (2008: 112–113).

the South negotiations, it was only after the creation of the MERCOSUR Parliament, in 2007, that some Brazilian legislators began to pay more sustained attention to their role in the integration process.[27]

Are New Opportunities for Domestic Action New Threats to Transnational Action?

In Latin America, the election of new Presidents that were more skeptical of the advantages of trade agreements than previous ones presented CSOs with new opportunities, but also with new challenges. More specifically, changes shifted the lines dividing what Bill Smith and Patricio Korzeniewicz have called "insiders" and "outsiders," that is, those that accepted dialogue with government officials and focused mainly on advancing demands to democratize negotiations and change part of the contents of agreements, and those for whom trade negotiations were an opportunity for contestation (Korzeniewicz and Smith 2003b; Smith and Korzeniewicz 2007). Contradictory interpretations of what was expected from these new administrations in trade negotiations coexisted within the countries and among CSOs in different countries, threatening the survival of the coalitions built in the last two decades. As the story of the U.S.–Peru free trade agreement showed at the beginning of this chapter, U.S. CSOs also had to face similar tensions after the Democrats regained the majority of seats in the U.S. Congress.

The election of Workers' Party leader Luis Inácio Lula da Silva as president of Brazil is a good example, because of the close ties between this political party and many of the most active CSOs in the domestic HSA chapter and in the Brazilian Campaign against the FTAA.[28] Many Brazilian and non-Brazilian trade challengers thought that the new administration would pull out of the FTAA and the World Trade Organization (WTO) negotiations, but that did not happen. As Lori Wallach, from the Washington-based NGO Public Citizen, expressed

[27] Brazilian political parties have not incorporated the Southern Cone regional integration process as part of their priorities. It remains, for them, an issue of foreign policy, and thus within the purview of the Executive branch (Vigevani et al. 2001).

[28] The foundation of the Workers' Party (PT) had the support of many labor leaders that also founded the Unified Workers' Federation (CUT-Brazil), including President Luis Inácio Lula da Silva himself. Other challengers of the FTAA, such as the Rural Landless Workers' Movement, also had historically close ties with the PT. For a review of the relationships between the PT and Brazilian social movements since the beginning of the 1980s, see, for example, Doimo (1995); Sader (1988).

her disappointment: "First, we thought: 'it's a miracle! [President] Lula is elected in the country that will decide the fate of globalization!' And, now, 'Oops, Lula is in the country that will decide the fate of globalization.'"[29]

Although some Brazilians shared these feelings, other disagreed. In fact, one of the main tensions within the Brazilian Campaign against the FTAA was about the different interpretations actors offered of what the election of President Lula represented for the country (Midlej e Silva 2008: 188–190). In Argentina, Bolivia, Ecuador, and Nicaragua, in spite of the many important differences among these cases, the national chapters of the Campaign and of the HSA were divided in similar ways between groups that were more sympathetic to the new administrations and groups that were more critical of them.[30] At the hemispheric scale, this tension was reflected in the suppression of clear references to the new governments in the documents produced by the Continental Campaign against the FTAA, as one Brazilian participant explains:

In Havana [during the Hemispheric Meeting against the FTAA], CUT [the Brazilian Unified Workers' Federation] and REBRIP [the Brazilian Network for the Integration of the Peoples] asked that Lula [President of Brazil] and Kirchner [President of Argentina] figure [in the final declaration] as examples of progressive governments that blocked the FTAA, but there was no consensus, and the final declaration was much more generic.[31]

These disagreements were even clearer during the Third Peoples' Summit, organized in parallel to the Mar del Plata Summit of the Americas, in 2005. For the first time, the civil society event had the active participation of political party and government leaders that were sympathetic to the arguments against the FTAA. These included the president of Venezuela, Hugo Chávez, and Argentinean and Cuban politicians. However, organizers of the Peoples' Summit were ill-prepared to deal with these actors, as one of them later recalled:

What happened in Mar del Plata forced us to think strategically about the delicate and complicated relationships among governments, political forces, and social

[29] Interview with Lori Wallach, Global Trade Watch, Public Citizen, Washington, D.C., September 2005.
[30] Interview with Gonzalo Berrón, Advisor, Trade Union Confederation of the Americas, São Paulo, February 2008.
[31] Interview with Roberto Leher, National Association of University Teachers–ANDES, Rio de Janeiro, May 2005.

movements. Insofar as more Southern governments that purport to be part of the popular field are elected, ... how can we take advantage of points of agreement and opportunities for dialogue and even interaction but prevent them from trying to control the social movements, ignoring their organizations and action repertoires, and violating their goals?[32]

Once more, a parallel can be traced to what happens in the debates about the World Social Forums. After the 2003 Forum, in which the Presidents of Brazil and Venezuela were both very visible participants, one key activist expressed her frustration in strong terms:

How on earth did a gathering that was supposed to be a showcase for new grassroots movements become a celebration of men with a penchant for three-hour speeches about smashing the oligarchy? ... For some, the hijacking of the World Social Forum by political parties and powerful men is proof that the movements against corporate globalization are finally maturing and "getting serious." But is it really so mature, amidst the graveyard of failed left political projects, to believe that change will come by casting your ballot for the latest charismatic leader, then crossing your fingers and hoping for the best?[33]

In some cases, the skepticism of activists and scholars about the prospects of new center-to-left administrations reflects an overly idealized view of transnational collective action that can be disconnected from political systems. For example, Yahia Said and Meghnad Desai, in their analysis of mobilizations against trade agreements, have argued that what they characterize as "the anti-capitalist movement" "has attracted some nasty fellow-travelers in the guise of nationalist leaders, Third World multinationals, and old left gurus. They are threatening to hijack the movement and blot out its most attractive features – openness, cosmopolitanism, informality, and popular appeal" (Said and Desai 2003: 82). However, this chapter has shown that most challengers of trade agreements maintain ties to political party leaders and government officials and are not about to sever them. At the same time, it has also shown that an important source of tensions within challengers' networks relates to the attempts by actors to juggle between domestic pressures and the continuous collaboration with foreign allies.

The new political landscape in Latin America in the first years of the twenty-first century helps us to understand that, in spite of different institutional frameworks for trade policy making, CSOs from the North and

---

[32] de la Cueva 2005: 91, author's translation.
[33] Klein (2003).

the South faced these tensions in similar ways. Again, the case of labor is enlightening. The political economy literature on sources of labor power usually specifies the greater presence of parties allied with organized labor in the Legislative and Executive branches of government as a key positive resource for labor movements (Robinson 1994: 659). Nevertheless, the increased strength of political allies may offer as many opportunities as threats for transnational collective action.

The case of the AFL-CIO's position on the U.S.–Peru free trade agreement provided a good example, and it is by no means an exceptional one. As one labor participant from Brazil admitted, trade agreement negotiations in the context of the rise to the Presidency of the coalition led by the Workers' Party could present CUT-Brazil with similarly difficult choices:

Let us imagine for a moment that the U.S. government accepts the main Brazilian demands, on agricultural subsidies and tariffs. It presents a proposal that the labor unions consider good, but conditions it to the introduction in the agreement of a social clause. President Lula's government will say no to the social clause, because that has been the Brazilian government's traditional position. In that case, CUT would find itself in a difficult situation.[34]

CUT-Brazil could find itself in a difficult situation because of its unwillingness to criticize openly the Lula administration, but it would feel the pressure to do so from its allies inside as well as outside the country. Of course, this situation never left the realm of conjectures, but it is interesting to note how aware this former labor leader was of the contradictory pressures actors may face due to their embeddedness in social networks and political systems across scales.

The cases of the AFL-CIO and CUT-Brazil are clear ones, because of their long-standing ties to the Democratic Party and to the Workers' Party, respectively, but other social movement organizations that are similarly politically embedded may be affected too. In a context of increasingly plural networks, in which various CSOs have made efforts at crossing sectoral lines by expanding their agendas and demands, what may be seen initially as positive changes in the political contexts can put these broad-based coalition-building efforts in jeopardy.

[34] Interview with Kjeld Jakobsen, former CUT-Brazil International Relations Secretary, Brasilia, January 2008.

11

Conclusions: Agency, Networks, and Collective Action

The dynamic contours of transnational collective action are the result of the continuous negotiation and reappraisal of choices made by actors, as they become part of new networks and react to changes in political contexts. These processes of negotiation and reappraisal happen within as well as among civil society organizations (CSOs) and inside as well as outside national boundaries. Their outcomes cannot be predetermined from a set of economic or political structures. Although structural analysis of the forces of globalization or capitalism can help in explaining the increased relevance of transnational collective action, they give us few clues on why CSOs differ in the ways in which they seek to be a part of a globalizing world, and how these pathways vary through time.

The agency-centered approach used in this book spotlights dimensions of transnational collective action that we cannot ignore if we want to understand how and why civil society's repertoires of contention are changing. In these conclusions, I will highlight two, whose importance has been asserted repeatedly throughout the book: (1) the national, or domestic, dimension, and (2) the asymmetry dimension, both of which I regard as constitutive of transnational collective action. These dimensions became visible because of the focus of the research on the relational and political embeddedness of CSOs, that is, the importance given to the analysis of actors' networks and their dynamic relationships, and the relevance attributed to the specific political contexts in which they build coalitions, define their goals, and articulate their frames.

The National Dimension

The most central organizations in the networks mapped are domestic CSOs that have remained nationally rooted even as they became increasingly engaged in transnational collective action through their participation in trade agreement debates. Trade was an issue that most of them did not follow closely before the 1990s, neither in the domestic nor in the international arenas. The social network data confirm that cross-national ties among challengers of trade agreements increased in number and became more diverse in the last twenty years because of trade-related activities, a finding that was corroborated in the literature and in the analysis of documents.

The research also showed that, in spite of this overall increased engagement, only a few of these actors took a sustained transnationalization pathway, in which they prioritized the creation of long-term transnational coalitions and engaged in efforts to produce common programs for action. Many continued to focus on domestic targets, even as they participated intermittently in transnational actions, in a yoyo-like movement that took them back and forth across the domestic-international boundaries. Most importantly, even among those that did reach higher levels of continuous transnationalization, the perception of new political opportunities for bargaining at the domestic scale may put their transnational collaboration in jeopardy

How can we make sense of this paradoxical situation of increased engagement in transnational collective action by CSOs that remain rooted in the domestic arena?

The framework used in this book allows for the reconciliation of these seemingly disparate empirical findings. The debate about local–global interactions underscores the need for a better understanding of the location of political life in general, and collective action in particular. Scholars remain trapped in an either/or framework, whereby political claims are either oriented toward a territorially bounded political community or toward universal values. The answer is not simply to bring the national back into our analysis as a separate site of action, nor to blur the boundaries across scales as though the place of origin did not matter. The challenge is to focus on the dynamic interactions and influences across the domestic and the international collective action scales, because, more often than not, transnational collective action entails an ambiguous combination of domestic and international targets, networks, discourses, and goals.

I approached this challenge by analyzing the multiple pathways actors used to crisscross boundaries, and by exposing the mechanisms CSOs used in their efforts to generate and sustain collective action. These mechanisms are deliberate responses provided by actors as they struggled to find common ground in very heterogeneous coalitions. The mechanisms of extension, suppression, and transformation of frames are attempts to provide a compatible platform across difference. Although contradictions and conflicts remain, actors have learned to show greater sensibility to the problem of how to combine various degrees of internationalization at different points in time, so as to avoid ruptures. National collective action has tended to become less autonomous from international politics, and CSOs in the Americas became conscious of this through debates about multilateral trade agreement negotiations.

The document "Alternatives for the Americas," analyzed in this book, provided examples of these mechanisms in play, as a group of actors made continuous attempts to create a common transnational project of change. Although there is no evidence that this document has proven itself useful as an alternative template to be presented by CSOs when they face specific negotiations, the dialogue that led to its writing has shown the willingness and the capacity of a broad cluster of CSOs from across the Americas to reach basic and provisional agreements on a common set of issues.

The mechanism of diffusion exemplifies another kind of attempt to find compatibility across scales. In the two decades of trade mobilizations studied in this book, repertoires of contentions and ideas flew in many directions: vertically from the domestic to the international and from the international to the domestic, and horizontally across domestic collective action arenas. The diffusion of a similar coalition form that initially was implemented in Canada to other countries throughout the hemisphere (first to the United States and Mexico, and subsequently elsewhere) was possible only because of the embeddedness of actors in new transnational networks. The Hemispheric Social Alliance (HSA), which brought together these arrangements under an international umbrella, was the result of a vertical diffusion of this coalition-building form to enable the coordination of actions at a higher scale. The movement of ideas from one country to another – for example, the influence of the Uruguayan Interunion Workers' Assembly–National Workers' Confederation (PIT-CNT)'s position on the Common Market of the South (MERCOSUR) in the internal debates of the Brazilian Unified Workers' Federation (CUT) – and from domestic to international arenas – the HSA's decision to oppose the Free Trade Area of the Americas (FTAA) negotiations –provides other examples of diffusion through social networks.

Diffusion, however, is not an automatic mechanism triggered by social networks. Although some ideas and repertoires travel well across borders, others do not. Some CSOs choose to adopt them, whereas others offer resistance. Furthermore, diffusion does not entail simple reproduction. As the comparison of the functioning of the national chapters of the HSA showed, in each case actors adapted this organizational format to their specific contexts, with different results. The networks that were the basis for these coalitions were at the same time the result of the history of relationships within that country and of the new ties generated by the political context of challenges to trade agreements. The institutionalization of dialogue across scales through brokers helped to sustain the flow of information and resources among a great number of actors; at the same time, it led to the introduction of asymmetries among actors engaged in transnational collective action.

The Asymmetry Dimension

A second constitutive dimension of transnational collective action relates to the asymmetries that characterize the relationships among actors. Once again, the research has yielded apparently disparate findings. On the one hand, the network data confirmed what the literature on transnationalism has argued: that cross-sectoral, multi-issue collaborative ties have become more common in the past decades, reflecting the greater presence in the international arena of a more plural set of actors that are both member-based and not, that come from the North as well as from the South, and that espouse different interests and goals. On the other hand, there is no empirical support for the idea that the relationships among these actors are either horizontal or reciprocal. As the sociograms of networks among close allies showed in the cases of Brazil, Chile, Mexico, and the United States, although some actors acquired greater visibility and populated the center of networks, others remained on the periphery, and still others were absent.

The analysis of the efforts to institutionalize ties through coalition-building initiatives complemented the data on asymmetries from the social network maps. It showed that power imbalances among actors permeated the various attempts, but were clearer in the cases of affiliation-based coalitions. Within them, actors played different roles and had disparate access to information and resources. In Brazil, Chile, Mexico, and the United States, new organizational arrangements overcame, at least temporarily, the traditional difficulties of multisectoral collaboration. At the same time, they had to face the mounting criticism of those who felt excluded from internal decision-making processes and from access to financial resources. The difficulties in adapting organizational arrangements to guarantee a plural and sustained participation of challengers of trade agreements were the most important reasons behind the crisis of the HSA national chapters in countries such as Chile and Mexico.

At the domestic scale, tensions have pitted capital-based and local CSOs against each other, either because of the concentration of meetings and events in the capital city, or because of the top–down approach that some CSOs use when traveling around the country to implement their strategies. This kind of contention has been felt most strongly in the cases of the United States and Mexico.

A second source of tensions has been that between member-based organizations and nongovernmental organizations (NGOs). This relates to the issue of representation, as new transnational arenas were created, and as the number of international events requiring the participation of representatives of organizations increased. The decision of who could speak in the name of heterogeneous coalitions in international events led to episodes of contention among challengers of trade agreements, in all the countries studied. This has been felt most strongly in the cases of Chile and Mexico. In spite of efforts by CSOs to bridge these divides, and in spite of important differences in the ways in which these struggles were played out in each country, they remain key challenges for any sustainable and multisectoral coalition-building project.

However, the sources of asymmetries vary through time, as actors try to deal with them, and as the relationships and political contexts change. An answer within the HSA that tried to generate a better coordination across borders, without the creation of new centralized bureaucracies, has been the establishment of mediators, or brokers – a role played by organizations in charge of the secretariats of national chapters. These would act as gateways for overseas contacts and information. The comparison of the functioning of four domestic chapters of the HSA showed that the NGOs in charge of the Brazilian and U.S. chapters were more successful in this mediating role because not only were they willing to coordinate collective action, but they also were careful not to speak in the name of others. In these cases, a negotiated balance was struck between the consensus-based position espoused by all members of the coalition and the continuous autonomy of each organization to uphold specific propositions, on their own or with other allies.

Conclusions

In terms of asymmetries beyond national boundaries, this book showed the increased relevance of Southern organizations and of South–South ties in the construction of the transnational network of trade challengers. As argued in the introduction, the literature on transnational activism has tended to focus its attention on Northern-based organizations. In part, this bias results from a tendency to conflate the power of national states in the international system with the power of national civil societies. There is an unwarranted assumption in part of the literature that any attempt to influence multilateral negotiations will be most effective if focused on actors and decision-making arenas from the more developed countries, and, thus, that links to CSOs in the North will be the most relevant ones. However, this is not always the case.

Throughout the 1990s, Southern CSOs progressively became very active in the networks of trade challengers. Diffusion of experiences and information did not only flow from the North to the South, but also from the South to the South, and from the South to the North. Thus, although at the beginning of the 1990s North–South differences represented the key source of asymmetry in trade challengers' networks in the Americas, in the middle years of the first decade of the twenty-first century participation was more balanced across both regions. This is not to say that North–South differences have been erased, but CSOs' geographical origins are not the main analytical key to studying power relations among trade challengers.

In order to study the continuities and changes in the asymmetry dimension of transnational collective action, it was essential to use broad empirical lenses that provided not only a map of participants and their networks, but also information on the variation of participation through time. Through a combination of social network data and qualitative information, gathered through interviews with key actors and the analysis of documents, it was possible to investigate the flow of ties and to understand the building of transnational networks as a two-decade-long process. Had this study focused on the case of a specific campaign, it would have missed the relevance of previously established relationships and lessons learned, and of the overlaps of ties created in different trade-related contexts and initiatives.

For example, had this research been limited to analyzing the case of the Continental Campaign against the FTAA, it would have included a much narrower set of actors, because many participants of the field of trade challengers have not been active members of the Campaign. In fact, most

Chilean and Mexican actors would have been excluded from such a case study, given the little priority the FTAA has had on their agendas. Others, such as the Brazilian labor federations General Workers' Confederation (CGT) and Labor Force (Força Sindical), have been active participants at the MERCOSUR level, but not in the FTAA Campaign. The fact that different organizations use different pathways in specific negotiating arenas provides us with an important clue to the potentialities of sustainable transnational collective action.

Most importantly, a study based on a single campaign would have missed the variety of organizational and ideational pathways mapped. Case studies of short-lived and narrowly targeted campaigns face a greater difficulty in analyzing conflicts among its members. By definition, these campaigns are structured around common goals and against common targets. A longer-term approach to transnational collective action offers the possibility of studying how these campaigns relate to previous experiences, how sustained the relationships created around campaigns are, and whether interaction changes the ways actors think about themselves and about the goals and targets of collective action.

Have Trade Agreements Gone Too Far?

The wave of free trade negotiations in the Americas presented important new challenges not only for civil society activists, but also for scholars who study trade policy making and transnational collective action. Although the liberalization of international flows of goods and services remained at the core of these agreements, new negotiations included regulations on almost all public policy arenas. This change has transformed the debate about free trade and its alternatives into a much broader discussion about development and global governance. The politicization of trade was at the same time cause and consequence of the incorporation of trade in the agenda of a more diversified set of CSOs. These actors themselves contributed to the expansion of what has been understood as "trade-related," by analyzing the potential impacts of trade negotiations from an increasingly broad perspective, ranging from policy issues such as access to medicines to debates about the role of international investors in development.

In this context, the scholarly literature on trade policy making as a two-level game could not explain the more complicated dynamics of interaction between negotiators and nonstate actors that has become typical of negotiations in the Americas (and also at a global scale). Similarly, the literature on coalition building that focuses on the polarization between free traders and protectionists with clear and fixed interests does not present an accurate view of the more complex reality of interaction among civil society actors. Although labor and business organizations remain important actors, the rise of rural organizations, multi-issue NGOs, and others presents many new possibilities of different combinations of actors and demands at the domestic and international scales.

In such a heterogeneous environment, it is no surprise that challengers of trade agreements have not been able to present a common alternative to the treaties being negotiated in the region. However, they did find common ground on specific issues. Broadly speaking, trade agreement challengers shared the view that free trade agreement negotiations have gone too far. The most common joint critique presented by these actors related to the so-called democratic deficit of negotiations, followed by demands to enhance the transparency of decision-making processes. In this respect, challengers have been somewhat successful. In Brazil, for example, even before the government of Luis Inácio Lula da Silva was inaugurated, CSOs had been able to widen their domestic communication channels with state officials. The spaces for participation opened in the 1990s within the institutions of MERCOSUR, although primarily oriented to representatives of labor unions and business associations, remain a unique example in the region of sustained state–civil society dialogue about regional integration and its impacts.

A second issue that united most challengers of trade agreements in the Americas was investors' rights. Thanks to the experience in the North American Free Trade Agreement (NAFTA) region with cases of investor-state disputes and the subsequent mobilizations against the Multilateral Agreement on Investment (MAI), the one demand that had the greatest support across networks of challengers was the exclusion of the issue of investors' rights from trade negotiations. Even so, there was no consensus on alternative language to be adopted by negotiators.

Through the process of elaboration of the document "Alternatives for the Americas," members of the HSA were able to reach provisional agreements on a wider set of issues, such as labor rights. However, there was no consensus among labor organizations in the hemisphere on how to negotiate with national authorities the inclusion of a labor clause, nor on how this demand related to other contents of agreements that at least some of these actors (and their allies) also opposed.

After two decades of mobilizations, the progressive opening of new channels of negotiations and dialogue between civil society and state exposed the increasingly sophisticated critiques of the contents of trade agreements, but also the absence of a joint alternative template for hemispheric negotiations. A key obstacle to reaching a common set of demands is the unresolved tension between arguments in favor of more global governance and arguments in favor of the preservation of national sovereignty and the strengthening of nation-states. Actors located in the center-to-left of the political spectrum, in the North as well as in the South, have tended to frame this debate as a democracy issue. Although the need to preserve and strengthen national democracy gave differently positioned actors a common platform on which all could agree, it did not disentangle the controversies about the future of global governance. Such disagreements were most clearly seen when actors argued that free trade agreements have gone too far in the addition of regulation topics that should remain non-trade-related, such as investors' rights, while at the same time pushing for other issues to be included, such as labor rights and rules for environmental protection.

The future of collective action on trade remains uncertain. This book gives credence to the more cautious views about the potential impacts of transnational collective action, offering little empirical support for the more optimistic views about the emergence of a powerful "global civil society." Challengers of trade agreements remain divided with respect to the necessary reforms to the governance of trade, and the limited agreements reached by them at the hemispheric level are fragile. The difficulties encountered by trade coalitions seem to confirm the skepticism of those scholars who emphasize the obstacles to sustained coalition building across national borders. In part, these difficulties are related to the mainly reactive character of transnational collective action. Trade negotiations are intermittently in the political agenda, leading to moments of high mobilization, followed by steep declines in the attention given by CSOs and public opinion in general. Even as pathways to transnationality varied, the FTAA provided a common focal point for challengers of trade agreements. In the post-FTAA years, it has become harder to maintain a hemispheric basis for collective action.

At the same time, this book has also provided empirical evidence of the creation of new forms of transnational organization and common agendas that did not exist twenty years ago. It showed that innovative North–South forms of collaboration have been created that provide a basis for hemispheric action that, however fragile, was not imaginable before. More specifically, coalitions created in the context of trade debates shared one characteristic: they were sustained by a broad variety of types of organizations, ranging from tiny NGOs to organizations with millions of members. Because of their interaction, particular agendas became extended, issues in which there was no agreement were suppressed, and/or their contents were transformed. The analysis in this book has shown that these changes have not been easy ones, and that not all CSOs have felt the need to engage in negotiated interactions with other types of organizations. However, among those that did were some of the most powerful organizations in the hemisphere.

Coalition-building initiatives seemed to yield better results in terms of their sustainability through time when actors were able to adapt preexisting social networks, repertoires, and resources to deal with new challenges. That was the case of the Southern Cone Coordinator of Labor Federations, which became the most relevant (though not unique) space for labor dialogue in the MERCOSUR region, and that was the case of the Jubilee South Campaign, which incorporated the Campaign against the FTAA in Brazil by adding it to a previously agreed-upon agenda. In the cases of creation of new domestic trade coalitions, the experience showed that challenges to their role were avoided better when they were headquartered in a previously existing organization with a good reputation among those groups challenging free trade negotiations – such as the Development Group for Alternative Policies (D-GAP) in the United States or the Federation of Organisms for Social and Educational Assistance (FASE) in Brazil.

This study assumed that the boundaries among comparative politics, international relations, and transnational studies have long ago become obsolete. It engaged in a broad dialogue across disciplines that also considered the contributions by sociologists to the analysis of social networks and social movements. A multidisciplinary approach that is based on the agency of actors as they engage in transnational collective action through time helps us to go beyond the somewhat innocuous – but still popular – polarization between accounts that welcome a new world of global collective action and others that deny that any fundamental changes are happening. The case of challengers of trade agreements in the Americas has shown simultaneously the achievements of these actors and the dilemmas that haunt their transnational collective action. The middle road between disillusionment and euphoria may not be the easiest, but it is the most fruitful in the long term.

Main Abbreviations Used

ABIAIDS	Brazilian Interdisciplinary Aids Association (Brazil)
ACJR	Chilean Alliance for a Just and Responsible Trade (Chile)
AFL-CIO	American Federation of Labor–Congress of Industrial Organizations (U.S.)
AFSC	American Friends Service Committee (U.S.)
AFSCME	American Federation of State, County, and Municipal Employees (U.S.)
ALAMPYME	Latin American Association of Small and Medium Firms
ANAMURI	National Association of Rural and Indigenous Women (Chile)
ANDES	National Association of University Professors (Brazil)
ANEC	National Association of Rural Producers' Commercial Firms (Mexico)
ART	Alliance for Responsible Trade (U.S.)
CAFTA	U.S.–Central America Free Trade Agreement
CAPISE	Center for Political Analysis and Social and Economic Research (Mexico)
CECCAM	Center for Studies for Rural Change in Mexico (Mexico)
CEDM	Ecumenical Center Diego de Medellín (Chile)
CEE	Ecumenical Studies Center (Chile)

CEMDA	Mexican Center for Environmental Law (Mexico)
CENCOS	National Center for Social Communication (Mexico)
CENDA	Center for National Studies on Alternative Development (Chile)
CEPIS	Center for Popular Education – Institute Sedes Sapientiae (Brazil)
CETEBES	Confederation of Bank Workers (Chile)
CGT	General Workers' Confederation (Brazil)
CGT	General Workers' Confederation (Argentina)
CIEL	Center for International Environmental Law (U.S.)
CIEPAC	Center for Economic and Political Research for Community Action (Mexico)
CILAS	Center for Labor Research and Consulting (Mexico)
CIOAC	Independent Confederation of Farmworkers and Peasants (Mexico)
CLOC	Latin American Coordinator of Peasant Organizations
CNB	National Confederation of Bank Workers (Brazil)
CNM	National Steelworkers Confederation (Brazil)
CNOC	National Coordinator of Coffee Producers (Mexico)
CODEPU	Human Rights Defense Committee (Chile)
COMIEDES	Mexican Council for Sustainable Development (Mexico)
CONADECU	National Users and Consumers Corporation (Chile)
CONIECO	National Council of Environmental Industrialists (Mexico)
CONSTRAMET	Steelworkers Confederation (Chile)
CONTAG	National Confederation of Agricultural Workers (Brazil)

COPROFAM	Coordinator of Family Farm Organizations of MERCOSUR
CSO	Civil society organization
CTC	Citizens' Trade Campaign (U.S.)
CTM	Confederation of Mexican Workers (Mexico)
CTW	Change to Win Coalition (U.S.)
CUSFTA	Canada–U.S. Free Trade Agreement
CUT-Brazil	Unified Workers' Federation (Brazil)
CUT-Chile	Unitary Workers' Central (Chile)
CUT-Peru	Unitary Workers' Central (Peru)
CWA	Communication Workers of America (U.S.)
DECA-EP	Peoples' Team (Mexico)
D-GAP	Development Group for Alternative Policies (U.S.)
ECLAC	Economic Commission for Latin America and the Caribbean
EPI	Economic Policy Institute (U.S.)
FASE	Federation of Organizations for Social and Educational Assistance (Brazil)
FAT	Authentic Labor Front (Mexico)
FDC	Peasants' Democratic Front of Chihuahua (Mexico)
FOE	Friends of the Earth (U.S.)
FTAA	Free Trade Area of the Americas
GATT	General Agreement on Tariffs and Trade
GEA	Environmental Studies Group (Mexico)
HRW	Human Rights Watch (U.S.)
HSA	Hemispheric Social Alliance
IATP	Institute for Agricultural and Trade Policy (U.S.)
IBASE	Brazilian Institute of Social and Economic Analysis (Brazil)
IBT	International Brotherhood of Teamsters (U.S.)
ICFTU	International Confederation of Free Trade Unions
IEP	Institute of Political Ecology (Chile)

ILRF	International Labor Rights Fund (U.S.)
INESC	Institute of Socio-Economic Studies (Brazil)
IPS	Institute for Policy Studies (U.S.)
MAI	Multilateral Agreement on Investment
MERCOSUR	Common Market of the South
MSF	Doctors without Borders (Brazil)
MST	Landless Rural Workers' Movement (Brazil)
NAFTA	North American Free Trade Agreement
NFFC	National Family Farm Coalition (U.S.)
NGO	Nongovernmental organization
NRDC	National Resources Defense Council (U.S.)
NWF	National Wildlife Federation (U.S.)
ORIT	Inter-American Regional Organization of Workers
PACS	Alternative Policies for the Southern Cone (Brazil)
PIT-CNT	Interunion Workers' Assembly–National Workers' Confederation (Uruguay)
PO	Workers' Pastoral (Brazil)
PSI	Public Services International
REBRIP	Brazilian Network for the Integration of the Peoples (Brazil)
RECHIP	Chilean Action Network for Peoples' Initiative (Chile)
RMALC	Mexican Action Network on Free Trade (Mexico)
SME	Mexican Electrical Workers Union (Mexico)
SOF	Feminist Organization Sempre-Viva (Brazil)
SPM	Migrants' Pastoral Service (Brazil)
STRM	Mexican Telephone Workers Union (Mexico)
TUCA	Trade Union Confederation of the Americas
UAW	United Auto Workers (U.S.)
UE	United Electrical, Radio, and Machine Workers (U.S.)
UNCTAD	United Nations Conference on Trade and Development

Main Abbreviations Used

UNE	National Union of Students (Brazil)
UNITE	Union of Needletrades, Industrial and Textile Employees (U.S.)
UNORCA	National Union of Autonomous Regional Rural Organizations (Mexico)
UNT	National Union of Workers (Mexico)
USAS	United Students against Sweatshops (U.S.)
USBIC	United States Business and Industrial Council (U.S.)
USTR	United States Trade Representative
USWA	United Steelworkers of America (U.S.)
VC	Via Campesina
WOLA	Washington Office on Latin America (U.S.)
WSF	World Social Forum
WTO	World Trade Organization

Appendix A

Lists of Interviews

Three types of interviews were conducted for this study, most of them between May 2004 and August 2008, with actors from Brazil, Canada, Chile, Mexico, Peru, the United States, and Uruguay (see Table A1). Structured interviews using a social network questionnaire were done with informants from 123 civil society organizations (CSOs) from Brazil, Chile, Mexico, and the United States (listed in Tables A2 through A5). Semistructured and in-depth interviews were held with other civil society informants, government officials, parliamentarians, legislative staff, and international organization officials. Their names, affiliation, and the date and place of the interview are listed in Table A6, with the exception of interviewees that requested anonimity.

In many cases, more than one person from the same CSO was interviewed to answer the social network questionnaire. In other cases, individuals were interviewed more than once, and, sometimes, the same individuals were interviewed in more than one organization, as they switched jobs over the years. That is why the total number of questionnaires is different from the number of individuals interviewed in Table A1. The number of semistructured and in-depth interviews with CSOs is also different from the total number of interviews, which includes those undertaken with government officials, parliamentarians, legislative staff, and international organization officials (listed in Table A6). Some interviews were held with individuals when they were traveling overseas, which explains why in a few cases, for example, Americans were interviewed in Brazil or vice versa. The great majority of interviews were face-to-face (exceptions are noted in Table A6).

Table A1. *Total Number of Interviews, by Type of Interview, Number of Individuals, and Number of Civil Society Organizations*

Type of interview	Number of interviews	Number of CSOs
Social network questionnaire	148	123
Semistructured and in-depth interviews	87	35
Total	235	158

Table A2. *Organizations That Answered the Social Network Questionnaire in Brazil between February and May 2005*

Action Aid Brazil
Associação Brasileira Interdisciplinar de Aids (ABIAIDS)
Associação Nacional dos Docentes em Entidades de Ensino Superior (ANDES)
Cáritas Brasileira
Central Única dos Trabalhadores (CUT)
Centro de Educação Popular – Instituto Sedes Sapientiae (CEPIS)
Confederação Geral dos Trabalhadores (CGT)
Confederação Nacional dos Bancários (CNB)
Confederação Nacional dos Metalúrgicos (CNM)
Confederação Nacional dos Trabalhadores em Agricultura (CONTAG)
Federação de Órgãos para Assistência Social e Educacional (FASE)
Força Sindical
Instituto Brasileiro de Análises Sociais e Econômicas (IBASE)
Instituto Brasileiro de Desenvolvimento (IBRADES)
Instituto de Estudos Socioeconômicos (INESC)
Instituto Eqüit
Internacional do Serviço Público (ISP)
Médicos Sem Fronteiras (MSF)
Movimento dos Atingidos por Barragens (MAB)
Movimento dos Pequenos Agricultores (MPA)
Movimento dos Trabalhadores Rurais Sem-Terra (MST)
Oxfam Great Britain – Brazil Program
Pastoral Operária (PO)
Políticas Alternativas para o Cone Sul (PACS)
Sempre-Viva Organização Feminista (SOF)
Serviço Pastoral dos Migrantes (SPM)
Sindicato Nacional dos Auditores Fiscais da Receita Federal (Unafisco)
União Nacional dos Estudantes (UNE)
World Wildlife Fund (WWF)

Appendix A: Lists of Interviews

Table A3. *Organizations That Answered the Social Network Questionnaire in Chile between May and June 2005*

Alianza Chilena por un Comercio Justo y Responsable (ACJR)
Asociación Nacional de Mujeres Rurales e Indígenas (ANAMURI)
Central Unitaria de Trabajadores de Chile (CUT)
Centro de Estudios Nacionales de Desarrollo Alternativo (CENDA)
Centro Ecuménico Diego de Medellín (CEDM)
Colegio de Profesores
Comité de Defensa de los Derechos del Pueblo (CODEPU)
Confederación de los Trabajadores Metalúrgicos (CONSTRAMET)
Confederación de Trabajadores Bancarios (CETEBES)
Consumers International – Chile
Corporación Nacional de Consumidores y Usuarios (CONADECU)
Corporación Participa
Derechos Digitales
Fundación Terram
Instituto de Ecología Política (IEP)
LOM Editores
Oxfam Great Britain – Chile Program
Pastoral de los Trabajadores
Programa de Economía del Trabajo (PET)
Recursos e Investigación para el Desarrollo Sustentable (RIDES)
Servicio Paz y Justicia (SERPAJ)
Unidad Obrero Campesina (UOC)
Vivo Positivo

Table A4. *Organizations That Answered the Social Network Questionnaire in Mexico in August 2004 and August 2005*

Asociación Latinoamericana de Pequeños Empresarios/México (ALAMPYME)
Asociación Nacional de Empresas Comercializadoras de Productores del Campo, A.C. (ANEC)
Central Independiente de Obreros Agrícolas y Campesinos (CIOAC)
Centro de Análisis Político e Investigaciones Sociales y Económicas (CAPISE)
Centro de Derechos Humanos Miguel Agustín Pro Juárez
Centro de Estudios Ecuménicos (CEE)
Centro de Estudios para el Cambio en el Campo Mexicano (CECCAM)
Centro de Investigación Laboral y Asesoría Sindical (CILAS)
Centro de Investigaciones Económicas y Políticas de Acción Comunitaria (CIEPAC)
Centro Mexicano de Derecho Ambiental (CEMDA)
Centro Nacional de Comunicación Social (CENCOS)
Confederación de Trabajadores de México (CTM)
Consejo Mexicano para el Desarrollo Sustentable (COMIEDES)
Consejo Nacional de Industriales Ecologistas (CONIECO)
Coordinadora Nacional de Organizaciones Cafetaleras (CNOC)
DECA Equipo Pueblo
Frente Auténtico del Trabajo (FAT)
Frente Democrático Campesino de Chihuahua (FDC)
Fundación Heinrich Böll/México
Greenpeace México
Grupo de Estudios Ambientales (GEA)
Movimiento Ciudadano por la Democracia (MCD)
Mujer y Medio Ambiente
Mujeres para el Diálogo
Oxfam International – Mexico Program
Seminario Permanente de Estudios Chicanos y de Fronteras
Servicio y Asesoría para la Paz (SERAPAZ)
Sindicato de Telefonistas de la República Mexicana (STRM)
Sindicato Mexicano de Electricistas (SME)
Unión Nacional de Organizaciones Regionales Campesinas Autónomas (UNORCA)

Appendix A: Lists of Interviews

Table A5. *Organizations That Answered the Social Network Questionnaire in the United States between May 2004 and January 2006*

American Federation of Labor–Congress of Industrial Organizations (AFL-CIO)
American Federation of State, County and Municipal Employees (AFSCME)
American Friends Service Committee (AFSC)
American Welfare Institute (AWI)
Campaign for Labor Rights (CLR)
Center for Economic Justice (CEJ)
Center for Economic Policy Research (CEPR)
Center for International Environmental Law (CIEL)
Center of Concern
Church World Service (CWS)
Communications Workers of America (CWA)
Defenders of Wildlife
Development Group for Alternative Policies (D-GAP)
Earthjustice
Economic Policy Institute (EPI)
Esquel Foundation
Freedom House
Friends of the Earth (FOE)
Global Exchange (GE)
Human Rights Watch (HRW)
Institute for Agricultural and Trade Policy (IATP)
Institute for Policy Studies (IPS)
International Brotherhood of Teamsters (IBT)
International Labor Rights Fund (ILRF)
Maryknoll Office for Global Concerns
National Family Farm Coalition (NFFC)
National Resources Defense Council (NRDC)
National Wildlife Federation (NWF)
Oxfam America
Partners of the Americas
Public Citizen
Rural Coalition
Sierra Club
Union of Needletrades, Industrial and Textile Employees (UNITE)
United Auto Workers (UAW)
United Electrical, Radio and Machine Workers (UE)
United States Business and Industrial Council Educational Foundation (USBIC)
United States Council of Catholic Bishops (USCCB)
United Steelworkers of the America (USWA)
United Students against Sweatshops (USAS)
Washington Office on Latin America (WOLA)

Table A6. *Semistructured and In-Depth Interviews, by Country Where the Interview Was Conducted, Name, Affiliation, City, and Date*

Country	Name	Organization	City and date
Brazil	Alexandra Stricknert	Trade and Global Governance Program, Geneva Office, Institute for Agriculture and Trade Policy (IATP)	São Paulo, June 2004
	Anonymous	Legislative Staff – Brazilian House of Representatives	Brasilia, December 2004
	Florisvaldo Fier (Dr. Rosinha)	Congressman, President of the Joint MERCOSUR Commission – Brazilian House of Representatives	Brasilia, December 2004
	Antônio Ferreira Costa Filho	Secretary of the Joint MERCOSUR Commission – Brazilian House of Representatives	Brasilia, December 2004
	Víctor Báez Mosqueira	Secretary General, Inter-American Regional Organization of Workers (ORIT)	Belo Horizonte, December 2004
	Adriano Campolina	Americas' Regional Director, Action Aid International	Rio de Janeiro, March 2005
	Adhemar Mineiro	Interunion Department for Statistics and Socioeconomic Studies (DIEESE)	Rio de Janeiro, March 2005
	Lúcia Maduro	National Industry Confederation (CNI-Brazil)	Rio de Janeiro, March 2005
	Fátima Mello	International Relations Coordinator of FASE and Executive Secretariat of the Brazilian Network for the Integration of the Peoples (REBRIP)	Rio de Janeiro, March 2005
	Sérgio Schlesinger	Project Sustainable Brazil at FASE	Rio de Janeiro, March 2005
	Luis Alberto	International Relations Secretary, National Confederation of Agricultural Workers (CONTAG)	Brasilia, April 2005
	Luís Vicente Facco	Advisor, International Relations Secretariat, National Confederation of Agricultural Workers (CONTAG)	Brasilia, April 2005
	Rosilene Wansetto	Secretariat of the National and Continental Campaigns against the FTAA	São Paulo, April 2005

Appendix A: Lists of Interviews

Country	Name	Organization	City and date
	Rafael Freire Neto	Former International Relations Secretary, Unified Workers' Federation (CUT-Brazil)	São Paulo, April 2005
	Iara Pietricovsky	Executive Board, Institute of Socio-Economic Studies (INESC)	Brasilia, April 2005
	Jerry Fernández	International corporate campaigner, United Steelworkers of America (USWA)	Brasilia, April 2005
	Gonzalo Berrón	Advisor, Hemispheric Social Alliance and Continental Campaign against the FTAA Secretariats	São Paulo, April 2005
		Advisor for integration issues, Trade Union Confederation of the Americas (TUCA)	São Paulo, February 2008
	Edélcio Vigna	Advisor for Agrarian Reform and Food Sovereignty, Institute of Socio-Economic Studies (INESC)	Brasilia, February 2008
	Kjeld Jakobsen	Former International Relations Secretary, Unified Workers' Federation (CUT-Brazil)	Brasilia, May 2008
	Graciela Rodríguez	Equit Institute and Global Coordinator of the International Gender and Trade Network (IGTN)	Rio de Janeiro, May 2008
Canada	John Dillon	Program Coordinator, Global Justice Project, Kairos: Canadian Ecumenical Justice Initiatives	Toronto, September 2004
	Joseph Gunn	Director of Social Affairs at the Canadian Conference of Catholic Bishops	Ottawa, September 2004
	Ed Finn	General Editor, Canadian Centre for Policy Alternatives (CCPA)	Ottawa, September 2004
	Robert Baldwin	Social and Economic Policy Department, Canadian Labour Congress (CLC)	Ottawa, September 2004

(continued)

Table A6 *(continued)*

Country	Name	Organization	City and date
	Jean Yves-Lefort	Trade Campaigner, Council of Canadians	Ottawa, September 2004
	John Foster	North/South Institute	Montreal, September 2004
Chile	Etiel Moraga	Former President, Unitary Workers' Central (CUT-Chile)	Santiago, May 2005
	Manuel Baquedano	Institute of Political Ecology (IEP)	Santiago, May 2005
	Bernardo Reyes	Institute of Political Ecology (IEP)	Santiago, May 2005
	Pablo Lazo	General Direction of Economic International Relations (Direcon), Ministry of Foreign Affairs	Santiago, May 2005
	Anonymous	Advisor, Ministry of Labor	Santiago, June 2005
Mexico	Gustavo Alanis Ortega	President, Mexican Center for Environmental Law (CEMDA)	Mexico City, May 2001
	Alejandro Villamar	Member of the Mexican Action Network on Free Trade (RMALC)	Mexico City, May 2001 and August 2005
	Héctor de la Cueva	Director, Center for Labor Research and Consulting (CILAS), and member of the Mexican Action Network on Free Trade (RMALC)	Mexico City, August 2004 and August 2005
	María Atilano	General Coordinator, Mexican Action Network on Free Trade (RMALC)	Mexico City, August 2004 and August 2005
	Bertha Luján	Former coordinator of the Authentic Labor Front (FAT) and founder of the Mexican Action Network on Free Trade (RMALC)	Mexico City, August 2005
	Maureen Meyer	Former employee of the Human Rights Center Miguel Agustín Pro Juárez	Mexico City, August 2005
	Manuel Pérez-Rocha	Former employee of the Mexican Action Network on Free Trade (RMALC) and Oxfam-Mexico	Mexico City, August 2005

Appendix A: Lists of Interviews

Country	Name	Organization	City and date
	Gilberto Silvestre López	Central Independiente de Obreros Agrícolas y Campesinos (CIOAC)	Mexico City, August 2005
	Víctor Suárez	Congressman, House of Representatives	Mexico City, August 2005
Peru	José Marcos-Sánchez	Director, Labor Development Program – Programa Laboral de Desarrollo (PLADES)	Lima, July 2008
	Juan José Gorriti	General Secretary, General Workers' Confederation of Peru (CGTP)	Lima, July 2008
	Rosa Guillén	Gender and Economy Group, Global Women's March	Lima, July 2008
	Julio Cesar Bazán	President, Unitary Workers' Central United States (CUT-Peru)	Lima, July 2008
United States	Anonymous	Democratic trade staff, Ways and Means Committee of the House of Representatives	Washington, D.C., March 2004
	Jeff F. Hornbeck	Specialist in International Trade and Finance, Congressional Research Service, U.S. Congress	Washington, D.C., March 2004
	Anonymous	Congressional staff for Democratic Congressman	Washington, D.C., March 2004
	Anonymous	Republican staff, subcommittee on Western Hemisphere	Washington, D.C., April 2004
	Anonymous	Congressional staff for Republican Congressman	Washington, D.C., May 2004
	Anonymous	Democratic staff, U.S. Senate	Washington, D.C., May 2004
	Anonymous	Senior Policy Advisor to a Democratic Member of Congress, House of Representatives	Washington D.C., May 2004
	Timi Gerson	FTAA Coordinator, Global Trade Watch, Public Citizen	Washington, D.C., May 2004 and September 2005
	Sandy Levin	Congressman, U.S. House of Representatives	Washington, D.C., May 2004
	Alexandra Spieldoch	Senior Program Associate, Center of Concern	Washington D.C., May 2004
		Director of the Trade and Global Governance Program, Institute for Agriculture and Trade Policy (IATP)	Washington, D.C., March 2008

(continued)

215

Table A6 *(continued)*

Country	Name	Organization	City and date
	Jack Howard	Former assistant to the President in charge of international relations, American Federation of State, County and Municipal Employees (AFSCME)	Washington, D.C., June 2004
	John Cavanagh	Director, Institute for Policy Studies (IPS)	Washington, D.C., July 2004
	Thea Lee	Assistant Director for International Economic Policy (AFL-CIO)	Washington, D.C., August 2004
	Jeff Hermanson	Senior Advisor, American Center for International Labor Solidarity (The Solidarity Center)	Washington, D.C., September 2004
	Stan Gacek	International Affairs Assistant Director (AFL-CIO)	Washington, D.C., October 2004
	Fred Azcarate	Executive Director, Jobs with Justice	Washington, D.C., October 2004
	Rick Rowden	Policy Director, Action Aid U.S.	Washington D.C., January 2005
	Maria Sílvia Portella de Castro	Advisor to the International Relations Secretariat, Unified Workers' Federation (CUT-Brazil)	Washington, D.C., January 2005
	Átila Roque	Executive Director, Action Aid U.S.	Washington, D.C., February 2005
	Anonymous	State Department, U.S. Government	Over the phone, February 2005
	Anonymous	Labor Department, U.S. Government	Washington, D.C., March 2005
	Karen Hansen-Kuhn	Secretariat of the Alliance for Responsible Trade (ART)	Washington, D.C., September 2005
	Susan Ruether	Program Associate, Citizens' Trade Campaign (CTC)	Washington, D.C., September 2005
	Lori Wallach	Director, Global Trade Watch, Public Citizen	Washington, D.C., September 2005
	Larry Weiss	Executive Director, Citizens' Trade Campaign (CTC)	Over the phone, September 2005

Appendix A: Lists of Interviews

Country	Name	Organization	City and date
	Thomas Quigley	Policy Advisor, Latin American, Caribbean and Asian Affairs, U.S. Conference of Catholic Bishops (USCCB)	Washington, D.C., January 2006
	Steve Hellinger	President, Development-GAP (D-GAP)	Washington, D.C., March 2006
	Didier Jacobs	Special Adviser on Policy, Oxfam America	Boston, July 2006
	Sehar Raziuddin	State and Local Program Associate, Global Trade Watch, Public Citizen	Washington, D.C., November 2006
	Anonymous	AFL-CIO	Washington, D.C., February 2008
	Tom Loudon	Secretariat of the Alliance for Responsible Trade (ART), Quixote Center	Washington, D.C., February 2008
	Stephanie Weinberg	Oxfam America's Trade Policy Advisor	Washington, D.C., February 2008
	Jim McDermott	Congressman, U.S. House of Representatives	Washington, D.C., February 2008
	Manuel Pérez-Rocha	Institute for Policy Studies (IPS)	Washington, D.C., March 2008
	Todd Tucker	Research Director, Global Trade Watch, Public Citizen	Washington, D.C., March 2008
	Andy Gussert	Executive Director, Citizens' Trade Campaign (CTC)	Washington, D.C., March 2008
Uruguay	Álvaro Padrón	Interunion Workers' Assembly/National Workers' Confederation (PIT-CNT)	Montevideo, November 1999

217

Appendix B

Social Network Questionnaire (United States)

(A version of the same questionnaire translated into Spanish and Portuguese was administered to representatives of civil society organizations in Brazil, Chile, and Mexico)

I. GENERAL INFORMATION

1. Name of the organization
2. How long has your organization been involved in the debates about the consequences of trade agreements?

   a. Since before NAFTA ( ) Year:
   b. Since NAFTA ( ) Year:
   c. After NAFTA ( ) Year:

3. How long have you been following trade debates?

In this organization, since....... And before that, since......

4. In the table below, if your organization participates in the coalitions listed, please state the year when it began to participate. If your organization was a member of any of these coalitions/campaigns and is not involved anymore, please state the period during which it participated:

Coalition/Campaign	Participates since...	Period (years):
Citizen's Trade Campaign – CTC		
Alliance for Responsible Trade – ART		
Other domestic trade coalitions		
Hemispheric Social Alliance		
Continental Campaign against the FTAA		
Coalition for Justice in the *Maquiladoras*		
Maquiladora Health and Safety Support Coalition		
Other regional-level coalitions		
Our World Is Not for Sale		
International Forum on Globalization		
Other global-level coalitions		

5. Please mark with an "x" to which of the following events your organization has sent or will send representatives (as organizers, participants in official delegations, as organizers of parallel events, and/or other form of participation):

Event	Organizer of the event	Organizer of parallel event	Part of the U.S. official delegation	Other form of participation	No participation
Belo Horizonte FTAA Ministerial, 1997					
Buenos Aires FTAA Ministerial, 2001					

Appendix B: Social Network Questionnaire (United States)

Quito FTAA Ministerial, 2002					
Miami FTAA Ministerial, 2003					
First Summit of the Americas, Miami, 1994					
Second Summit of the Americas, Santiago, 1998					
Third Summit of the Americas, Québec, 2001					
WTO Ministerial Conference in Seattle, 1999					
WTO Ministerial Conference in Cancún, 2003					
First Hemispheric Meeting against the FTAA, Cuba, 2001					
Second Hemispheric Meeting against the FTAA, Cuba, 2002					
Third Hemispheric Meeting against the FTAA, Cuba, 2004.					
UNCTAD XI, São Paulo, 2004					

II. TIES

6. Which of the organizations listed below would you consider to be your closest allies (the ones you work most closely with and you most trust) in your current activities with respect to trade agreements' negotiations? Please mark as many as you wish with an "x".

Action Aid – U.S.	
AFL-CIO (includes Solidarity Center)	
The Alliance for Democracy	
The Alliance for Sustainable Jobs and the Environment	
American Lands Alliance	
American Welfare Institute	
Campaign for Labor Rights	
Carnegie Endowment for International Peace	
Center for Economic Justice	
Center for Economic and Policy Research – CEPR	
Center for International Environmental Law – CIEL	
Center of Concern	
Communications Workers of America – CWA	
Defenders of Wildlife	
Development Group for Alternative Policies D-GAP	
Earth Justice	
Esquel Foundation	
50 Years Is Enough	
Freedom House	
Friends of the Earth – FOE	
Global Exchange	
Greenpeace	
Institute for Agriculture and Trade Policy – IATP	
Institute for International Economics – IIE	

Institute for Policy Studies – IPS	
Institute for Social Ecology	
International Brotherhood of Teamsters	
International Forum on Globalization	
International Gender and Trade Network	
International Labor Rights Fund – ILRF	
International Trade Union Federal Public Services International – PSI	
Jobs with Justice	
Mexican Solidarity Network	
National Family Farm Coalition	
National Wildlife Federation – NWF	
Oxfam	
Partners of the Americas	
Public Citizen	
Rural Coalition	
UAW	
UE – United Electrical, Radio and Machine Workers	
UNITE – Union of Needletrades, Industrial and Textile Employees	
United States Business and Industrial Council Educational Foundation	
United Students against Sweatshops – USAS	
USWA (Steelworkers)	
Washington Office on Latin America – WOLA	

Are any missing from the list? If so, which ones?

7. Of these, please name between 3 and 5 organizations with which you currently most *share goals and strategies with respect to the FTAA negotiations*:

   7a. How long have you been working with each of them on trade-related issues?

Organization	Over 10 years	Over 5 years	Less than 5 years
1			
2			
3			
4			
5			

8. If your organization participated also in the NAFTA debates:

Were the organizations you just nominated also your closest allies during the NAFTA debates? If not, please list the ones that were:

9. The next two questions are about the relationship of your organization with other prominent organizations in the field.

   a. Here are a number of prominent organizations in the field. Specifically with respect *to your organization's goals* (ultimate ends) in the trade debates, how would you characterize your organization's current relationship with:

Organization:	*Very close* (agree on most important strategies)	*Close* (agree on some strategies)	*Distant* (agree on minor strategies)	*Very distant* (do not agree on strategies)	*Don't know*
AFL-CIO					
Public Citizen					
Human Rights Watch					
Institute for Agriculture and Trade Policy					
Global Exchange					
Friends of the Earth					
International Labor Rights Fund					

National Wildlife Federation					
OXFAM					
Esquel Foundation					

b. With respect to the same prominent organizations, how do you characterize your relationship with them with respect to *strategies chosen* (the ways in which you choose to achieve your goals) in trade-related activities:

Organization:	*Very close* (agree on most important strategies)	*Close* (agree on some strategies)	*Distant* (agree on minor strategies)	*Very distant* (do not agree on strategies)	*Don't know*
AFL-CIO					
Public Citizen					
Human Rights Watch					
Institute for Agriculture and Trade Policy					
Global Exchange					
Friends of the Earth					
International Labor Rights Fund					
National Wildlife Federation					
OXFAM					
Esquel Foundation					

10. When searching for partners and allies to influence trade policy, which of the following criteria do you consider most important in these different arenas? Check the three most important ones:

a) In looking for partners to work at the U.S. Congress:

( ) Common goals
( ) Coincidence of strategies to achieve these goals
( ) Need to strengthen mobilization capacity
( ) Need to incorporate different issue areas
( ) Common political orientation
( ) Others:

b) In looking for partners to influence the Executive:

( ) Common goals
( ) Coincidence of strategies to achieve these goals
( ) Need to strengthen mobilization capacity
( ) Need to incorporate different issue areas
( ) Common political orientation
( ) Others:

c) In looking for partners to participate in a domestic coalition:

( ) Common goals
( ) Coincidence of strategies to achieve these goals
( ) Need to strengthen mobilization capacity
( ) Need to incorporate different issue areas
( ) Common political orientation
( ) Others:

d) In looking for partners to participate in an international coalition:

( ) Common goals
( ) Coincidence of strategies to achieve these goals
( ) Need to strengthen mobilization capacity
( ) Need to incorporate different issue areas
( ) Common political orientation
( ) Others:

III. TRANSNATIONAL TIES

MEXICO

11. If your organization has contacts with civil society organizations in Mexico:
How would you characterize your relationship with:

Organization/ coalition	Very close (agree on all the most important goals and strategies)	Close (agree on some goals and strategies)	Distant (agree on minor goals and strategies)	Very distant (do not agree on goals and strategies)	Don't know
Red Mexicana de Acción Frente al Libre Comercio (RMALC)					
Frente Auténtico del Trabajo (FAT)					
Via Campesina					
Centro Mexico de Derecho Ambiental (CEMDA)					
Central de Trabajadores de México (CTM)					
Unión Nacional de Trabajadores (UNT)					
Others:					

( ) No contacts with Mexican organizations.

11a. Do you recall when your organization started having contact with Mexican organizations to debate trade issues?

( ) Before NAFTA
( ) During NAFTA debates
( ) After NAFTA
( ) No contact
( ) I don't know

11b. Can you tell me the story of when your organization first met with Mexican organizations to debate trade issues?

12. Suppose the next Ministerial meeting of the FTAA will be held in Mexico and you need to discuss a strategy for participating in it with Mexican organizations. Do you:

( ) Get in touch with them directly. If so, which organizations would you first contact:
( ) Get in touch through domestic coalitions, such as ART or CTC. If so, through which one:
( ) Get in touch through other U.S. organizations. If so, through which ones:
( ) Get in touch through regional coalitions. If so, through which one:
( ) I don't know.

13. Does your organization help finance organizations and/or activities in Mexico?

( ) Yes   ( ) No
If so, how much is sent and to whom?

Organization	Amount	Year

14. Do you also have established contacts with members of the Legislative and Executive powers of this country? When someone

from your organization goes to Mexico, do you also meet with members of the Legislative and the Executive to discuss trade?

BRAZIL

15. If your organization has contacts with civil society organizations in Brazil:

How would you characterize your relationship with:

Organization/ coalition	Very close (agree on all the most important goals and strategies)	Close (agree on some goals and strategies)	Distant (agree on minor goals and strategies)	Very distant (do not agree on goals and strategies)	Don't know
Central Única dos Trabalhadores (CUT)					
FASE					
INESC					
Movimento dos Trabalhadores Rurais Sem-Terra (MST)					
IBASE					
Jubileu Sul					
REBRIP – Rede Brasileira pela Integração dos Povos					
Others:					

( ) No contacts with Brazilian organizations.

16. Do you recall when your organization started having contact with Brazilian organizations to debate trade issues?

    ( ) Before FTAA
    ( ) During FTAA negotiations

( ) No contacts
( ) I don't know.

16a. Can you tell me the story of when your organization first met with Brazilian organizations to debate trade issues?

17. Suppose the next Ministerial meeting of the FTAA will be held in Brazil and you need to discuss a strategy for participating in it with Mexican organizations. Do you:

> ( ) Get in touch with them directly. If so, which organizations would you first contact:
> ( ) Get in touch through coalitions, such as ART or CTC If so, through which one:
> ( ) Get in touch through other U.S. organizations. If so, through which ones:
> ( ) Get in touch through regional coalitions. If so, through which one:
> ( ) I don't know.

18. Does your organization help finance organizations and/or activities in Brazil?

> ( ) Yes   ( ) No

If so, how much is sent and to whom?

Organization	Amount	Year

19. Do you also have established contacts with members of the Legislative and Executive powers of this country? When someone from your organization goes to Brazil, do you also meet with members of the Legislative and the Executive to discuss trade?

CHILE

20. If your organization has contacts with civil society organizations in Chile:

How would you characterize your relationship with:

Appendix B: Social Network Questionnaire (United States)

Organization/ coalition	*Very close* (agree on all the most important goals and strategies)	*Close* (agree on some goals and strategies)	*Distant* (agree on minor goals and strategies)	*Very distant* (do not agree on goals and strategies)	*Don't know*
Central Única de los Trabalhadores (CUT/Chile)					
Instituto de Ecología Política (IEP)					
Chile Sustentable					
Recursos e Investigación para el Desarrollo Sustantable, RIDES					
Corporación Participa					
Corporación de Promoción y Defensa de los Derechos del Pueblo, CODEPU					
Alianza Chilena por un Comercio Justo y Responsible – ACJR					
Others:					

( ) No contacts with Chilean organizations.

21a. Do you recall when your organization started having contact with Chilean organizations to debate trade issues?

( ) Before debates about U.S.–Chile FTA
( ) During debates about U.S.–Chile FTA
( ) After debates about U.S.–Chile FTA
( ) During FTAA negotiations
( ) No contacts
( ) I don't know.

21b. Can you tell me the story of when your organization first met with Chilean organizations to debate trade issues? Who introduced your organization?

22. Suppose the next Ministerial meeting of the FTAA will be held in Chile and you need to discuss a strategy for participating in it with Chilean organizations. Do you:

( ) Get in touch with them directly. If so, which organizations would you first contact:

( ) Get in touch through domestic coalitions, such as ART or CTC. If so, through which one:

( ) Get in touch through other U.S. organizations. If so, through which ones:

( ) Get in touch through regional coalitions. If so, through which one:

( ) I don't know.

23. Does your organization help finance organizations and/or activities in Chile?

( ) Yes   ( ) No

If so, how much is sent and to whom?

Organization	Amount	Year

24. Do you also have established contacts with members of the Legislative and Executive powers of this country? When someone from your organization goes to Chile, do you also meet with members of the Legislative and the Executive to discuss trade?

III. OTHER TIES

25. Back to the U.S.: does your organization meet with members of the USTR to debate trade policy? And for what purpose?

( ) Yes, frequently
( ) Yes, occasionally
( ) Rarely
( ) Never
( ) I don't know

26a. What kinds of activities does your organization promote in Congress, if any?

For example, does your organization:

( ) Send letters to members
( ) Help staff and members in drafting legislation
( ) Answer requests for information from members and/or staff
( ) Participate in public hearings
( ) Meet with members to discuss trade policies

Others:

26b. Has your organization been able to directly influence legislation? Can you give me an example?

27. If your organization is not a business organization:

Has your organization been exchanging information or collaborating in any form with business organizations on trade issues?

( ) Yes ( ) No

If yes, with which ones?

Business organization	Type of activity

Bibliography

Aaronson, Susan Ariel (2001), *Taking Trade to the Streets: The Lost History of Public Efforts to Shape Globalization*. Ann Arbor, the University of Michigan Press.

Adamovsky, Ezequiel (2006), The World Social Forum's new project: "The Network of the World's Social Movements." http://www.nadir.org/nadir/initiativ/agp/free/wsf.htm, accessed January 19, 2006.

Adler, Glenn, and James H. Mittelman (2004), Reconstituting "common-sense" knowledge: Representations of globalization protests. *International Relations* 18(2): 189–211.

Agnew, John (1994), The territorial trap: The geographical assumptions of international relations theory. *Review of International Political Economy* 1(1): 53–80.

Akça, Ismet (2003), "Globalization" and labour strategy: Towards a social movement unionism, in: Gordon Laxer and Sandra Halperin (eds.). *Global Civil Society and Its Limits*. Hampshire, Palgrave Macmillan, 210–228.

Alternate Forum for Research in Mindanao et al. (1997), "Joint NGO Statement on the MAI." Paris. October 27. http://www.c3.hu/~bocs/igaz-a-1.htm, accessed March 1, 2009.

Anheier, Helmut, Marlies Glasius, and Mary Kaldor (2001), Introducing global civil society, in: Helmut Anheier, Marlies Glasius, and Mary Kaldor (eds.). *Global Civil Society 2001*. Oxford, Oxford University Press, 3–23.

Anheier, Helmut, and Nuno Themudo (2002), Organisational forms of global civil society: Implications of going global, in: Marlies Glasius, Mary Kaldor, and Helmut Anheier (eds.). *Global Civil Society 2002*. Oxford, Oxford University Press, 191–216.

Anner, Mark (2003), Industrial structure, the state, and ideology: Shaping labor transnationalism in the Brazilian auto industry. *Social Science History* 27(4): 603–634.

235

Anner, Mark, and Peter Evans (2004), Building bridges across a double divide: Alliances between U.S. and Latin American labour and NGOs. *Development in Practice* 14(1 & 2): 34–47.

Ayres, Jeffrey M. (1998), *Defying Conventional Wisdom: Political Movements and Popular Contention against North American Free Trade*. Toronto, Toronto University Press.

Balassa, Bela (1961), *The Theory of Economic Integration*. Homewood, IL, Richard D. Irwin.

Beck, Ulrich (2003), The analysis of global inequality: From national to cosmopolitan perspective, in: Mary Kaldor, Helmut Anheier, and Marlies Glasius (eds.). *Global Civil Society 2003*. Oxford, Oxford University Press, 45–55.

Bédoyan, Isabelle, Peter Van Aelst, and Stefaan Walgrave (2004), Limitations and possibilities of transnational mobilization: The case of EU Summit protesters in Brussels, 2001. *Mobilization* 9(1): 39–54.

Bello, Walden (2002a), *Deglobalization: Ideas for a New World Economy*. London, Zed Books.

(2002b), The Oxfam debate: From controversy to common strategy. www.maketradefair.com, accessed September 18, 2006.

(2002c), What's wrong with the Oxfam trade campaign. www.maketradefair.com, accessed September 18, 2006.

Bennett, W. Lance (2005), Social movements beyond borders: Understanding two eras of transnational activism, in: Donnatella della Porta and Sidney Tarrow (eds.). *Transnational Protest and Global Activism*. Landham, Rowman and Littlefield, 203–226.

Bensusán, Graciela, and Marisa von Bülow (1997), Reforma de los sistemas de relaciones laborales en México y Brasil. *Perfiles Latinoamericanos* (11): 185–229.

Berrón, Gonzalo (2007), Identidades e Estratégias Sociais na Arena Transnacional: o caso do movimento social contra o livre comércio nas Américas, unpublished dissertation, Department of Political Science, University of São Paulo.

Bethell, Leslie (ed.) (1985), *The Cambridge History of Latin America: From Independence to c. 1870*. Cambridge, Cambridge University Press.

Bielschowsky, Ricardo (1998), Cincuenta años del pensamiento de la CEPAL: Una reseña, in: Ricardo Bielschowsky (ed.). *Cincuenta años de pensamiento en la CEPAL: textos seleccionados*. Santiago, CEPAL/Fondo de Cultura Económica, 1: 9–61.

Bleyer, Peter (2001), Cross-movement coalitions and political agency: The popular sector and the pro-Canada/Action Canada Network, unpublished dissertation, London School of Economics and Political Science.

Blyth, Mark (2002), *Great Transformations: Economic Ideas and Political Change in the Twentieth Century*. Cambridge, Cambridge University Press.

Bognanno, Mario F., and Jiangfeng Lu (2003), NAFTA's labor side agreement: Withering as an effective labor law enforcement and MNC compliance strategy? in: William Cooke (ed.). *Multinational Companies and Global Human Resource Strategies*. Westport, CT, Quorum Books, 369–399.

Borgatti, Stephen P., et al. (2002), Ucinet for Windows: Software for social network analysis, Harvard, MA, Analytic Technologies.

Bibliography

Borgatti, Stephen P., and Pacey C. Foster (2003), The network paradigm in organizational research: A review and typology. *Journal of Management* 29(6): 991–1013.

Borras Jr., Saturnino, Marc Edelman, and Cristóbal Kay (2008), Transnational agrarian movements: origins and politics, campaigns and impact . *Journal of Agrarian Change* 8 (2–3): 169–204.

Brooks, David, and Jonathan Fox (2002), Movements across the border: An overview, in: David L. Brooks and Jonathan Fox (eds.). *Cross-Border Dialogues – U.S.-Mexico Social Movement Networking.* San Diego, Center for U.S. Mexican Studies at the University of California, 1–68.

Brown, L. David, and Jonathan Fox (1998), Accountability within transnational coalitions, in: Jonathan Fox and L. David Brown (eds.). *The Struggle for Accountability: The World Bank, NGOs, and Grassroots Movements.* Cambridge, MA, MIT Press, 439–483.

Buffenbarger, R. Thomas (2007), Letter by IAM's international president to the U.S. Congress, Washington, D.C. August 2.

Carter, Miguel (2005), *The Landless Workers Movement (MST) and Democracy in Brazil.* Oxford, Centre for Brazilian Studies Working Paper CBS-60-05, University of Oxford.

Castells, Manuel (2000), Materials for an exploratory theory of the network society. *British Journal of Sociology* 51(1): 5–24.

CCSCS (1993), Projeto de Carta dos Direitos Fundamentais do MERCOSUL, Buenos Aires. October 23.

CEPAL (1949), *Estudio Económico de América Latina.* Santiago, Naciones Unidas.

(1959), *El Mercado Común Latinoamericano.* Santiago, Naciones Unidas.

CGT (1992), *Conclusiones.* Seminario sobre el Mercosur, Buenos Aires, Argentina, November.

Chaison, Gary (2007), The AFL-CIO split: Does it really matter? *Journal of Labor Research* 28(2): 301–311.

Charnovitz, Steve (2000), Opening the WTO to non-governmental interests. *Fordham International Law Journal* 24: 173–216.

Clemens, Elisabeth S. (2005), Two kinds of stuff: The current encounter of social movements and organizations, in: Gerald F. Davis, Doug McAdam, W. Richard Scott, and Mayer N. Zald (eds.). *Social Movements and Organization Theory.* Cambridge, Cambridge University Press, 351–365.

Colás, Alejandro (2002), *International Civil Society – Social Movements in World Politics.* Cambridge, Polity.

Comparato, Bruno Konder (2001), A ação política do MST. *São Paulo em Perspectiva* 15(4): 115–118.

Continental Campaign against the FTAA (2002). "Estrategia de lucha contra el ALCA." II Hemispheric Meeting against the FTAA, Havana, November 28.

Costa, Hermes Augusto (2005a), A política internacional da CGTP e da CUT: etapas, temas e desafios. *Revista Crítica de Ciências Sociais* (71): 141–161.

(2005b), Sindicalismo global ou metáfora adiada? Os discursos e as práticas transnacionais da CGTP e da CUT, unpublished dissertation, University of Coimbra.

Curtis, Russell L., and Louis A. Zurcher (1973), Stable resources of protest movements: The multi-organizational field. *Social Forces* 52: 53–61.

CUT (1991), Resolução do 4° Congresso Nacional da Central Única dos Trabalhadores, São Paulo.

(1997), O sindicalismo continental e a ALCA. *Textos para Debate Internacional* (9): 2–8.

Dagnino, Evelina (ed.) (2002), *Sociedad Civil, Esfera Pública y Democratización en América Latina: Brasil*. Mexico City, Editora UNICAMP and Fondo de Cultura Económica.

Dalton, Russell (1994), *The Green Rainbow: Environmental Groups in Western Europe*. New Haven, Yale University Press.

de la Cueva, Héctor (2005), Mar del Plata: el ALCA no pasó – una victoria de la Cumbre de los Pueblos. *OSAL* 6(18): 81–91.

Degenne, Alain, and Michel Forsé (1999), *Introducing Social Networks*. London, Sage Publications.

della Porta, Donatella (2005), Multiple belongings, tolerant identities, and the construction of "another politics": Between the European Social Forum and the local social fora, in: Donatella della Porta and Sidney Tarrow (eds.). *Transnational Protest and Global Activism*. Lanham, MD, Rowman & Littlefield, 175–202.

della Porta, Donatella, and Sidney Tarrow (2005a), Transnational processes and social activism: An introduction, in: Donatella della Porta and Sidney Tarrow (eds.). *Transnational Protest and Global Activism*. Lanham, MD, Rowman & Littlefield, 1–17.

della Porta, Donatella, and Sidney Tarrow (eds.) (2005b), *Transnational Protest and Global Activism*. Lanham, MD, Rowman & Littlefield.

Desai, Meghnad, and Yahia Said (2001), The new anti-capitalist movement: Money and global civil society, in: Helmut Anheier, Marlies Glasius, and Mary Kaldor (eds.). *Global Civil Society 2001*. Oxford, Oxford University Press, 51–78.

Desmarais, Annette-Aurélie (2002), The Vía Campesina: Consolidating an international peasant and farm movement. *Journal of Peasant Studies* 29(2): 91–124.

(2003), The Vía Campesina: Peasants resisting globalization, unpublished dissertation, Department of Geography, University of Calgary.

Destler, I. Mac (2007), *American Trade Politics in 2007: Building Bipartisan Compromise*. Washington, D.C., Policy Brief, Peterson Institute for International Economics.

Destler, I. Mac, and Peter J. Balint (1999), *The New Politics of American Trade: Trade, Labor, and the Environment*. Washington, D.C., Institute for International Economics.

Devlin, Robert and Paolo Giordano (2004), The old and new regionalism: benefits, costs, and implications for the FTAA, in: Antoni Estevadeorda, Dani Rodrik, Alan M. Taylor, and Andrés Velasco (eds.). *Integrating the Americas: FTAA and beyond*. Cambridge, MA, Harvard University David Rockefeller Center for Latin American Studies, 143–186.

Bibliography

Diani, Mario (2003a), Introduction: Social movements, contentious actions, and social networks: "From metaphor to substance"? in: Mario Diani and Doug McAdam (eds.). *Social Movements and Networks: Relational Approaches to Collective Action*. Oxford, Oxford University Press, 1–18.

(2003b), "Leaders" or brokers? Positions and influence in social movement networks, in: Mario Diani and Doug McAdam (eds.). *Social Movements and Networks: Relational Approaches to Collective Action*. Oxford, Oxford University Press, 105–122.

(2005), *The Structural Bases of Movement Coalitions: Multiple Memberships and Networks in the February 15th 2003 Peace Demonstrations*. American Sociological Association Centenary Meeting, Philadelphia, August 13–16.

Diebold, W., Jr. (1993 [1952]), The End of the WTO, in: Kym Anderson and Bernard Hoekman (eds.). *The Global Trading System: The Genesis of the GATT*. London, I. B. Tauris, 1: 81–111.

Doimo, Ana Maria (1995), *A vez e a voz do popular: movimentos sociais e participação política no Brasil pós-70*. Rio de Janeiro, Relume Dumará.

Doucet, Marc G. (2005), Territoriality and the democratic paradox: The Hemispheric Social Alliance and its *Alternatives for the Americas*. *Contemporary Political Theory* 4(3): 275–295.

Doyle, Michael W. (1983), Stalemate in the North-South debate: Strategies and the New International Economic Order. *World Politics* 35(3): 426–464.

Dreiling, Michael (2001), *Solidarity and Contention: The Politics of Security and Sustainability in the NAFTA Conflict*. New York, Garland Publishing.

Dreiling, Michael, and Ian Robinson (1998), Union responses to NAFTA in the U.S. and Canada: Explaining intra and international variation. *Mobilization* 3(2): 163–184.

Eade, Deborah, and Alan Leather (eds.) (2005), *Development NGOs and Labor Unions: Terms of Engagement*. Bloomfield, Kumarian Press.

Edelman, Marc (2003), Transnational peasant and farmer movements and networks, in: Mary Kaldor, Helmut Anheier, and Marlies Glasieu (eds.). *Global Civil Society Yearbook 2003*. Oxford, Oxford University Press, 185–193.

(2005), Bringing the moral economy back in … to the study of 21st-century transnational peasants movements. *American Anthropologist* 107(3): 331–345.

Elliott, Kimberly Ann (2007), Treatment of labor issues in U.S. bilateral trade agreements, Policy Brief 07-5. Washington, D.C., Peterson Institute for International Economics.

Emirbayer, Mustafa, and Jeff Goodwin (1994), Network analysis, culture, and the problem of agency. *American Journal of Sociology* 99(6): 1411–1454.

Emirbayer, Mustafa, and Ann Mische (1998), What is agency? *American Journal of Sociology* 103(4): 962–1023.

Ezzat, Heba Raouf (2005), Beyond methodological modernism: Towards a multicultural paradigm shift in the social sciences, in: Helmut Anheier, Marlies Glasius, and Mary Kaldor (eds.). *Global Civil Society 2004/5*. London, Sage Publications, 40–58.

FCES (1997), Recomendação N° 1/97 Tema: ALCA, Asunción, April 22.

Foster, John (2005), The trinational alliance against NAFTA: sinews of solidarity, in: Joe Bandy and Jackie Smith (eds.). *Coalitions across Borders: Transnational Protest and the Neoliberal Order.* Lanham, Rowman & Littlefield Publishers, 209–229.

Fox, Jonathan (2002), Lessons from Mexico-U.S. civil society coalitions, in: David Brooks and Jonathan Fox (eds.). *Cross-Border Dialogues – U.S.-Mexico Social Movement Networking.* San Diego, Center for U.S.-Mexican Studies at the University of California, 341–418.

(2005), Unpacking "transnational citizenship." *Annual Review of Political Science* 8: 171–201.

Fox, Jonathan, and L. David Brown (eds.) (1998), *The Struggle for Accountability: The World Bank, NGOs, and Grassroots Movements.* Cambridge, MA, MIT Press.

Francia, Peter (2006), *The Future of Organized Labor in American Politics.* New York, Columbia University Press.

Freeman, Linton C. (2004), *The Development of Social Network Analysis: A Study in the Sociology of Science.* Vancouver, Empirical Press.

French, John (1994), NAFTA and Mexican labor, in: John French, Jefferson Cowie, and Scott Littlehale (eds.). *Labor and NAFTA: A Briefing Book.* Durham, Paper prepared for the Conference on "Labor, Free Trade, and Economic Integration in the Americas: National labor union responses to a transnational world," 120–154.

Friedman, Debra, and Doug McAdam (1992), Collective identity and activism: Networks, choices, and the life of a social movement, in: Aldon Morris and Carol McClurg Mueller (eds.). *Frontiers in Social Movement Theory.* New Haven, Yale University Press, 156–173.

Friedman, Elisabeth Jay, Kathryn Hochstetler, and Ann Marie Clark (2005), *Sovereignty, Democracy, and Global Civil Society.* Albany, State University of New York.

Furtado, Celso (1976), *Economic Development of Latin America: Historical Background and Contemporary Problems.* Cambridge, Cambridge University Press.

Garcia, Frank J. (2003), *Trade, Inequality, and Justice: Toward a Liberal Theory of Just Trade.* Ardsley, Transnational Publishers.

Giugni, Marco, Marko Blandler, and Nina Eggert (2006), *The Global Justice Movement – How Far Does the Classic Social Movement Agenda Go in Explaining Transnational Contention?* Geneva, Civil Society and Social Movements Programme no. 24, United Nations Research Institute for Social Development.

Glasius, Marlies, Mary Kaldor, and Helmut Anheier (2005), Introduction, in: Marlies Glasius, Mary Kaldor, and Helmut Anheier (eds.). *Global Civil Society 2005/6,* London, Sage Publications, 1–34.

Glick Schiller, Nina (1997), The situation of transnational studies. *Identities* 4(2): 155–166.

Goodwin, Jeff, and James Jasper (1999a), Caught in a winding, snarling vine: The structural bias of political process theory. *Sociological Forum* 14(1): 27–54.

(1999b), Trouble in paradigms. *Sociological Forum* 14(1): 107–125.

Bibliography

Gould, Kenneth A., Tammy L. Lewis, and J. Timmons Roberts (2004), Blue-green coalitions: Constraints and possibilities in the post 9–11 political environment. *Journal of World-Systems Research* 10(1): 91–116.

Gould, Roger, and Roberto M. Fernández (1989), Structures of mediation: A formal approach to brokerage in transaction networks. *Sociological Methodology* 19: 89–126.

Granovetter, Mark (1985), Economic action and social structure: The problem of embeddedness. *American Journal of Sociology* 91(3): 481–510.

Grassroots Global Justice (2005), Briefing Paper for Lessons of Trade Campaign Meeting, October 14–15. http://www.ggjalliance.org/system/files/GGJ BriefingPaperFall05.doc, accessed March 1, 2009.

Halperin, Sandra, and Gordon Laxer (2003), Effective resistance to corporate globalization, in: Gordon Laxer and Sandra Halperin (eds.). *Global Civil Society and Its Limits*. Hampshire, Palgrave Macmillan, 1–21.

Hathaway, Dale (2000), *Allies across the Border: Mexico's 'Authentic Labor Front' and Global Solidarity*. Cambridge, MA, South End Press.

Hemispheric Social Alliance (1998), Alternatives for the Americas. Mimeo.

(2001), Alternatives for the Americas. Mimeo.

(2002), Alternatives for the Americas. Mimeo.

(2005), Alternativas para las Américas. Mimeo.

(2007a), Conclusiones de la reunión del Consejo Hemisférico de la ASC. São Paulo, February 15–17.

(2007b), Propuesta de Tesis para la Nueva Etapa de la Alianza Social Continental. Havana, May 3–5.

Herkenrath, Mark (2006), *Unity and Diversity in Transnational Social Movement Networks – A Case Study on the Hemispheric Campaign against the FTAA*. International Studies Association Annual Meeting, San Diego, CA, March 22–25.

Hernández Navarro, Luis (2002), Globalization and transnational coalitions in the rural sector, in: David Brooks and Jonathan Fox (eds.). *Cross-Border Dialogues: U.S.-Mexico Social Movement Networking*. La Jolla, Center for U.S.-Mexican Studies of the University of California, 145–166.

Hertel, Shareen (2006), *Unexpected Power: Conflict and Change among Transnational Activists*. Ithaca, Cornell University Press.

Hiscox, Michael J. (2002), *International Trade and Political Conflict: Commerce, Coalitions, and Mobility*. Princeton, Princeton University Press.

Hobsbawn, Eric J. (1988), Working-class internationalism, in: Frits van Holthoon and Marcel van der Linden (eds.). *Internationalism in the Labour Movement 1830–1940*. Leiden, E. J. Brill, 1: 3–16.

Hochstetler, Kathryn (2003), Fading green: Environmental politics in the Mercosur Free Trade Agreement. *Latin American Politics and Society* 45(4): 1–32.

Huyer, Sophia (2005), Challenging relations: A labor-NGO coalition to oppose the Canada-U.S. and North American Free Trade Agreements, 1985–1993, in: Deborah and Alan Leather Eade (eds.). *Development NGOs and Labor Unions: Terms of Engagement*. Bloomfield, Kumarian Press, 51–67.

241

ILO (2006), Origins and history. http://www.ilo.org/global/About_the_ILO/ Origins_and_history/lang--en/index.htm, accessed February 17, 2006.

Imig, Doug, and Sidney Tarrow (eds.) (2001), *Contentious Europeans: Protest and Politics in an Emerging Polity*. Lanham, MD, Rowman & Littlefield.

Jakobsen, Kjeld (1999), Uma visão sindical em face da ALCA e de outros esquemas regionais, in: Yves Chaloult and Paulo Roberto de Almeida (eds.). *Mercosul, NAFTA e ALCA: A dimensão social*. São Paulo, LTr, 232–248.

(2007), A Rede da Aliança Social Continental: Um estudo de caso, unpublished paper, São Paulo.

Jasper, William F. (2002), Erasing our borders. *New American* 18(9).

Juris, Jeffrey S. (2008), Spaces of intentionality: Race, class, and horizontality at the United States Social Forum. *Mobilization* 13(4): 353–371.

Kaiser, Karl (1969), Transnationale Politik: Zu einer Theorie der multinationale Politik, in: Erns-Otto Czempiel (ed.). *Die anachronistische Souveränität: Zum Verhältnis von innen- und aussen-politik*. Cologne, Westdeutscher Verlag, 80–109.

(1971), Transnational relations as a threat to the democratic process. *International Organization* 25(3): 706–720.

Kaldor, Mary, Helmut Anheier, and Marlies Glasius (2005), Introduction, in: Helmut Anheier, Marlies Glasius, and Mary Kaldor (eds.). *Global Civil Society 2004/5*. London, Sage Publications, 1–22.

Keck, Margaret (2006), Review of Sidney Tarrow's *The New Transnational Activism*. *Mobilization* 11(1): 117–119.

Keck, Margaret, and Kathryn Sikkink (1998), *Activists beyond Borders: Advocacy Networks in International Politics*. Ithaca, Cornell University Press.

Kelly, Dominic, and Wyn Grant (2005), Introduction: Trade politics in context, in: Dominic Kelly and Wyn Grant (eds.). *The Politics of International Trade in the Twenty-First Century: Actors, Issues and Regional Dynamics*. Hampshire, Palgrave Macmillan, 1–10.

Keohane, Robert O., and Joseph Nye (eds.) (1971), *Transnational Relations and World Politics*. Cambridge, MA, Harvard University Press.

Klein, Naomi (2003), Cut the Strings. *The Guardian*, February 1. http://www.guardian.co.uk/politics/2003/feb/01/greenpolitics.globalisation, accessed March 1, 2009.

Klotz, Audie (2002), Transnational activism and global transformations: The anti-apartheid and abolitionist experiences. *European Journal of International Relations* 8(1): 49–76.

Kobrin, Stephen J. (1998), The MAI and the clash of globalizations. *Foreign Policy* (112): 97–109.

Koo, Jah-Hon (2001), Maintaining an international social movement coalition: The case of the Hemispheric Social Alliance, unpublished dissertation, School of Social Work, McGill University.

Korzeniewicz, Roberto Patricio, and William C. Smith (2003a), *Mapping Regional Civil Society Networks in Latin America*, Report for the Ford Foundation.

(2003b), Redes transnacionales de la sociedad civil: Entre la protesta y la colaboración, in: Diana Tussie and Mercedes Botto (eds.). *El ALCA y las Cumbres de las Américas: Una nueva relación público-privada?* Buenos Aires, Editorial Biblos and FLACSO/Argentina, 47–74.

Krasner, Stephen (1985), *The Third World against Global Liberalism: A Structural Conflict.* Berkeley, University of California Press.

Kriese, Hanspeter, Ruud Koopmans, Jan Willem Duyvendak, and Marco G. Giugni (1995), *New Social Movements in Western Europe – A Comparative Analysis.* Minneapolis, University of Minnesota Press.

Lambert, Jacques (1968), *Latin America: Social Structure and Political Institutions.* Berkeley, University of California Press.

Laurie, Peter (1990), Ah-hah! GATT-fly. *New Internationalist* (204).

Laxer, Gordon (2003), The defeat of the Multilateral Agreement on Investment: National movements confront globalism, in: Gordon Laxer and Sandra Halperin (eds.). *Global Civil Society and Its Limits.* Hampshire, Palgrave Macmillan, 169–188.

Lehman, Karen (2002), Farmer organizations and regional integration in North America, in: David Brooks and Jonathan Fox (eds.). *Cross-Border Dialogues: U.S.-Mexico Social Movement Networking.* La Jolla, Center for U.S.-Mexican Studies of the University of California, 167–186.

Lenin, V. I. ([1902] 1969), *What Is to Be Done? Burning Questions of Our Movement.* New York, International Publishers.

Lipschutz, Ronnie (2005), Power, politics and global civil society. *Millennium* 33(3): 747–769.

MacDonald, Laura (2005), Gendering transnational social movement analysis: Women's groups contest free trade in the Americas, in: Joe Bandy and Jackie Smith (eds.). *Coalitions across Borders: Transnational Protest and the Neoliberal Order.* Lanham, MD, Rowman & Littlefield, 21–41.

Marsden, Peter V. (1982), Brokerage behavior in restricted exchange networks, in: Peter V. Marsden and Nan Lin (eds.). *Social Structure and Network Analysis.* Beverly Hills, CA, Sage, 201–218.

(1990), Network data and measurement. *Annual Review of Sociology* 16: 435–463.

(2005), Recent developments in network measurement, in: Peter Carrington, John Scott, and Stanley Wasserman (eds.). *Models and Methods in Social Network Analysis.* Cambridge, Cambridge University Press, 8–30.

Marx, Karl, and Friedrich Engels ([1847] 1998), *The Communist Manifesto.* New York, Signet Classic.

Massicotte, Marie-Josee (2003), "Local" organizing and "global" struggles: Coalition-building for social justice in the Americas, in: Gordon Laxer and Sandra Halperin (eds.). *Global Civil Society and Its Limits.* Hampshire, Palgrave Macmillan, 105–125.

(2004), Mexican sociopolitical movements and transnational networking in the context of economic integration in the Americas, unpublished dissertation, Department of Political Science, York University.

McAdam, Doug (1999), *Political Process and the Development of Black Insurgency, 1930–1970.* Chicago, University of Chicago Press.

McAdam, Doug, Sidney Tarrow, and Charles Tilly (2001), *Dynamics of Contention.* Cambridge, Cambridge University Press.

McCarthy, John D., and Mayer N. Zald (1977), Resource mobilization and social movements: A partial theory. *American Journal of Sociology* 82: 1212–1241.

Melucci, Alberto (1996), *Challenging Codes – Collective Action in the Information Age.* Cambridge, Cambridge University Press.

Meyer, David, and Catherine Corrigall-Brown (2005), Coalitions and political context: U.S. movements against wars in Iraq. *Mobilization* 10(3): 327–346.

Midford, Paul (1993), International trade and domestic politics: Improving on Rogowski's model of political alignments. *International Organization* 47: 535–564.

Midlej e Silva, Suylan (2008), "Ganhamos a batalha, mas não a guerra": A visão da Campanha Nacional contra a ALCA sobre a não-assinatura do acordo, unpublished dissertation, Department of Sociology, University of Brasilia.

Mische, Ann (2003), Cross-talk in movements: Reconceiving the culture-network link, in: Mario Diani and Doug McAdam (eds.). *Social Movements and Networks: Relational Approaches to Collective Action.* Oxford, Oxford University Press, 258–280.

(2008), *Partisan Publics: Communication and Contention across Brazilian Youth Activist Networks.* Princeton, Princeton University Press.

Munck, Ronaldo (2002), Global civil society: Myths and prospects. *Voluntas* 13(4): 349–361.

Murillo, Maria Victoria (2001), *Labor Unions, Partisan Coalitions, and Market Reforms in Latin America.* Cambridge, Cambridge University Press.

Murphy, Craig (1984), *The Emergence of the NEIO Ideology.* Boulder, Westview Press.

Myconos, George (2005), *The Globalization of Organized Labour: 1945–2005.* Hampshire, Palgrave Macmillan.

O'Brien, Robert, Anne Marie Goetz, Jan Aart Scholte, and Marc Williams (2000), *Contesting Global Governance: Multilateral Economic Institutions and Global Social Movements.* Cambridge, Cambridge University Press.

Ong, Aihwa (1999), *Flexible Citizenship – The Cultural Logics of Transnationality.* Durham, Duke University Press.

ORIT et al. (1997), Declaração conjunta do movimento sindical e organizações sociais aprovada pelo Fórum dos Trabalhadores das Américas. Belo Horizonte, May 15.

Ostry, Sylvia (ed.) (2002), *The Trade Policy-Making Process Level One of the Two Level Game: Country Studies in the Western Hemisphere.* Working Paper 13. Buenos Aires, Inter-American Development Bank/Munk Centre/Inter-American Dialogue.

Oxfam (2002a), Oxfam's response to Walden Bello's article. www.maketradefair.com, accessed September 18, 2006.

(2002b), *Rigged Rules and Double Standards: Trade, Globalisation, and the Fight Against Poverty.* Oxford, Oxfam International.

Bibliography

Padrón, Álvaro (1998), El Foro Consultivo Económico-Social del Mercosur, in: *Participación de la Sociedad Civil en los Procesos de Integración*. Montevideo, CLAEH/CEFIR/ALOP, 245–254.

Panfichi, Aldo (ed.) (2002), *Sociedad Civil, Esfera Pública y Democratización en América Latina: Andes y Cono Sur*. Mexico City, Pontifícia Universidad Católica del Perú and Fondo de Cultura Económica.

Pecci, Antonio (1994), Los trabajadores ante el Mercosur, CUT/Paraguay, Asunción. May.

Peytavi, Claire (2003), Annie Besant and the 1888 London matchgirls strike. http://anglais.u-paris10.fr/spip.php?article84, accessed February 12, 2008.

Pianta, Mario (2001), Parallel summits of global civil society, in: Helmut Anheier, Marlies Glasius, and Mary Kaldor (eds.). *Global Civil Society 2001*. Oxford, Oxford University Press, 169–194.

(2002), Parallel summits of global civil society: An update, in: Marlies Glasius, Mary Kaldor, and Helmut Anheier (eds.). *Global Civil Society 2002*. Oxford, Oxford University Press, 371–377.

Portella de Castro, Maria Sílvia (1994), *Mercosul e Ação Sindical*. Conference on Labor, Free Trade and Economic Integration in the Americas: National labor union responses to a transnational world, Durham, N.C., August 25–27.

(2002), Contribuição ao Grupo de Reflexão Prospectiva sobre o Mercosul: Propostas para ação e debate, in: Clodoaldo and Carlos Henrique Cardim Hugueney Filho (eds.). *Grupo de Reflexão Prospectiva sobre o Mercosul*. Brasilia, FUNAG-IPRI-Ministério das Relações Exteriores/SGIE-MRE, BID, 63–76.

(2007), El sindicalismo frente al Mercosur. *Nueva Sociedad* (211): 66–80.

Portes, Alejandro, Luis E. Guarnizo, and Patricia Landolt (1999), the study of transnationalism: Pitfalls and promise of an emergent research field. *Ethnic and Racial Studies* 22(2): 217–237.

Powell, Walter W. (1990), Neither market nor hierarchy: Network forms of organization. *Research in Organizational Behavior* 12: 295–336.

Prebisch, Raúl (1964), *Hacia una política comercial en pro del desarrollo. Informe del Secretario General de la Conferencia de las Naciones Unidas sobre Comercio y Desarrollo*. New York, United Nations.

Pries, Ludger (2005), Configurations of geographic and societal spaces: A sociological proposal between "methodological nationalism" and the "spaces of flows." *Global Networks* 5(2): 167–190.

Putnam, Robert (1988), Diplomacy and domestic politics: The logic of two-level games. *International Organizations* 42(3): 427–460.

Ramonet, Ignacio (2006), Never give up on that other world. *Le Monde Diplomatique*, February 8.

REBRIP (2007). Balanço do período 2005–2007: Roteiro para avaliação e debate, Rio de Janeiro.

Risse, Thomas, and Kathryn Sikkink (1999), The socialization of international human rights norms into domestic practices, in: Thomas Risse, Stephen Ropp, and Kathryn Sikkink (eds.). *The Power of Human Rights: International Norms and Domestic Politics*. Cambridge, Cambridge University Press, 1–38.

Ritchie, Mark (1996), Cross-border organizing, in: Jerry Mander and Edward Goldsmith (eds.). *The Case against the Global Economy and for a Turn toward the Local*. San Francisco, Sierra Club Books, 494–500.

RMALC (1992), Memoria de Zacatecas (results of the International Forum: The Public Opinion and the NAFTA Negotiations: Citizens' Alternatives), Mexico City. February.

(1993), Nacimiento y Desarrollo de la Red Mexicana de Acción Frente al Libre Comercio (RMALC). Mexico City.

Robinson, Ian (1994), NAFTA, social unionism, and labour movement power in Canada and the United States. *Relations Industrielles* 49(4): 657–695.

Rogowski, Ronald (1989), *Commerce and Coalitions – How Trade Affects Domestic Political Alignments*. Princeton, Princeton University Press.

Roof, Tracy (2008), Can the Democrats deliver for the base? Partisanship, group politics, and the case of organized labor in the 110th Congress. *PS: Political Science and Politics* 41(1): 83–87.

Rootes, Christopher (2005), A limited transnationalization? The British environmental movement, in: Donatella della Porta and Sidney Tarrow (eds.). *Transnational Protest and Global Activism*. Lanham, MD, Rowman & Littlefield, 21–43.

Rosenau, James (1969a), Introduction: Political science in a shrinking world, in: James Rosenau (ed.). *Linkage Politics: Essays on the Convergence of National and International Systems*. New York, Free Press, 1–17.

(1969b), Toward the study of national-international linkages, in: James Rosenau (ed.). *Linkage Politics: Essays on the Convergence of National and International Systems*. New York, Free Press, 44–63.

Ruggie, John Gerard (2004), Reconstituting the global public domain – Issues, actors, and practices. *European Journal of International Relations* 10(4): 499–531.

Rütters, Peter, and Rüdiger Zimmermann (eds.) (2003), *On the History and Policy of the IUF*. Bonn, Friedrich Ebert Stiftung.

Sader, Eder (1988), *Quando novos personagens entram em cena: experiências, falas e lutas dos trabalhadores da Grande São Paulo, 1970–80*. Rio de Janeiro, Editora Paz e Terra.

Sáez, Sebastián (2005), *Trade Policy Making in Latin America: A Compared Analysis*. Economic and Social Research Institute International Workshop on Free Trade Agreements, Japan, March 16.

Saguier, Marcelo I. (2007), The Hemispheric Social Alliance and the Free Trade Area of the Americas Process: The challenges and opportunities of transnational coalitions against neo-liberalism. *Globalizations* 4(2): 251–265.

Said, Yahia, and Meghnad Desai (2003), Trade and global civil society: The anti-capitalist movement revisited, in: Mary Kaldor, Helmut Anheier, and Marlies Glasius (eds.). *Global Civil Society 2003*. Oxford, Oxford University Press, 59–85.

Scholte, Jan Aart (2003), *Democratizing the Global Economy – The Role of Civil Society*. Coventry, Centre for the Study of Globalisation and Regionalisation, University of Warwick.

Bibliography

Shiva, Vandana (2002), Export at any Cost: Oxfam's free trade recipe for the Third World. www.maketradefair.com, accessed September 18, 2006.

Sikkink, Kathryn (2005), Patterns of dynamic multilevel governance and the insider-outsider coalition, in: Donatella della Porta and Sidney Tarrow (eds.). *Transnational Protest and Global Activism*. Lanham, MD, Rowman & Littlefield, 151–173.

Silver, Beverly (2003), *Forces of Labor – Workers' Movements and Globalization since 1870*. Cambridge, Cambridge University Press.

Silverglade, Bruce (1999), *The WTO Agreement on Sanitary and Phytosanitary Measures – Weakening Food Safety Regulation to Facilitate Trade?* Conference on Incorporating Science, Economics, Sociology and Politics in Sanitary and Phytosanitary Standards and International Trade, Irvine, CA.

Singer, J. David (1969), The global system and its sub-systems: A developmental view, in: James Rosenau (ed.). *Linkage Politics: Essays on the Convergence of National and International Systems*. New York, Free Press, 21–43.

Smith, Jackie (2005), Globalization and transnational social movement organizations, in: Geral F. David, Doug McAdam, W. Richard Scott, and Mayer N. Zald (eds.). *Social Movements and Organization Theory*. Cambridge, Cambridge University Press, 226–248.

Smith, Russell, and Mark Healey (1994), *Labor and Mercosur: A Briefing Book*. Conference on Labor, Free Trade and Economic Integration in the Americas: National labor union responses to a transnational world, Durham, N.C., August 25–27.

Smith, William C., and Roberto Patricio Korzeniewicz (2007), Insiders, outsiders, and the politics of civil society, in: Gordon Mace, Jean-Phillipe Thérien, and Paul Haslam (eds.). *Governing the Americas: Assessing Multilateral Institutions*. Boulder, Lynne Rienner Publishers, 151–172.

Snow, David, and Robert Benford (1988), Ideology, frame resonance and participant mobilization, in: Bert Klandermans, Hanspeter Kriesi, and Sidney Tarrow (eds.). *International Social Movement Research: From Structure to Action Comparing Social Movement Research across Cultures*. London, JAI Press, 1: 197–217.

Snow, David, E. Burke Rochford, Steven Worden, and Robert Benford (1986), Frame alignment processes, micromobilization, and movement participation. *American Sociological Review* (51): 464–481.

Staggenborg, Suzanne (1986), Coalition work in the pro-choice movement: organizational and environmental opportunities and obstacles. *Social Problems* 33(5):374–390.

Stédile, João Pedro (2002), Landless batallions: The Sem Terra movement of Brazil. *New Left Review* 15: 77–104.

Stillerman, Joel (2003), Transnational activist networks and the emergence of labor internationalism in the NAFTA countries. *Social Science History* 27(4): 577–561.

Tarrow, Sidney (1998), *Power in Movement: Social Movements and Contentious Politics*. Cambridge, Cambridge University Press.

(1999), Paradigm warriors: Regress and progress in the study of contentious politics. *Sociological Forum* 14(1): 71–77.

(2005), *The New Transnational Activism*. Cambridge, Cambridge University Press.

Tarrow, Sidney, and Donatella della Porta (2005), Conclusion: "Globalization," complex internationalism, and transnational contention, in: Donatella della Porta and Sidney Tarrow (eds.). *Transnational Protest and Global Activism*. Lanham, MD, Rowman & Littlefield, 227–246.

Taylor, Rupert (2002), Interpreting global civil society. *Voluntas* 13(4): 339–347.

Tieleman, Katia (2002), Negotiation as transformation: Tracing the failure of the multilateral agreement on investment (MAI): agency and change in international negotiations, unpublished dissertation, European University Institute.

Tilly, Charles (1978), *From Mobilization to Revolution*. Reading, MA, Addison-Wesley.

(1984), *Big Structures, Large Processes, Huge Comparisons*. New York, Russell Sage Foundation.

(1999), Wise quacks. *Sociological Forum* 14(1): 55–61.

Tonelson, Alan (2000), *The Race to the Bottom: Why a Worldwide Worker Surplus and Uncontrolled Free Trade Are Sinking American Living Standards*. Boulder, Westview Press.

Twyford, Phil (2002), Oxfam's Response to Vandana Shiva's Article. www.maketradefair.com, accessed September 18, 2006.

Urquidi, Víctor L. (1993), Free trade experience in Latin America and the Caribbean. *Annals of the American Academy of Political and Social Science* 526: 58–67.

Via Campesina (2002), Proposals for Family Farm Based, Sustainable Agriculture. Presented during the World Summit on Sustainable Development, Johannesburg, August.

Vigevani, Tullo, Karina Pasquariello Mariano, and Marcelo Fernandes de Oliveira (2001), Democracia e atores políticos no Mercosul, in: Gerónimo de Sierra (ed.). *Los rostros del Mercosur: el difícil camino de lo comercial a lo societal*. Buenos Aires, CLACSO, 183–228.

von Bülow, Marisa (2003a), El medio ambiente y la participación de la sociedad civil, in: Diana Tussie and Mercedes Botto (eds.). *El ALCA y las Cumbres de las Américas: una nueva relación público-privada?* Buenos Aires, Editorial Biblos/ FLACSO Argentina, 77–103.

(2003b), *Labor organizations in a changed world: A comparison of labor responses to NAFTA and MERCOSUL*. XXIX International Congress of the Latin American Studies Association, Dallas, March 27–29.

(2009), Networks of trade protest in the Americas: Toward a new labor internationalism? *Latin American Politics and Society* 51(2): 1–28.

Wachendorfer, Achim (2007), Hacia una nueva arquitectura sindical en América Latina? *Nueva Sociedad* (211): 32–49.

Walker, R. B. J. (1994), Social movements/World politics. *Millennium* 23(3): 669–700.

Wallach, Lori (2004), Introduction: It's not about trade, in: Lori Wallach and Patrick Woodall (eds.). *Whose Trade Organization? A Comprehensive Guide to the WTO*. Washington, D.C., Public Citizen, 1–17.

Bibliography

Wallach, Lori, and Patrick Woodall (2004), *Whose Trade Organization? A Comprehensive Guide to the WTO*. Washington, D.C., Public Citizen.

Wasserman, Stanley, and Katherine Faust (1994), *Social Network Analysis: Methods and Applications*. Cambridge, Cambridge University Press.

Whitaker, Chico (2005), *Desafios do Fórum Social Mundial: um modo de ver*. São Paulo, Fundação Perseu Abramo/Edições Loyola.

White, Harrison C. (1992), *Identity and Control: A Structural Theory of Social Action*. Princeton, Princeton University Press.

Wilkinson, Rorden (2005), Managing global civil society: The WTO's engagement with NGOs, in: Randall D. and Michael Kenny Germain (eds.). *The Idea of Global Civil Society: Politics and Ethics in a Globalizing Era*. London, Routledge, 156–174.

Williams, Marc (2005), Civil society and the world trading system, in: Dominic Kelly and Wyn Grant (eds.). *The Politics of International Trade in the Twenty-First Century: Actors, Issues and Regional Dynamics*. Hampshire, Palgrave Macmillan, 30–46.

Zahniser, Steven, and William Coyle (2004), *U.S.-Mexico Corn Trade in the NAFTA Era: New Twists to an Old Story*. Washington, D.C., U.S. Department of Agriculture.

Index

abolitionist movement, 40
Action Aid, 72, 146–147
Action Canada Network (ACN), 131
actors. *See also* civil society organizations
 anti-globalization, 13, 27, 47, 166
 nonstate actors, 4
 range of, 6
agency, 8, 199
 agency-centered view/approach, 8, 190
agricultural subsidies, 95–96, 103, 113, 189
Alliance for Responsible Trade (ART),
 57, 142–145, 178, 183, *See also* trade
 coalitions, United States
 as an affiliation-based trade
  coalition, 133
 as transnational broker, 108, 143
 centrality in transnational network of
  closest allies, 132–133
 critiques of, 144–145
 differences with CTC, 142–143
Alternative Policies for the Southern Cone
 (PACS), 104
 and MERCOSUR, 104–106
 and the mechanism of extension, 110
Alternatives for the Americas, 34, 156–160
 and ideational pathways to
  transnationality, 161
 and the debate about labor clauses,
  166–167
 on national sovereignty, 165–175
American Federation of Labor-Congress of
 Industrial Organizations (AFL-CIO)
 and Alliance for Responsible Trade
  (ART), 142
 and NAFTA, 53, 55

and the Cold War, 83
and the FTAA, 89
centrality in domestic network of closest
 allies, 74
centrality in transnational network of
 closest allies, 77
change in pathway to transnationality,
 92, 189
critiques of, 113
debate about social alliances, 91
new relational embeddedness of, 112
organizational pathways to
 transnationality, 118
pathway to transnationality, 87–90
position on the United States-Peru Free
 Trade Agreement, 176–178
relationships with Latin American
 allies, 164
Andean Community, 51
Argentina, 59, 98, 148, 187
Authentic Labor Front (FAT), 60, 84
 and NAFTA, 56
 and RMALC, 134
 centrality in domestic network of closest
  allies, 74
 centrality in transnational network of
  closest allies, 77
 debate about social alliances, 90–91
 pathway to transnationality, 83

bilateral agreements. *See* Chile-U.S. Free
 Trade Agreement, U.S.-Peru Free
 Trade Agreement
Bolivia, 98, 187
boomerang effect, 182–184

Brazil, 6, 13–15, *See also* Brazilian Network
for the Integration of the Peoples
(REBRIP)
and challengers of trade agreements, 67
and GATT, 42
and labor organizations, 73–79, 81
and MERCOSUR, 53, 59–61
and networks of closest allies, 72, 73–79,
112–113
and NGOs, 104, 106
and organizational pathways to
transnationality, 146–152
and rural organizations, 107–109
and the consultation on the FTAA, 148
and the HSA, 122, 125–127, 131
and the World Social Forums, 129
and trade coalitions, 132–133
Chamber of Deputies, 185
Brazilian Institute of Social and Economic
Analysis (IBASE)
centrality in transnational network of
closest allies, 77
Brazilian Network for the Integration of the
Peoples (REBRIP), 146
and the election of new governments, 187
as an affiliation-based trade coalition,
131–133
as transnational broker, 149
centrality in transnational network of
closest allies, 132–133, 146
internal organization of, 147–148
brokerage/brokers, 18, 35, 76, 107–109, 118,
128, 151, 183, 194
and trade coalitions, 139–142, 143,
149, 193
definition of, 108
business organizations
and civil society, 5–6
and coalition building, 197
and MERCOSUR, 58, 61–62, 64, 106, 197
and NAFTA, 182
and networks of closest allies, 69, 72, 74
and the debate about labor clauses, 159
and the FTAA, 123
and the GATT, 42
and the WTO, 45, 162
participation in trade debates, 10, 41, 50

campaign. *See also* Continental Campaign
against the FTAA, Jubilee South

Campaign, organizational pathways to
transnationality
as coalition building mode, 119–121
single-issue/issue-based, 24–25, 28, 103
Canada, 14, 16, 49, 148, *See also* Canada-
United States Free Trade Agreement
(CUSFTA), Action Canada Network,
Pro-Canada Network
and civil society networks during the
NAFTA debates, 54–58
and GATT, 42
and NAFTA, 54, 56–57, 96
and the anti-MAI campaign, 21
Canada-United States Free Trade
Agreement (CUSFTA), 11, 51–54
Canadian Jesuit Center, 57
Canadian Labour Congress (CLC)
and the search for allies in the NAFTA
region, 53, 55
debate about social alliances, 89, 91
Catholic Church. *See also* faith-based
organizations
and the Brazilian Campaign Against the
FTAA, 148
Center for Labor Investigation and
Consulting (CILAS)
centrality in domestic network of closest
allies, 74
Center for Studies for Rural Change in
Mexico (CECCAM)
position in domestic network of closest
allies, 101
Center of National Studies on Alternative
Development (CENDA)
and the mechanism of extension, 110
and transnational brokerage, 109
position in domestic network of closest
allies, 101
Change to Win Coalition (CTW)
position on the U.S.-Peru Free Trade
Agreement, 178
Chávez, Hugo, 183, 187
Chile, 6, 13–15
and labor organizations, 82
Chile Action Network for Peoples' Initiative
(RECHIP), 135–136
Chilean Alliance for a Just and Responsible
Trade (ACJR) 103–104, 120, 156, 183,
See also trade coalitions, Chile
as an NGO, 104, 136

as an affiliation-based trade coalition,
132–142
centrality in domestic network of closest
allies, 74
centrality in transnational network of
closest allies, 77, 132–134
weakening of, 134–138
Citizens' Trade Campaign (CTC), 120
and the HSA, 145–146
as transnational broker, 143
differences with ART, 142–143
ideational pathways to transnationality,
161
citizenship
new forms of, 24
civil society. *See also* civil society
organizations
definition of, 6
increased interest in trade negotiations,
9–11, 39–41
participation in trade debates before the
1990s, 50
civil society organizations, 8,
See also organizational pathways to
transnationality, ideational pathways to
transnationality
and ideational pathways to
transnationality, 32–34
and NAFTA, 54–58
and organizational pathways to
transnationality, 30–31
and the FTAA, 11
and the WTO, 45–47
as challengers of trade agreements, 6, 13
as participants in the anti-MAI
campaign, 20
as targets of transnational collective
action, 5
critiques of trade agreements, 12
definition of, 6
grassroots. 7
in networks of closest allies, 67–80
internationalization of, 5
interviews with, 16
member-based, 72
non member-based, 72
pathways to transnationality, 3, 6–7, 17
relationship with political parties and
national governments, 9, 180, 189
responses to structural changes, 16

claims
and ideational pathways to
transnationality, 33–34
coalition building, 27–32,
See also organizational pathways to
transnationality, trade coalitions
definition of, 28
modes of, 28–31
patterns and dynamics of, 150–152
collective action. *See* transnational
collective action
Colombia, 148
Common Market of the South
(MERCOSUR), 4, 12, 48, 51, 53
and labor organizations, 58–62
and legislators, 186
and NGOs, 106–107
and rural organizations, 98
lack of interest in, 62–63
lessons from, 58–64
Social-Labor Declaration, 86
Communist Party (Cuba), 185
Confederation of Mexican Workers
(CTM), 86
and NAFTA, 55, 56
pathway to transnationality, 84
ties with the AFL-CIO, 87
Confederation of National Unions (CSN)
and NAFTA, 56
constructivist approach, 7
Continental Campaign against the FTAA,
118, 120, 127, 128–130, 137, 146, 150
as campaign coalition building
mode, 119
as example of periodic
transnationalization, 161
Brazilian chapter of the, 148
Mexican chapter of the, 139
national chapters of the, 29
public consultations on the FTAA, 129
relationship with national
governments, 187
ties to political parties, 185
Coordination of Southern Cone Labor
Federations (CCSCS)
and MERCOSUR, 54, 59–60, 88
creation of, 53, 120
Coordinator of Family Farm Organizations
of MERCOSUR (COPROFAM),
98–100

Cuba
 meetings of the Continental Campaign
   against the FTAA, 129–130

democracy
 and coalition building, 30, 31, 59
 and the debate about national sovereignty,
   20, 157, 198
 transitions to, 43, 50, 53–54, 56, 58, 63, 82
Democratic Party, 176–177, 186
 ties with the AFL-CIO, 189
Development-GAP (D-GAP)
 as transnational broker, 108
 new relational embeddedness of, 112
diffusion, 15
 as a type of relational mechanism, 17
 definition of, 35
 in "Alternative for the Americas",
   158–159, 184
 of ideas, 63
 of organizational repertoires, 63, 117, 131
Doctors Without Borders, 104

Economic Commission for Latin America
   and the Caribbean (ECLAC)
 and regional integration in Latin
   America, 51
embeddedness
 "argument of embeddedness", 7
 double embeddedness of actors in social
   networks and political contexts, 6–9,
   13, 21, 23, 27, 35, 67, 179, 189, 190,
   192
 in political contexts, 179
 in social networks, 48, 86, 88
 labor organizations' double
   embeddedness in social networks
   and political contexts, 82
 political, 7, 17
environmental organizations
 and CTC, 142
 and debates about national sovereignty, 166
 and domestic networks of closest allies,
   69, 72
 and MERCOSUR, 62
 and NAFTA, 96
 and the debate about genetically modified
   organisms, 101–102
 centrality in transnational network of
   closest allies, 78

participation in trade debates, 10
Environmental Studies Group (GEA)
 position in domestic network of closest
   allies, 101
extension
 as a type of relational mechanism, 17
 definition of, 35
 example of, 113
 in "Alternatives for the Americas", 158
 of issues and agendas, 91, 108–109, 110

faith-based organizations, 6
 and domestic networks of closest
   allies, 72
 and NAFTA, 56–57
 and the search for allies in the NAFTA
   region, 56
 ties with rural organizations in Brazil and
   the United States, 100
Federation of Organisms for Social and
   Educational Assistance (FASE), 104
 as transnational broker, 108–109
 centrality in domestic network of closest
   allies, 74
free trade
 and anticommunism, 49
 and the creation of a global trade
   regime, 45
 and the World Trade Organization
   (WTO), 44–45
 between the United States and
   Canada, 49
 interfaces with other issue areas, 39–41
 negotiations in the Americas, 4
Free Trade Area of the Americas (FTAA), 4,
   11, 29, 57, 67, 76, 100, 146, 149, 162,
   See also Continental Campaign against
   the FTAA
 and labor organizations, 83, 84, 88
 Belo Horizonte Ministerial Meeting,
   53–54, 108, 121
 Miami Ministerial Meeting, 122
Friends of the Earth (FOE)
 centrality in domestic network of closest
   allies, 74
 position in transnational network of
   closest allies, 78

G-20
 and the WTO, 95

Index

gender organizations. *See also* International
Gender and Trade Network (IGTN)
and challengers of trade agreements, 11
participation in trade coalitions, 118
General Agreement on Tariffs and Trade
(GATT), 11, 54, 96
differences with the WTO, 44–45
history of, 42–44
General Workers' Confederation
(CGT-Argentina)
and MERCOSUR, 60, 61
General Workers' Confederation
(CGT-Brazil)
and MERCOSUR, 60, 88
and the FTAA, 196
pathway to transnationality, 83
global civil society, 6
and the anti-MAI campaign, 21
and the relevance of actors'
embeddedness in political
contexts, 23
Global Exchange, 9
global governance, 13, 107, 198
and "Alternatives for the Americas",
165–175
and ideational pathways to
transnationality, 32
and trade, 10, 44, 113, 196
globalization, 10, 13, 22, 31, 187, 188, 190
Grassroots Global Justice, 144
Greenpeace (Mexico)
and the debate about genetically modified
organisms, 102
position in domestic network of closest
allies, 101

Hemispheric Social Alliance (HSA),
89, 113, 147, 150, 185
and "Alternatives for the Americas",
34, 167
as affiliation-based coalition
mode, 119
as example of sustained
transnationalization, 161
as transnational broker, 140
creation of, 89
critiques of, 125–127
internal organization of, 123–125
phases of, 121–122
Human Rights Watch (HRW), 104

ideational pathways to transnationality, 18,
32–34
and "Alternatives for the Americas",
156–161
and diffusion, 184
diffusion of, 63
typology of, 32–33, 160–161
variety of, 156
identity, 89, 91
building and "Alternatives for the
Americas", 156
Institute for Policy Studies (IPS)
and CUSFTA, 53
and the search for allies in the NAFTA
region, 54
centrality in domestic network of closest
allies, 74
Institute of Political Ecology (IEP)
centrality in transnational network of
closest allies, 77
position in transnational network of
closest allies, 78
Institute of Socio-Economic Studies
(INESC); 104
and MERCOSUR, 106
Institutional Revolutionary Party (PRI), 97
Inter-American Regional Organization of
Workers (ORIT) 54, 136
and MERCOSUR, 62
and the HSA, 122
debate about social alliances, 89–92
International Brotherhood of Teamsters
(IBT)
and the HSA, 146
International Confederation of Free Trade
Unions (ICFTU), 54, 55
International Gender and Trade Network
(IGTN)
as affiliation-based coalition mode,
119–121
International Labor Organization (ILO), 40
and the debate about labor clauses, 89
International Trade Organization (ITO), 42
Interunion Workers' Assembly-National
Workers' Confederation (PIT-CNT)
and MERCOSUR, 60–61

Jubilee South Campaign, 148
centrality in transnational network of
closest allies, 132–133

Keynesianism, 50

Labor Force
　and MERCOSUR, 88
　and the FTAA, 196
　pathway to transnationality, 83
labor organizations
　and domestic networks of closest allies, 69
　and MERCOSUR, 58–62, 64
　and the mechanism of extension, 108–109
　centrality in social networks, 81–82
　new relational embeddedness of, 86–92
　participation in trade debates in the
　　Americas, 83–86
Landless Rural Workers' Movement
　　(MST), 93
　centrality in domestic network of closest
　　allies, 74, 94
　centrality in transnational network of
　　closest allies, 77, 79
　position in transnational network of
　　closest allies, 78
Latin American Coordination of Rural
　　Organizations (CLOC)
　and the FTAA, 98
Latin American Workers' Federation
　　(CLAT)
　and MERCOSUR, 62

mechanisms, 7, *See also* extension,
　　suppression, diffusion, transformation
　in "Alternatives for the Americas",
　　158–159
　typology of relational mechanisms,
　　17, 35–36
Mexican Action Network on Free Trade
　　(RMALC), 57
　as transnational broker, 139–142
　centrality in transnational network of
　　closest allies, 132–133
　critiques of, 136–139
Mexican Center for Environmental Law
　　(CEMDA)
　position in transnational network of
　　closest allies, 78
Mexican Labor Congress
　and NAFTA, 56
Mexico, 6, 13–15, 148
　and civil society networks during the
　　NAFTA debates, 55–58

　and labor organizations, 82
　and NAFTA, 54
monkeywrenching tactics, 184
Multilateral Agreement on Investment (MAI)
　campaign against the, 20–22

National Association of Rural and
　　Indigenous Women (ANAMURI)
　centrality in domestic network of closest
　　allies, 74, 94
National Association of Rural Producers'
　　Commercial Firms (ANEC)
　position in domestic network of closest
　　allies, 101
National Confederation of Workers in
　　Agriculture (CONTAG)
　and the WTO, 95
　and REBRIP, 146–147
National Family Farm Coalition (NFFC)
　and commodity prices, 95
　centrality in domestic network of closest
　　allies, 94
National Peasants' Confederation (CNC)
　and NAFTA, 97
national sovereignty
　and global governance, 164
　and states, 22
　and transnational actors, 22
　as a transnational collective action
　　dilemma, 161–175
　defended by civil society organizations,
　　21, 22
　flexible framing of, 21
　Southern views on, 164
　threats to, 161–164
National Union of Autonomous Regional
　　Rural Organizations (UNORCA)
　centrality in domestic network of closest
　　allies, 94
　centrality in transnational network of
　　closest allies, 77
　position in domestic network of closest
　　allies, 101
National Union of Workers (UNT), 84
　pathway to transnationality, 84
new regionalism, 51
nongovernmental organizations (NGOs), 6, 13
　and domestic networks of closest allies, 69
　and the mechanism of extension, 109–110
　brokerage roles of, 108–109

eligible to attend WTO Ministerials,
    45–47
increased participation in trade debates,
    106–107
multi-issue, 103–106
North American Commission for
    Environmental Cooperation (CEC)
    contamination of maize fields, 102
North American Free Trade Agreement
    (NAFTA), 4, 11, 48
    agrarian chapter of the, 101
    and investment regulations, 21
    and NGOs, 107
    Labor Side Agreement, 86
    lessons from, 63–64
North-South
    divide, 12
    interactions among civil society
        organizations, 13

organizational pathways to transnationality,
    28–31
    and organizational repertoire, 17
    campaign coalition building mode,
        119–121
    diffusion of, 11, 35, 57, 63, 131–132
    main affiliation-based trade coalitions,
        131–133
    new and old, 117–118
    typology of, 28–31
Oxfam International/America/Great
    Britain, 147
    and domestic networks of closest allies, 72
    and the mechanism of transformation,
        102, 113
    report on rules of trade, 95

Paraguay, 53, 59, 98, 148
    and MERCOSUR, 61
pathways to transnationality, 3, 15,
    See also organizational pathways
        to transnationality, ideational
        pathways to transnationality,
        periodic internalization, periodic
        transnationalization, sustained
        internalization, sustained
        transnationalization
    and changing political opportunities, 9
    and scales of action, 17
    changes in, 92

definition of, 6, 25
typology of, 25–27
variation of, 13
Peoples' Team (DECA-EP), 104
    and the mechanism of extension, 110
    centrality in domestic network of closest
        allies, 74
periodic internalization
    as pathway to transnationality, 27, 160
periodic transnationalization
    as pathway to transnationality, 26, 161
Peru. See United States-Peru Free Trade
    Agreement
political opportunities
    and the political embeddedness of actors,
        189
    definition of, 8
    domestic and international, 9, 24, 179
political parties, 6, 8, 59, 137, 179, 181, 188
    and the Brazilian Campaign against the
        FTAA, 148–149
    and the Continental Campaign against
        the FTAA, 128
    ties with challengers of trade agreements,
        185
Pro-Canada Network (PCN), 51, 57
projects
    and ideational pathways to
        transnationality, 33–34
protectionism
    in Latin America, 49–50
Public Citizen
    and the HSA, 145
    and the mechanism of extension, 110
    centrality in domestic network of closest
        allies, 74
    centrality in transnational network of
        closest allies, 77
    critiques of, 111–112, 113
    new relational embeddedness of, 112
    participation in trade debates, 110–112

relational mechanisms. See mechanisms
repertoires of contention, 24, 190
rural organizations
    and domestic networks of closest
        allies, 69
    and NAFTA, 96
    and the FTAA, 100
    density of ties, 100

rural organizations *(cont.)*
increased interest in trade
negotiations, 96
new relational embeddedness of, 96–103

Sierra Club
and the HSA, 145
Silva, Luis Inácio Lula da, 92, 149, 183, 186
social movements, 4, 6
and frames, 32
and social network analysis, 7
and the political process approach, 8
social network analysis. *See* social networks
social networks, 17
and domestic networks of closest allies,
67–76
and the political contexts in which actors
live, 8
and transnational network of closest
allies, 75–80
asymmetric distribution of ties in
domestic networks, 72–73
asymmetric distributions of ties in
transnational network, 77–79
boundaries of, 15
definition of, 7
density in domestic networks of closest
allies, 73–76
density in transnational network of
closest allies, 79
embeddedness of actors in, 7–8
heterogeneity of, 69
metaphorical use of, 29–30
missing ties and nodes in, 112–114
questionnaire, 67, 76, 81
social network analysis techniques, 13
South Korean Federation of Farmers and
Fishermen
and protests against the WTO, 92
Stop CAFTA Coalition, 118
as campaign coalition building mode, 119
Summit of the Americas
Mar del Plata, 187
Santiago, 91, 93
suppression
as a type of relational mechanism, 17
definition of, 35
example of, 113
in "Alternative for the Americas", 159
sustained internalization

as pathway to transnationality. 26, 161
sustained transnationalization
as pathway to transnationality. 26–27,
161

trade coalitions, 15, 27–32, *See also* coalition
building, organizational pathways to
transnationality
domestic, 131–152
transnational, 117–130
Trade Promotion Authority (TPA), 181
transformation
as a type of relational mechanism, 17
definition of, 35
example of, 102, 113
in "Alternative for the Americas", 159
transnational collective action, 3
and changing political opportunities, 189
and political contexts, 17
and social networks, 17
conditions for the creation of, 63
definition of, 5
increased relevance of, 16
longer-term approach to the study of,
24–25
multidisciplinary approach to, 9
precedents of, 39
variety and dynamics of, 4

Unified Workers' Federation (CUT-Brazil)
and MERCOSUR, 59–61, 88
and ORIT, 88
centrality in domestic network of closest
allies, 74
centrality in transnational network of
closest allies, 77, 79
debate about social alliances, 89–91
new relational embeddedness of, 112
pathway to transnationality, 83
relationship with Lula government, 189
relationship with NGOs, 147
Unitary Workers' Central (CUT-Chile)
and MERCOSUR, 60–61
and the 1998 Summit of the Americas,
91, 93
centrality in domestic network of closest
allies, 74
pathway to transnationality, 84
Unitary Workers' Central (CUT-Paraguay)
and MERCOSUR, 60, 61

Index

Unitary Workers' Central (CUT-Peru), 178
Unified Workers' Socialist Party
    (PSTU), 185
Union of South American Nations
    (UNASUR), 51
United Nations Conference on Trade and
    Development (UNCTAD), 42
United States, 6, 13–15, 148
    and civil society networks during the
        NAFTA debates, 58–62
    and labor organizations, 82
    Congress, 43, 50, 92, 110, 143, 145, 163,
        165, 176–177, 181–182, 184, 186
    trade policy making, 181
United States Business and Industrial
    Council (USBIC), 162
United States Catholic Conference of
    Bishops, 163
United States Trade Representative
    (USTR), 182
United States-Central America Free
    Trade Agreement (CAFTA), 102, 176,
    See also Stop CAFTA Coalition
United States-Chile Free Trade Agreement,
    113, 136
United States-Peru Free Trade Agreement,
    16, 176–178, 189
Uruguay, 53, 59, 98

Via Campesina, 103, *See also* rural
    organizations
    affiliates in social networks, 100
    and NGOs, 94
    and the debate about food
        sovereignty, 94
    and the WTO, 93–94
    as transnational broker, 100
    organizational pathways to
        transnationality, 103
    participation in trade debates, 95–96

Workers' Party (PT)
    ties with CUT-Brazil, 189
World Social Forum, 28, 143
    and ideational pathways to
        transnationality, 33–34
    and the Continental Campaign against
        the FTAA, 129
    relationship with national governments,
        188
World Trade Organization (WTO)
    and civil society, 45–47
    and global agreement on investments, 20
    Cancun Ministerial Meeting, 92–94
    creation of a global trade regime, 44–45
    Doha Round, 12
    Seattle Ministerial Meeting, 11, 46, 90